Time and memory in reggae music

Music and Society

Series editors Peter J. Martin and Tia DeNora

Music and Society aims to bridge the gap between music scholarship and the human sciences. A deliberately eclectic series, its authors are nevertheless united by the contention that music is a social product, social resource, and social practice. As such it is not autonomous but is created and performed by real people in particular times and places; in doing so they reveal much about themselves and their societies.

In contrast to the established academic discourse, *Music and Society* is concerned with all forms of music, and seeks to encourage the scholarly analysis of both `popular' styles and those which have for too long been marginalised by that discourse – folk and ethnic traditions, music by and for women, jazz, rock, rap, reggae, muzak and so on. These sounds are vital ingredients in the contemporary cultural mix, and their neglect by serious scholars itself tells us much about the social and cultural stratification of our society.

The time is right to take a fresh look at music and its effects, as today's music resonates with the consequences of cultural globalisation and the transformations wrought by new electronic media, and as past styles are reinvented in the light of present concerns. There is, too, a tremendous upsurge of interest in cultural analysis. *Music and Society* does not promote a particular school of thought, but aims to provide a forum for debate; in doing so, the titles in the series bring music back into the heart of sociocultural analysis.

The land without music: music, culture and society in twentieth-century Britain   *Andrew Blake*
Music and the sociological gaze: art worlds and cultural production   *Peter J. Martin*
Sounds and society: themes in the sociology of music   *Peter J. Martin*
Popular music on screen: from the Hollywood musical to music video   *John Mundy*
Popular music in England 1840–1914: a social history (2nd edition)   *Dave Russell*
The English musical renaissance, 1840–1940: constructing a national music   (2nd edition)   *Robert Stradling and Meirion Hughes*

Sarah Daynes

Time and memory in reggae music
The politics of hope

Manchester University Press

Copyright © Sarah Daynes 2010

The right of Sarah Daynes to be identified as the author of this work has been asserted by her in accordance with the Copyright, Designs and Patents Act 1988.

Published by Manchester University Press
Altrincham Street, Manchester M1 7JA, UK
www.manchesteruniversitypress.co.uk

British Library Cataloguing-in-Publication Data is available

Library of Congress Cataloging-in-Publication Data is available

ISBN 978 1 7849 9280 4 *paperback*

First published by Manchester University Press in hardback 2010

This paperback edition first published 2016

The publisher has no responsibility for the persistence or accuracy of URLs for any external or third-party internet websites referred to in this book, and does not guarantee that any content on such websites is, or will remain, accurate or appropriate.

Printed by Lightning Source

Contents

List of tables and boxes	*page*	vii
List of figures		ix
Acknowledgements		xi
Introduction		1

Part I A study in elective affinity: Music, religion, memory

1	Reggae and Rastafari: A short history	21
2	Interpreting songs: Notes on methodology	36
3	A diachronic analysis of Jamaican reggae charts, 1968–2000	54
4	The construction of a musical memory	69

Part II Remembering the past

5	Slavery and the diaspora: Temporal and spatial articulations	85
6	The construction of a religious chain of memory	105

Part III Revealing the future

7	Messianism, between past and future	125
8	Hope and redemption	141
9	The eschatology as future-present	154
10	The construction of a socio-political memory	169

Part IV From revelation to revolution

11 Rhetoric of oppression and social critique ... 191
12 Only rasta can liberate the people: resistance and revolution ... 205

Part V Conclusion

13 Time and memory ... 231

Appendices:

Annex 1: List of songs mentioned, by artist ... 265

Annex 2: Albums in the corpus ... 271

Bibliography ... 274

Index ... 291

Tables and boxes

Tables

2.1	Examples of semantic vehicles in Buju Banton's Inna Heights (1997)	page 44
3.1	Rasta artists with more than one charted hit during the two peaks of Rastafari influence, in decreasing order	64
3.2	Artists linked to Rastafari with more than one charted hit during the two peaks of Rastafari influence, in decreasing order	65
3.3	Categories for the year 1978, Jamaican charts	66
3.4	Categories for the year 1999, Jamaican charts	66
6.1	References to the Bible in Bob Marley & the Wailers	117

Boxes

2.1	Examples of proverbs used in reggae lyrics	40
2.2	Albums used in this study	50

Figures

3.1	Evolution of the content of the songs	page 59
3.2	Evolution in terms of the artists and their link with Rastafari	62
3.3	Cumulated categories A and B (rasta artists and artists linked to Rastafari)	63
5.1	Representations of Africa	103
13.1	Memory in reggae music	232
13.2	Close past and close future	233
13.3	Continuity and discontinuity in the representation of time	237
13.4	The temporal process of memory	240
13.5	Sacred and profane articulations in the representation of time	241
13.6	Myths, rites, and historical time	247
13.7	Vernant's distinctions between time, and memory and history	261

Acknowledgements

This book is a largely revised version of my Ph.D. dissertation, defended at the École des Hautes Études en Sciences Sociales. It would have never been completed without the assistance of my committee: Danièle Hervieu-Léger, Marie-Claire Lavabre, Laënnec Hurbon, Pete Martin, and Erwan Dianteill; I am grateful for their guidance during my doctoral studies. I most warmly thank my colleagues Orville Lee, Linden Lewis, Alexander Riley, and Terry Williams for their careful reading and enlightening feedback. By mentioning Vernant, Marie-Claire Lavabre allowed my reflection to pursue a path that had felt uncertain before. I also thank Andrew Arato and Sharon Hays, whose friendship and support in difficult times has meant a great deal to me; and my colleagues at the University of North Carolina for their warm collegiality, especially Ken Allan and Sarah Wagner.

A special mention goes to my graduate students at the New School for Social Research, in particular Rina Bliss, Monica Brannon, Keerati Chenpitayaton, John Giunta, Adrian Leung, Marisol López-Menéndez, Ritchie Savage, Dan Sherwood, Héctor Vera, Wendy Washington, and Katia Yurguis: our shared intellectual inquiry greatly enriched my reflection on time and memory.

I also thank my editors and staff at Manchester University Press, especially Rob Byron, Tom Dark, and Andrew Kirk for working with me on the paperback edition. The photograph on the book cover is by Patrick Cariou, who chose it and graciously allowed us to use it; his powerful photographic work can be found in his books *Yes Rasta, Gypsies,* and *Surfers,* published in the United States by powerHouse Books.

Above all, my love and gratitude goes to my family: my parents, sister, niece and nephews, my very good friends A. and F., and of course T., my companion, for making me feel at home in the world.

Il me semble parfois que mon sang coule à flots,
Ainsi qu'une fontaine aux rythmiques sanglots.
Je l'entends bien qui coule avec un long murmure,
Mais je me tâte en vain pour trouver la blessure.

Baudelaire, *Les fleurs du mal*

Introduction

Since the late 1990s, memory has become one of the most studied themes in the social sciences. An exponential increase of scholarly work on memory has been accompanied by a parallel in other fields (from literary criticism to social policy) but also by the wide use of the terms "memory" and "collective memory" in the media and in the language spoken by governments, policymakers, and non-governmental organizations; in the words of Barbara Misztal, we have been witnessing an "astonishing burst of interest in social memory" (2004: 126). And yet the growing use of the term, in and out of academia, has also been accompanied by a definitional vagueness, despite the multiplication of both theoretical and empirical studies on memory; this might well be the fate of all "successful" concepts, which often lose in precision what they gain in use. And within a flourishing field of inquiry, an interesting surprise comes from the limited scholarship on a notion closely related to memory: time.[1] The analysis of time developed at the beginning of the twentieth century within the Durkheimian school did not found a field of study; instead, after a pause of more than forty years, the sociological interest in time only reemerged in the seventies, and has since remained marginal (Bergmann 1992: 126). And while memory studies rely on Durkheimian sociology through the foundational status given to Maurice Halbwachs, they also underplay the fact that he was actually part of a collective project that included a strong emphasis on social time, and in particular on

---

1 An interesting illustration is found in teaching: while courses on collective memory flourish, there are but a couple of courses on the sociology of time *per se* taught in the United States today.

the distinction between its sacred and profane dimensions, found in the work of Durkheim, Hubert, Mauss, and later Caillois. In this book, I offer a case study in social memory that also opens onto the articulation between sacred and profane time. Hence, this book should be read as a typical study in collective memory that serves as a point of entry into a reflection upon the relationship between, and conceptualization of, memory and time, by using the classical Durkheimian alley of the binary opposition between the sacred and the profane. In other words, my argument will use Halbwachs and social memory as a point of departure; but, following the incursions of time in the empirical case study that it focuses on, it will lead to the early Durkheimian school and social time.

Forgetting is also a marginal focus in sociological studies.[2] The general understanding of memory seems to imply a normative judgment that sees remembering as good, and forgetting as bad—this is especially visible in the media, as well as in public discourse, whether governmental or non-governmental. Every group claims its right to remember, to conserve its past, to commemorate its heroes; forgetting has become the evil that results from domination, genocide, war, or ignorance. It seems as though the positive function of forgetting has indeed been forgotten; and yet, the dialectic between remembrance and forgetting can be said to be inherent to group-building, in particular to groups said to be "in diaspora": indeed history is not a continuous flow anymore, expressed by an uninterrupted transmission, but a time broken in a before and an after; and the familiar place, in which history spontaneously grounds itself, is not lived day after day but replaced by an imagined elsewhere that is "put in memory." African slaves and their descendants had to face a geographical dispersal that happened in two stages (towards the slave states during the trade, and then, through ulterior migrations, towards Europe and the Americas) and was accompanied by a brutal rupture from their land of origin. This geographical rupture also implied a more or less clear separation from traditions, languages, religious practices or kinship systems, which were intently endangered by the system of slavery (Patterson 1967). This rupture, both geographical and socio-cultural, has shaped the progressive construction of the African diaspora since the time of slavery, and strongly marked the transmission of history

---

[2] Notable works on forgetting include Zerubavel (2006).

and memory by making it difficult and partial. And one could argue that it is precisely when it is rendered difficult that the transmission of memory actually matters, as if its very absence, or partiality, brought it to the forefront in the preoccupations of the group; in the case of the slaves' descendants, the issue of memory occupies a central place, not simply because of a more or less partial rupture in the continuity of society, but also because of the symbolic life of this rupture in collective representations. Hence the issue is not really whether culture (and social life) has survived—we know it both has and hasn't—but rather the space that the idea of rupture symbolically occupies in the formation of the group and in the way it conceives of itself.

Through the case of reggae music, this book looks at the construction, transmission and use of collective memory, and therefore at the symbolic space occupied by the idea of a historical discontinuity, within a specific context that includes a difficult past, characterized by forced uprooting and the experience of slavery. Reggae music claims a role of transmission—specifically, of a history that was broken by slavery and falsified by the slavemasters, and of a memory both to be conserved and built—and articulates the question of collective identity in relation to the construction of the African diaspora. I will therefore focus on the notion of memory and look at the way in which music participates in its dynamic transmission. But before going further, I wish to problematize the concepts needed for my inquiry, and the way in which they articulate.

Social memory and collective identity

The terms *history* and *memory* have here a specific meaning, situated within the Durkheimian framework, in particular in the work of Maurice Halbwachs. A student of both Bergson and Durkheim, Halbwachs was the first sociologist to work specifically on the notion of memory, breaking with the philosophical and psychological debates of his time, a rupture that is visible in the three major axes of his work on collective memory: the social frameworks of memory, the distinction between individual and collective memories, and the distinction between history and memory. Halbwachs is probably best known for the notion of social frameworks, which he discusses in detail in his book *The Social Frameworks of Memory*, originally published in 1925.[3] According to him, memory is fundamentally structured by the social, by what he calls the social frameworks of memory: "It is in society that people normally acquire their memories. It is also in society that they recall, recognize, and localize their memories ... it is to the degree that our individual thought places itself in these frameworks and participates in this memory that it is capable of the act of recollection" (1992: 38). Thus, Halbwachs places the social at the very heart of the processes of remembering and forgetting: indeed, there cannot be any individual recollection made in a social vacuum, and according to him individuals use the support of the social group in order to remember, even for their most intimate memories.[4] In a page not translated in the English version, he argues that "any memory, as personal it can be, even the memory of events that we alone have witnessed, even of thoughts and feelings that we did not express, is in relationship with a whole ensemble of notions that not only us but many others possess, with persons, groups, places, dates, words and linguistic forms, with even some ways of thinking and ideas, that is, with the entire material and moral life of the societies of which we are, or have been, a part" (1994: 38). Hence the social frameworks of memory are a collection of elements that induce and organize individual memories: spatial and temporal markers, historical, geographical, biographical and political notions, everyday experiences, representations and worldviews. Here Halbwachs also asserts the necessary link between recollection, language, and society:

> people living in society use words that they find intelligible: this is the precondition for collective thought. But each word (that is understood) is accompanied by recollections. There are no recollections to which words cannot be made to correspond. We speak of our recollection before calling them to mind. It is language, and the whole system of social conventions attached to it, that allows us at every moment to reconstruct our past. (1992: 173)

---

[3] It is worth mentioning that the English translation of Halbwachs' book has been heavily cut (*On Collective Memory*, 1992). When missing in the English text, references will be made to the French text (*Les cadres sociaux de la mémoire*, 1994).

[4] See the case Blondel presented to Halbwachs: his childhood memory of having fallen in a waterhole. Halbwachs' response was straightforward: "in reality, we are never alone" (1997: 52); the child still thought with and through his family, however absent.

It is therefore only to the extent that individuals are part of a society, and therefore of its language and system of representation, that they are *able* to remember. The frameworks of memory are to be considered as a tool that individuals use, a system on which they rely, which not only organizes and frames their memories, but also allows the process of recollection itself.

This focus on collective memory as being what enables individual memory is not simply deterministic. Halbwachs does not imply that society "creates" individual memories, nor that individuals have no active role in this process. The individual process of remembering is done in interaction with collective representations; hence, individual memories are unique. Collective memory—that is, the memory of the group—is not reducible to the sum of individual memories, even though each of them contributes to it; *the group does not remember by itself, but individuals need the group in order to remember*: this is one of Halbwachs' strongest assertions. Here is found the second major axis of his work, which questions the distinction between individual and collective memories. Each group has its own (collective) memory, its own system of reference and frameworks, which depend not only on space (through the boundaries of the group's identity in the present) but also on time (since these boundaries might change over time, but also since the interests and goals of the group might vary). There are thus two levels of interaction between individual and collective memories: on one level, each individual belongs to different groups, and therefore his or her memory lies at the unique intersection between these groups; on a second level, individuals play an active role in defining and building collective memories, as much as the latter shapes and organizes individual memories. In his later book *Collective Memory*,[5] Halbwachs indeed defines individual memory as "a point of view on collective memory," and notes that this point of view "changes depending on the position that one occupies and ... this position itself changes depending on the relations that one has with other milieus (1997: 94–95). By introducing the notion of "point of view," Halbwachs therefore gives a central place to the dynamic process of interpretation: individuals indeed use a tool that they have in common (the frameworks of memory), but they do so each in their own way, which depends on the groups they belong

---

[5] Which was published posthumously, as Halbwachs died in Buchenwald in 1945.

or have belonged to and at what moment in their life. Individual memories, therefore, build on collective memory, but they do so in an active way. Collective memory becomes primarily equated with the interpenetration of collective consciousnesses, a term that also reflects the earlier work of Durkheim and Mauss on collective representations and society as being embodied in individuals. Additionally, collective memory is not a simple sum of individual memories, in the same way that society is more than a simple sum of individuals. The frameworks of memory assume a normative function: they are a system of meaning, a system of representation that provides symbolic frames, but into which individuals dynamically inscribe themselves. But systems of meaning change: what matters for the group at some point might become secondary at another time, and it will therefore be set aside, ignored, forgotten. Here we reach an important point in Halbwachs' perspective on collective memory: the fact that the present produces the past, as opposed to a movement from the past to the present.[6] I will come back to this point in detail later on.

Halbwachs also distinguishes between collective memory and what he calls historical memory or history. He is very clear on these definitions: history is "dead memory," while memory is alive. "In general history starts at the point where tradition ends, at the moment where social memory dies and decays. As long as a memory subsists, it is useless to fix it in writing, or even to fix it at all," he says (Halbwachs 1997: 129). History is decayed tradition, dead memory; moreover, it is memory that has not been lived: "it is not on learned history that our memory is grounded, but on lived history" (Halbwachs 1997: 105). Memory then has a fundamentally alive and experienced character; it is dynamic, and has what Halbwachs calls a "natural" continuity: "It is a continuous current of thought, a continuity that has nothing artificial, since it retains from the past only what is still alive or able to live in the conscience of the group. By definition, it does not go beyond the limits of this group" (Halbwachs 1997: 132). Since individuals die or are born, since the group is perpetually changing and its boundaries are moving, collective memory itself is changing and multiple—in contrast to history, which Halbwachs qualifies as being "one." Here Halbwachs means history in a very specific sense: as a discipline, and moreover

---

[6] Hence Coser describes Halbwachs' work as "a presentist approach" (in Halbwachs 1992: 25).

as the discipline it was at the time he was writing. Today, one could debate the validity of the opposition set up by Halbwachs in the light of new developments in the field, which emphasize the constructed and dynamic character of history. However, his clear-cut opposition between history and memory remains useful in so far as it allows for a working definition of memory that can be used in a study that does not specifically focus on "historical knowledge."

The term memory will mean here a sort of "lived history," and will therefore have a fundamentally subjective and dynamic character—which implies that it is selective. Individual and collective memories are linked and in permanent interaction; collective memory is a mix of historical facts, feelings, opinions and consensus, which work at the symbolic level. It will also be considered as functioning within a dynamic double movement: both the present of the past and the past of the present, both being present in the past and past in the present, both from the past to the present and from the present to the past. Indeed memory is not only the *trace of the past*, it is also and above all a *narrative of the past*, which can be a reconstruction or even a reinvention. The movement from the present to the past is actually most important to memory, according to Halbwachs: what the group retains and builds from its past is what constitutes its memory—not simply what is imposed by the past. This hypothesis is important because it implies that the past can influence and shape the present, but also that this influence is always dependent on a symbolic construction that operates in the opposite direction, from the present to the past.

Recently, the link between memory and identity has become central in the scholarship—even if Halbwachs' work on the memory of the family or Mannheim's on generations prefigured it. As Huglo, Mechoulan and Moser point out (2000: 8), "memory cannot be understood as a simple psychic faculty anymore ... It is, before anything else, a matter of communities." Furthermore, for Marie-Claire Lavabre, the sense of belonging participates in the definition of memory in the sense that it specifies this narrative of the past that is memory; groups produce a narrative of the past that participates in their identity.[7] Indeed, memory, as the production of a continuity, necessarily takes part into the construction of individual and collective

---

[7] Unpublished; seminar at the Ecole des Hautes Etudes en Sciences Sociales, Paris, 1996–1997.

memories: to belong to a human community is to situate oneself in relationship to its past, even if it is by rejecting it (Hobsbawm 1972). Therefore, memory is about a dialectical relationship between the present and the past, but it is also ascribed within a relationship with the future. Indeed, whether it breaks with the past, maintains it by transmitting it, or reinvents it, memory always builds a continuity that is necessary to the sense of belonging (or of non-belonging) to the group. In other words, as both Ricoeur (2006) and Gadamer (2003) have pointed out, forgetting is, just like remembrance, a component of collective memory: both are at the heart of *memory at work*. As Gadamer says,

> Memory must be formed; for memory is not memory for anything and everything. One has a memory for some things, and not for others; one wants to preserve one thing in memory and banish another. It is time to rescue the phenomenon of memory from being regarded merely as a psychological faculty and to see it as an essential element of the finite historical being of man. In a way that has long been insufficiently noticed, forgetting is closely related to keeping in mind and remembering; forgetting is not merely an absence and a lack but, as Nietzsche in particular pointed out, a condition of the life of mind. (2003: 16)

Indeed, whether it allows continuity or discontinuity, whether it favors forgetting or remembrance, collective memory always sets up a *temporal progression* that allows the group to be situated both in time and space, therefore participating in the composition and recomposition of collective identities. Even when memory is an attempt to conserve what, in the past, makes sense, and is considered as having been lost, collective memory always remains an interpretation of the past. The selective process itself depends on meaning attribution: collective memory does not attempt to conserve what does not matter for the group in the present; what matters is what is meaningful. This reconstruction of the past—if only by ignoring some elements and retaining others—therefore operates within a movement that takes place from the present to the past: in other words, the group asserts that: "Here is what we see in the past, here is how it makes sense to use, here is what we wish to conserve because we need it today."[8] From Halbwachs' Durkheimian memory,

---

[8] Echoing Jorge Luis Borges in "The Garden of the Forking Paths": "Then I reflected that all things happen to *oneself*, and happen precisely, precisely

a shift towards a Weberian conception of the social world appears fruitful: the social frameworks that surround the memorialization process find their legitimacy (and their efficiency) *in the meaning that is attributed to them*. The essential mechanism here, hence, is that memory as the trace of the past owes its social reality only to memory as the narrative of the past; that is, to the way in which it is charged with meaning. Unmeaningful past, indeed, is simply forgotten.[9]

At this point, one might wonder why the issue of memory seems to have become overwhelming at the end of the twentieth century, to the point of seeing memory accepted as a commonplace term, used by the media, individuals, groups, communities, social movements, nations and diasporas alike. There might be one answer, among others, to be found in the importance of international morality and responsibility grounded in Kantian ethics (which would for instance push for the public recognition of collective crimes perpetrated in the past, such as slavery, genocide, or forced displacement). The omnipresence of "claims of memory" can also be linked to an increasing and unprecedented mobility said to be characteristic of the end of the twentieth century (Clifford 1997): the construction of international spaces, the resurgence of conflicts, the increasing mobility of individuals, the simultaneous reinforcement and weakening of nation-states, have as a consequence the complexification of the "here" and "there," and a permanent redefinition of identities and symbolic boundaries. From individuals to groups to communities to nations, memory plays a crucial role in this (re)definition. What is at stake is articulated around the conservation, restoration and reappropriation of a history that has been fragilized or complexified by mobility, around its construction, its invention and its reinvention; around its transmission or lack of transmission after conflicts that are difficult to resolve. Hannah Arendt (1993: 5) wrote that "without tradition—which selects and names, which hands down and preserves, which indicates where the

---

now. Century follows century, yet events occur only *in the present*; countless men in the air, on the land and sea, yet everything that truly happens, happens to me..." (1998: 120).

[9] Although this book will focus on the claim for "rescuing" a memory that is considered as having been "lost," and therefore on the dynamic and inventive process of remembrance, I cannot but point out the fact that remembrance is always accompanied by forgetting.

treasures are and what their worth is—there seems to be no willed continuity in time and hence, humanly speaking, neither past nor future, only sempiternal change of the world and the biological cycle of living creatures in it." Hence memory—tradition, in her own terms—is a necessary condition of social life, because no continuity can exist without an apprehension of the past, present and future, and therefore without the construction of a memory. According to her, memory "chooses and names ... transmits and conserves ... indicates where the treasures are and what their value is"; memory can be taken for granted: individuals are surrounded by signs, by objects, by reminders of who they are and where they come from: their family and friends, the places in which they live as well as the objects which inhabit them, all are charged with their past and present ways of life.[10] But in situations of mobility, these signs rarefy,[11] while individuals have to adapt to a way of life that might be extremely different from before. What means do they have to keep present what is now far away? Music is easy to transport, and it also has an immediate and powerful ability of evocation; as Stokes says, "the musical event ... evokes and organises collective memories and present experiences of place with an intensity, power and simplicity unmatched by any other social activity" (1994: 3). This is my point of entry into the role, function and uses of music in diasporic situations, and its relationship with memory and identity.

Articulating music, religion and memory

Music is one of those things that are taken for granted, because of its omnipresence; indeed, it has become an essential and permanent component of Western societies. However, this has not always been the case, and the massive diffusion of music is a recent phenomenon: it is only after World War II—with technological innovations in terms of sound recording, conservation and diffusion—that access

---

[10] Comte suggests that "our mental balance depends in a great part on the objects with which we are in daily contact and which do not change, or almost, therefore offering an image of permanence and stability" (in Connerton 2000: 57). Connerton adds, "individuals remember events of the past together because together they occupy certain narrative places ... Our environment is not a simple external image, it is inseparable from the history of our identities and is incorporated to it."
[11] For Connerton this is a characteristic of the modern world.

to music became easier to all. Just as the banalization of music makes one forget that it is not that easy to diffuse it, its permanent presence gives it a character of evidence and naturalness. Everybody knows what music is, and still it is difficult to define what it is exactly. Does the definition of music not vary from one individual to the other? For some, heavy metal is certainly not music, but noise at the most. Others would consider as musical some sounds that do not require human intervention. What will matter here will not be to come up with an exhaustive definition of music; it will be enough to consider it as *the production of a sound recognized as musical*. This definition, in appearance very simple, nonetheless implies fundamental theoretical choices, which are at the heart of the evolution of contemporary sociology of music.

According to Seeger (1994: 3), "social scientists rarely consider music in discussions of group formation." To be sure, music has been considered as a simple cultural expression, and its social dimension neglected. Even today, working on music is largely considered as a secondary hobby—and this is especially true of the sociologist of popular music, as opposed to "high" musical forms. Adorno himself recognized that his interest was not inclusive: for him, music "meant above all the composed works produced in Western Europe during the period from Monteverdi to Schoenberg" (Martin 1995: 103). Adorno's main hypothesis is that "music not only reflects the social totality but reformulates social conflicts and contradictions within its own structure" (Martin 1995: 98). Thus, the "truth" of a musical composition depends on its capacity to symbolically express the social structure in which it emerges, and with it the conflicts, tensions and contradictions that form its reality. This is reminiscent of Kandinsky's reflections on painting, which describe the internal necessity of the artist: "Each artist, as a creator, must express what is specific to himself ... as a child of his era, [he] must express what is specific to this era ... as a servant of art, [he] must express what is specific to art in general" (1989: 132–133). Art therefore has to be able to express the social structure; its author is only secondary, in the sense that if the piece only expresses individual realities, it is not worthy of interest. This conception implies, of course, that art *must* be a symbolic expression of society, a permanent reformulation of the conflicts it goes through, and a crystallization of its structure—but also, as it was dear to Kandinsky, the expression of an ideal, the prefiguration of a better future and of a "new man." More recently, the essential hypothesis for sociologists of music concerns the socially constructed character of music, in relation with the social group and the interactions that define it. I was saying earlier that music was taken for granted; but this "taking-for-granted" itself varies depending on cultures and societies. As Martin (1995: 60) suggests, "the simple but fundamental point is that what people take for granted as the normal and reasonable organisation of sounds, indeed what they take for granted as 'music', is culturally variable." Musical genres are to be considered as systems understood and used by a given group in a specific context; they hold meanings for the people—a meaning that can, or even must, be foreign to someone who does not belong to the group—and are therefore subjected to a process of permanent interpretation: "listening to music, just like listening to speech, involves an *active* process of interpretation" (Martin 1995: 56). In order to communicate, individuals rely on the assumption that the gestures and language used are the same for all the parties involved, and the same goes for music: as Halbwachs (1997: 31) puts it, "the musical language is a language like any other, that is, it presupposes a prior agreement between those who speak it." For Shepherd (1977: 7), "any significance assigned to music must be ultimately and *necessarily* located in the commonly agreed meanings of the group or society in which the particular music is created." Music is a medium of communication that holds and transports meaning, and this is especially true of popular music: "the music of the people" can therefore become a powerful tool for control (which was Adorno's main criticism), as well as for resistance.

This implies that there is no instinctive definition, nor listening, nor understanding, of music. Although an individual can be touched by foreign music because it conveys universal human feelings, the meanings held by music "emerge and become established (or changed or forgotten) as a consequence of the activities of groups of people in particular cultural contexts" (Martin 1995: 57). This suggests two essential comments. First, music is a *dynamic symbolic system*, built and maintained in action and interaction, able to express emotions but also meanings, whether cultural or social. Second, this symbolic system is deeply rooted in, and dependent on, the cultural and social context in which it emerges and grows. As a result, it is pertinent to work on the role that music plays in the construction of the social group: as a symbolic system that conveys meaning, it contributes to collective identity. As Seeger (1994: 3) points out, music can be used "to say who you are and ... to interpret who other people are and to indicate what a community aspires to." Bourdieu (1986: 18) asserts that "nothing more clearly affirms one's `class', nothing more infallibly classifies, than taste in music." Additionally, it is important to examine the social and cultural roles assumed by music, beyond its ability to express the whole range of human emotions. These roles, as shown by several scholars, are numerous and varied; Merriam (1964: 219–226), for instance, speaks of at least ten functions. According to Manuel (1995: 243), a specialist in Caribbean and South American music, "through music, men and women can voice aspirations and ideals, strengthen group solidarity, and transcend adversity by confronting it and transmuting it into song." Some scholars have explained the richness, importance and vitality of the music of the African diaspora by the fact that it was the only means of expression: because they did not have any access to writing and reading, slaves would have privileged an oral mode of expression. But things are more complex: music has always been an unmatched mode of expression, explanation, or even survival. As Behague (1994: v) puts it, "as one of the most highly structured human cultural expressions, music encapsulates social groups' most essential values affecting individual members' worldviews and cosmovisions."

A focus on meaning, on the symbolic dimension of music, opens up analysis on the dynamic use of music: how do people attribute meaning to music? How do they identify with it? How do they use it in order to build or consolidate their identity? Martin (1999, personal communication) notes that individuals tend more and more to remain faithful to one musical style to which they deeply identify and which becomes an essential part of their way of life, even as they travel, move, or change jobs. This faithfulness could be considered as a way of building permanence in an everyday life that is more and more mobile, unstable and changing. Additionally, it seems that what matters most is not a search for the inherent content of music, but to take into account what people do with music. The focus on dynamically attributed, not inherent, meaning is fundamental because it implies a different understanding of music, and allows sociologists to understand and explain why the same song or the same musical style can have different meanings for different individuals and groups.

Religion, just like music, "makes sense" for individuals as well as for groups. To use Behague's terms again (1994), religion "encapsulates" worldviews, ways of life, and identities like music does. The main focus of my approach will therefore be, as might already be clear, the dynamism of social representations. Many scholarly works have been concerned with the religious movements of African slaves and their descendants, using terms such as syncretism, cultural interpenetration, acculturation or transculturation; several have been articulated around the issue of the survival (or disappearance) of African elements within,[12] and around the degree of *métissage* between the African and European origins. Caribbean religious movements indeed mix, in a syncretic manner, elements that come from different traditions, giving place to a new and original construct. For instance, the cult of the saints, present in the Caribbean and across Latin America, is not a simple cultural adaptation but an original creation connected not only with its European origin but also with indigenous, African, or Hindu traditions.[13] While the issue of survival is interesting, it neglects the process of symbolic shaping that takes place from the present towards the past, in order to focus on the historical tracing of an element from the past towards the present. As already emphasized in the case of music, my analysis focuses on representations and identifications, not on the element itself; in other words, what matters is not "real Africaness," but what one could call "attributed Africaness."

Chevannes (1995: 38–40) asserts that Rastafari should be analyzed as a cultural movement—that is, in all its dimensions and without focusing on one aspect only. Because the Rastafari movement has no dogma, no churches, and no institutions, it fits well within Grace Davie's model of "believing without belonging" (1997). But does the social and cultural influence of Rastafari, the way in which it can be used as a philosophy and "unvested of its gods," allow us to speak of a "belonging without believing"? It has millenarian and messianic aspects (De Albuquerque 1977, among others), but also a revolutionary dimension (Campbell 1985); working on the notions

---

[12] See in particular the debate that took place between anthropologist Melville Herskovits, who argued for survival (1941), and sociologist Franklin Frazier, who argued for disappearance (1997 [1955]).
[13] The "use of saints" is a fascinating phenomenon, from Our Lady of Guadalupe in Mexico to Cuban Santeria or Haitian Vaudou. See for instance Lafaye (1987) or Metraux (1989).

of millenarism and messianism by focusing on the construction of collective memory, as I propose to do, is one of the ways of approaching religious modernity in the plurality and simultaneity of its dimensions, by relating them to each other and showing how they work dynamically together. This stems from a necessary rather than an analytical choice: after having spoken of "the loss of religion" and then "the return of God" and "religion everywhere," sociologists of religion now emphasize the deregulation of the religious phenomena in modernity, in parallel with religious institutions' decreasing control over the "goods of salvation," and the latter's proliferation: "Beliefs are disseminating. They less and less conform themselves to established models. They less and less command institutions-controlled practices. These tendencies are the major symptoms of the process of 'deregulation' that characterizes the institutional religious field at the end of the twentieth century" (Hervieu-Léger 1999: 53). Individuals tend to construct (*bricoler*) their own religious system, which might borrow from different traditions. Within a process of autonomization of the individual, which characterizes Western modernity, religious beliefs and practices become chosen rather than imposed. However, simultaneously, there is a reinforcement of the communal dimensions of religion: forging one's own "personal God" does not imply the disappearance of collective identities; on the contrary, it has as a consequence a stronger social identification, since it is the result of a dynamic and voluntary choice. Additionally, while individuals "do it themselves," they also intensely refer to a lineage, to a "chain of memory" (Hervieu-Léger 2000), to a religious tradition in which they actively ascribe themselves. This tension between a privatization of beliefs and collective identities, individualism and communalism, personal choice and ascription within a tradition, can seem paradoxical; but it can also be analyzed as a characteristic of, and an adaptation to, modernity. The Rastafari movement shows both an emphasis on individualism (an autonomous subject, free to choose her practices and even her beliefs) and communalism (through a strong sense of the collective and the foundation of communities). The strength of the ascription within a tradition is at the heart of the Rastafari movement, but it is a dynamic ascription made that is constructed from the present to the past at least as much as from the past to the present.

At this point, the question of memory gains great analytical importance. If music makes sense, if it says—or is thought to say—something about the group, if it "encapsulates" values and worldviews, then part of this process can be considered memorial and/or historical. This will form the starting point of my argument: a reappropriated, revisited or even reinvented memory, associated with reggae music. Following methodological choices further explained below, reggae music will be limited, in this study, to the musical production linked to the Rastafari movement, in the seventies and in the late nineties.

The first, introductory part, "A study in elective affinity," provides a descriptive basis for the book, including a historical sketch of reggae music, the methodology used for interpreting songs, a short quantitative analysis of reggae charts, and finally a preliminary consideration of the issue of memory, through the case of reggae's own musical memory. The goal of this first part, beyond situating the topic and introducing the reader to reggae music and the Rastafari movement, is to provide a basis for the pertinence of analyzing their point of meeting; in other words, it is an attempt to show the intersections between the music (reggae) and the religious movement (Rastafari). That roots reggae or conscious reggae exists is not an issue for reggae fans; but the extent of the influence of Rastafari on reggae music, and the elaboration of a corpus of songs, proves worthy to think about as a point of departure for this study.

In the second part, "Remembering the past," I will focus on the construction of a collective memory and the (re)interpretation of the past in reggae music. I will show how the time of slavery is recalled and remembered, in articulation with present collective identities that include the formation of a sense of being in diaspora. I will then look at the construction of a religious symbolic kinship, as it appears in reggae music.

In the third part, "Revealing the future," I will turn to the relationship between this rescued past and an imagined future, through the categories of hope and redemption. I will examine how the Rastafari movement builds a religious future and articulates the three temporal tenses—past, present and future—within an apocalyptic conception of history. Finally, I will look at the categories produced, in the present, by the latter, showing that the notions of Good and Evil are dynamically conceptualized to include both profane and sacred time on the basis of an apocalyptic reading of the present.

In the fourth part, "Politicizing redemption," I will analyze the relationship between the sacred and the profane, between the belief in an apocalyptic future and the need for revolution here on earth. I will show that the traditional view of millenarian movements as being passive and escapist—that is, as having a strong other-worldly dimension—is, in the case of the Rastafari movement, mistaken. I will attempt to demonstrate that it is precisely apocalyptic beliefs that induce and nourish a political commitment in the present; hence this fourth part will bring together the second and third parts of the book, by showing that it is precisely the articulation between the past and the future, through the work of memory, that nourishes present actions and thoughts and makes action possible in the present.

In other words, this book will discuss a series of questions that relate to, as Marie-Claire Lavabre would put it, the uses of memory, the uses of history, and the uses of the past. With the exception of the first, introductory, part, each part asks a question, which is essential to the general understanding of memory at work: How is the past remembered in the present? How does remembering the past allow the imagination of the future? How does collective memory participate into the historical grounding of collective identity? And finally, what is the relationship between tradition and revolution, between the recollection of the past and the imagination of the future, between passivity and action? From this case study in what can be seen as memory at work, I will open up on a theoretical problem raised by my empirical case, namely the issue of time and its relationship with memory. I will explore the problems raised by the conceptualization of social time, of the relationship between sacred and profane time, and of the intersection (or lack thereof) between time and memory. My argument will therefore culminate in a theoretical discussion, with which I do not hope to resolve such a complex question as time and memory; rather, I wish to explore some of the alleys in what seems to be a theoretical labyrinth: the relationship between time and memory, sacred and profane, coercion and agency, as well as epistemological issues linked to the rise of memory claims in the contemporary world.

Part I

A study in elective affinity: Music, religion, memory

1

Reggae and Rastafari: A short history

> Some say dem a Jehovah Witness
> Some say dem a Adventist
> Some say dem a Anglican
> I am the Rastaman
> The Wailing Souls, "They don't know Jah," 1977

Reggae music is seldom analyzed without a reference to the Rastafari movement, which makes it difficult to organize a bibliography that would clearly distinguish the works on Rastafari from the ones on reggae. Indeed, even Hepner (1998), who criticizes the space given to reggae in the Rastafari scholarship and calls for studies of Rastafari "through and beyond" reggae, still spends a lot of time speaking about the latter. This is due to the close ties that exist between the religious movement and the music as much as to the methodological choices of scholars. I argue that both reggae and Rastafari can (and should) be studied independently, but also that they can (and should) be studied together; in other words, both approaches are pertinent. For my part, I have chosen to examine the relationship between reggae and Rastafari, using the former as the starting point. This choice implies a focus on the points of contact, on the intersections, between reggae and Rastafari; and on the latter only insofar as it appears in the former.[1]

Speaking of a meeting point between a religious movement and a musical style implies that both also *overflow* this specific space, and have an existence independently of each other. On the Rastafari

---

[1] This is a crucial characteristic of this study, which is not about the Rastafari movement, but about reggae music at the point where it meets Rastafari.

side, there is independence at the level of both the individuals and the movement: not all rastas listen to reggae, and further the specificity of Rastafari is not to be found solely in its attachment to reggae. On the reggae music side, a large part of the musical production does not refer to Rastafari at all—a fact that is widely ignored by many scholars, to echo Hepner. Beyond the double romanticization of reggae music as a socially engaged popular music rooted in Rastafari and of Rastafari as a musicalized, fashionable religious movement, my approach still remains based on the existence of a point of meeting between the two, which, although commonly taken for granted, has rarely been systematically studied. I will argue that one could speak of a relationship of *elective affinity* found between reggae and Rastafari. The term has a long history. It was used in alchemy to express the attraction and fusion of two elements; Goethe transposed it to human beings in his novel *Die Wahlverwandtschaften* (1802), in which he defines it as follows:

> The tendency of those elements which, when they come into contact, at once take hold of, and act on one another, we call "affinity." The alkalis and the acids reveal these affinities in the most striking way—although by nature opposites, perhaps for that very reason they select one another, take hold of and modify each other eagerly; and then together form an entirely new substance. (Goethe 1963: 39)

> And those cases are indeed the most important and remarkable, wherein this attraction, this affinity, this separating and combining, can be demonstrated, the two pairs, as it were, crossing over; where four elements, until then joined in twos, are brought into contact and give up their former combination to enter a new one. In this dissociating and taking possession, this flight and seeking, we actually imagine we see some higher pre-determination; we believe these elements capable of exercising some sort of willpower and selection, and feel perfectly justified in using the term "elective affinities"! (Goethe 1963: 42)

It is with Max Weber that the term came to be developed as a sociological concept, with which he explains the complex relationship between the protestant ethic and capitalism, a relationship that does not involve any clear causality but rather an attraction that draws two kinds of "ethos" to each other (Weber 2002). The notion of elective affinity is one of Weber's great contributions to social thought; with it, he means that there exists some sort of "affinity of meaning" between two "mentalities," between two practical ways of conducting one's life. These two elements are attracted by each other "naturally," as if there was some powerful mutual attraction that drew each to the other; when they come into contact, they attract ineluctably and are able to interact in such a way that the two prior configurations may form a new configuration. We can turn to Goethe once again:

> Imagine an A so closely connected with a B that the two cannot be separated by any means, not even by force; and imagine a C in the same relation to a D. Now bring the two pairs into contact. A will fling itself on D, and C on B, without our being able to say which left the other first, or which first combined itself with the other. (Goethe 1963: 43)

Once the mutual attraction that draws the two elements to one another has produced a new configuration, it becomes impossible to say which has influenced the other, and to what extent. The two elements are in a situation of elective affinity—that is, their relationship is multi-directional. No exclusive unidirectional causal relationship can be distinguished. A relationship of elective affinity implies that there is a special affinity, a special attraction between two "practical systems of value" that enrich each other in a very complex, and rich, way. Michael Löwy offers the following definition: "It is the process by which two cultural forms (religious, literary, political, economic, etc), on the basis of some analogies or structural correspondences, enter a relationship of reciprocated influence, mutual choice, convergence, symbiosis, and even in some case fusion."[2] I would argue, then, for a relationship of elective affinity between a religious form and a musical form, namely the Rastafari movement and reggae music; indeed, we witness two independent cultural forms that have an existence of their own, but also a point at which these two forms meet; and this point of meeting has come from, indeed, a "special attraction," an affinity that seemed natural and ineluctable; in turn, it has produced such a complex relationship

---

2   Löwy 1999: 44. "Il s'agit du processus par lequel deux formes culturelles—religieuses, littéraires, politiques, économiques, etc.—entrent, à partir de certaines analogies ou correspondences structurelles, en un rapport d'influence réciproque, choix mutuel, convergence, symbiose et même, dans certains cas, fusion."

that it has become difficult to say which cultural form has influenced the other first, or most. In this first chapter, I will briefly give an historical account of both cultural forms, by focusing on their point of meeting. In chapter 2, I will describe the methodology I have used to select and analyze the material that forms the basis of my analysis. In chapter 3, I will test the validity of looking at the relationship between reggae music and the Rastafari movement by analyzing the evolution of Jamaican reggae charts since the early seventies. Finally, in chapter 4, I will introduce the issue of memory by analyzing the construction of a musical memory within reggae music.

A brief account of Rastafari

The founding event of the Rastafari movement was the coronation of Haile Selassie, Emperor of Ethiopia, which took place on November 2, 1930. In Jamaica, some interpreted it as the fulfillment of the prophecy announced by Marcus Garvey before his departure for the United States: "Look to Africa when a Black king shall be crowned, for the day of deliverance is near." Four Jamaicans started preaching: Howell in West Kingston, Hibbert and Hinds in the parish of St. Andrew, and Dunkley in Port Antonio.[3] All four essentially raised the question of the identity of God and affirmed his blackness: this

---

[3] Leonard Howell (1898–1981), influenced by Garvey and Padmore, founded a community of believers, first in St. Thomas in 1933, then in the parish of St. Catherine in 1940, at Pinnacle Estate. Life at Pinnacle, organized under the charismatic leadership of Howell, was based on collective work; although founded in a spirit of self-sustainability, the community had relationships with the outside world (for school, business, and to vote). It was destroyed by the police in 1941 because of cannabis culture, rebuilt in 1943, and then finally dismantled in 1954; meanwhile, Howell and other members were jailed on a regular basis. Joseph Hibbert, who lived in Costa Rica for a while and whose doctrine was greatly influenced by occultism, and Archibald Dunkley, who preached in Port Antonio, are less well known. What is certain is that both made the link between Garveyism and the coronation of Selassie, and had disciples. As for Robert Hinds, who admired Bedward and Garvey, he founded the "King of Kings Mission," organized like a Revival group and of which one of the most important rituals was baptism. As early as the 1940s, internal problems, mostly in terms of leadership, caused the Mission to lose many members. It is worth noting that "all four leaders ... ruled over their organization with charismatic authority. Hinds was the only one to share authority with his lieutenants" (Chevannes 1994: 142).

was the great innovation of the Rastafari movement compared to other religious movements of this era, an innovation that directly attacked the colonial Christian God. At the end of the forties, following the widespread rural exodus, the faith expanded to the ghettos of Kingston, such as Back'O'Wall and Trenchtown, where some members of Howell's dispersed community settled. Young rastas then moved away from existing groups and emphasized the notion of "spiritual struggle";[4] according to Chevannes (1994: 152–170), the major difference between "traditional" rastas and these youth, whom he calls "dreadlocks," was the aggressive position the latter adopted against the surrounding world, which they called Babylon; he argues that, hostile to any hierarchy and institution, they established the foundations of the contemporary Rastafari movement.[5]

Rastafari remained marginal until the seventies, when it benefited from the international success of reggae music, which made it known beyond Jamaica; today, from Harlem to Brixton, from Dakar to Tokyo, from Trenchtown to La Chapelle, one can see men, women and children with red, gold and green garments, wearing their hair in dread locks. Academic inquiry followed the same pattern: the work of Simpson in the fifties was followed by a report written by scholars from the University of the West Indies in Jamaica; however, in the seventies, several scholars showed an interest in this seemingly strange and paradoxical religious movement that considers the Emperor of Ethiopia a messiah, associates the West with Babylon the Great, promotes the use of "ganja," calls on the war against oppressors as much as universal peace, and expresses itself in a language which plays with words and is filled with metaphors, parables, and mystical and biblical symbols. The contemporary scholarship on the Rastafari movement is widespread, and cuts across disciplines. The works produced are very diverse, due to the different fields involved but also because the Rastafari movement seems inherently resistant

---

[4] *Nyabinghi*, a ritual based on Burru dances and drums in which God is invoked to kill oppressors, appeared at this time. The term *nyabinghi* originated in an African religious movement from the Great Lakes region, which resisted the Europeans until the 1930s.

[5] In the fifties one of them took the lead of a community: Prince Emmanuel and his group of "Bobo Shanti," who settled in Ackee Walk until 1968, then in Rose Town, Trenchtown, and finally Bull Bay, where they still live today. It is worth noting that several contemporary reggae artists, such as Anthony B or Sizzla, claim links to the Bobo Shanti.

to any easy attempt at classification: it has simultaneous religious, political, social and cultural dimensions; it is closely linked with a popular music, reggae, but has also developed its own music, Rastafarian chants. Moreover, its polymorphous character implies a great variety within the movement itself. It is characterized by a quasi-complete absence of institutions (Yawney 1976, Chevannes 1994, Cashmore 1994, Homiak 1995): while there exist a few organizations, such as the Twelve Tribes of Israel or the Nyabinghi Order, there is no equivalent of a clergy, nor are there any official theologians. Consequently, within their own group rastas retain a freedom of thought that leads to a great variability of practices and even beliefs. As Cashmore notes, Rastafari's "dynamic is in its heterogeneity of commitment and expression ... No one will ever create a definite version of what Rastas *should* believe" (Cashmore 1994: 193; emphasis in the original). Therefore, two scholars can work in two different locations and come up with two "versions" of the Rastafari movement that might contradict each other but nonetheless accurately represent two of its facets.

Some scholars have proposed an analysis centered on religion, usually based on the Jamaican case (Owens 1976, Johnson-Hill 1994) and focused on sacred practices, and the beliefs in which they are grounded. As Chevannes notes (1994: 20), Rastafari has been variously described as escapist, nativist, millenarian, visionary, or as a revitalization movement; although it indeed possesses millenarian tendencies, Chevannes holds that a strict focus on Rastafari's religious dimension limits analysis. To be sure, the dynamic character of the movement tends to elude these religious approaches because they are usually based on the study of communities that can be considered as the religious side of Rastafari, and therefore do not take into account the multitude of individuals who adhere to the movement without belonging to any specific group. However, their detailed analysis of symbolic processes, of the construction of the movement's own concepts, and of the elaboration of a worldview and its interaction with practices, make these studies extremely valuable. Edmond's recent book stands out by its analysis centered on Weber's ideal-type of charismatic authority and its routinization; he attempts to show that Rastafari can be seen as a movement which has routinized in the "third way" mentioned by Weber—that is, "routinization as cultural formation" (Edmonds 2003: 26). This work stands at the crossroads between studies which focus on religion, and those which see Rastafari as a cultural and social movement.

In contrast with the religion-focused approach, other scholars have considered the Rastafari movement from a socio-political standpoint, emphasizing its historical emergence in relation to a context of domination and its articulation around the key notion of liberation; these works usually concern the Jamaican case, and often represent a Marxist approach, using terms such as neo-colonialism, social stratification, economic deprivation and racial prejudice (Llewelyn-Watson 1973 and 1974, Campbell 1980b and 1985, Lewis 1986 and 1994). Llewelyn-Watson, for instance, compared Rastafari and the Nation of Islam, and concluded that

> religion *per se* is not their major attraction. Both are social protests which move on a semi-religious vehicle, with emphasis on social action geared to transforming their objective life situations ... close examination of these movements reveal that they are, among other things, the stirrings of socio-political movements explicable in terms of the *logic of the social situation*." (1973: 199, 201; emphasis in the original)

Others have proposed an analysis of Rastafari as sub-culture: these were mostly British scholars who worked in urban neighborhoods such as Brixton in London or Handsworth in Birmingham and looked at both reggae and Rastafari (Cashmore 1979b, Hebdige 1979, Back 1996). For Caribbean scholars, it is essential to situate the Rastafari movement within a socio-cultural history of the Caribbean—which implies that one must locate the continuities between Africa and Caribbean cultural constructs as well as in between Rastafari and ulterior religious movements; Alleyne, for instance, produced a remarkable work on the formation of Caribbean culture and the persistence of traditions of African origin within Jamaican religious movements (Alleyne 1988). Chevannes, in his analysis of Rastafari and Revival, proposes to consider the movement as an "African-derived religion in Jamaica and the Caribbean" that should be considered the "fulfillment" of Revival and understood as a "worldview" and a "cultural movement" (1994: 38-39).

After forty years of extensive scholarship on Rastafari, most authors agree that Rastafari is a religious and socio-political movement of resistance (Campbell 1985), which possesses a revolutionary strength (underestimated by Cashmore 1979b), the ability to create an original culture (Cashmore 1983, Hurbon 1986, Taylor 1990, Chevannes 1994) and to build a "black" identity (Nettleford 1972, Cashmore 1983, Hurbon 1986) that articulates ethnic and diasporic dimensions. By taking into account its relationship with reggae music, it seems correct to say that Rastafari has become a full trans-Caribbean cultural element, as emphasized by Tafari (1980), Campbell (1980a), and especially Besson (1995b: 310), who argues that "Rastafari is also advancing a pan-Caribbean creole identity out of a tradition of cultural resistance"; additionally, it has been able to flourish outside of the Caribbean space, and to appeal to individuals from every culture, color, or class.

Indeed, the great turning point in the evolution of the Rastafari movement took place at the end of the sixties. In 1962, Jamaica gained independence, an event that provoked a social and political explosion that resulted in a phase of intense cultural creativity together with the idea of freedom and the affirmation of Jamaican identity. This period gave birth to reggae music, which has since become one of the strongest emblems of Jamaica. It is rare to find a relationship between a young profane musical style and an already existing religious movement as fitting and fruitful as the one between reggae and Rastafari. Because popular music and rastas coexisted in the same neighborhoods, they quickly came together; but it is only with reggae music that the relationship became so close-knit that it is difficult to say which one influenced the other, at which point and in which direction, although they remained autonomous from each other and the tightness of the relationship fluctuated in time. What is certain is that reggae helped Rastafari to cross social, racial, and national boundaries, and therefore to emerge out of the marginal status it had occupied until the seventies. This relationship might have allowed each to survive, the former by providing a medium of communication and identification to the latter, and the latter by giving an irreplaceable ideological, social and cultural basis to the former.

The birth of reggae music

It is well known that Caribbean musical styles mix European and African musical traditions. But they are not a simple agglomerate of these traditions: they are original creations which, by the end of the nineteenth century, were already stabilized as genres, and have become specific constructs which are not European nor African, but Caribbean. Today, with increasing mobility and communication, musical exchanges are even easier and enrich already existing genres; musical styles now mix without losing their own specificity, giving birth to new categories (merengue-rap, samba-reggae, etc). As Manuel says, the Caribbean is therefore characterized by a paradox between unity and diversity. It is formed on the basis of three distinct linguistic ensembles, and still "the entire region shares a set of basic sociomusical attributes, including the presence of an Afro-Caribbean cultural common denominator; a history of musical syncretization; the strength of oral traditions; and the emergence of lower-class, African-influenced worksongs, religious musics, Carnival traditions, and creole, duplemetered dance-music genres" (Manuel 1995: 233). Religious rituals of African origin (including Yoruba, Fon, Ashanti, Congo, but also Bantu), which make a central use of drums, have deeply influenced Caribbean popular music.[6]

The term *reggae* is commonly used to designate the music that emerged in Jamaica at the end of the 1960s, and in which the most famous artist is Bob Marley. It is characterized by the prominence and freedom of the bass line, and by a back-beat rhythmic guitar (sometimes replaced by a piano or keyboard). Reggae is the product of multiple influences: African percussion (Burru drums)[7] and

---

[6] Examples of recordings concerning Jamaica include *Drums of Defiance: Maroon Music from the Earliest Free Black Communities in Jamaica*, Smithsonian/Folkways, and *From Kongo to Zion: Three Black Musical Traditions from Jamaica*, Heartbeat Records.

[7] Burru drums include the fundeh and bass drums, which provide the rhythmic foundation on which the repeater plays solo. According to Reckord (1977: 13), the Burru structure is found in reggae music, the bass line corresponding to the bass drum, the rhythmic guitar to the fundeh, and the solo guitar to the repeater. Rastafarian chants, as they have developed since the forties, mix Burru percussions, other instruments such as the harmonica or tambourin, and religious songs usually of Protestant origin with modified words. Count Ossie is a good example of this fusion. According to Reckord (1977: 11), the bass drum symbolizes the end of oppression; the fundeh, with its soft binary rhythmic, peace and love; and the repeater symbolizes struggle, since it defies through its solos the order set by the bass and fundeh drums. Constant (1982: 48) argues that Rastafarian chants can be said to be "nothing but a development of Burru rhythms. The musical structure is the same." And for Zips (1994: 46), the Kromanti songs of the Burru and Kumina drums, the maroon chants that they accompany, rasta music and reggae music, are part

Rastafarian chants, North-American rhythm'n'blues, Jamaican mento,[8] as well as diverse folk traditions linked to religion (Myal, Pukumina) or to work (slaves' worksongs); but it is to the tradition of sound-systems that reggae music owes its birth. During the World War II, American troops were stationed in Jamaica, and brought their music with them, in particular New Orleans jazz, characterized by its back beat. After the troops' departure in the forties, Jamaicans invented the sound systems, which traveled around the island and featured a "selector," who played the records, accompanied by an assistant who introduced the songs and encouraged the audience. In fact, the major goal of the sound system is to make people dance. Each sound system has its own sound, and therefore its own fans; it is "just like a mobile club, and people follow it wherever it plays" (Back 1987: 214). Among the first sound systems were Clement Dodd's *Coxsone Downbeat* and Dickie Wong's *Dickie's Dynamic*. The fast success of sound systems had three main consequences for the Jamaican music scene: first, a massive production of single records, because, unlike albums, they are played in sound systems; second, a great number of singers on the local scene; and third, a predilection for technical manipulation and post-recording mixing, over live music. Chude-Sokei (1994: 96) has also remarked that "sound systems are one of the black diaspora's most enduring and frequently unacknowledged cultural institutions," although they possess numerous and varied social functions (Stolzoff 2000) and are essential to reggae music, not only because they have assumed an increasing importance with the success of reggae dancehall since the mid-eighties, but also because it is through them new songs are first played, and new artists discovered. Moreover, they have played a central role in the evolution of styles and techniques: for instance, the movement of sound-engineers from their sound systems' turntables to recording studios' mixing desks resulted in the birth of ska, rock steady and then reggae, and the development of dub.

At the end of the fifties, the owners of the biggest sound

---

of the same ensemble characterized by "the collective remembrance of Africa, as well as by their defiance against European cultural colonization."

[8] Mento is a sort of Jamaican rural calypso with a syncope on the last beat of each measure, which appeared in the forties and was at first played with cheap instruments (spoons, bottles, rhumba box) to which were added banjo, flute, guitar, violin, and percussion; in the fifties, it started being recorded in studios, in particular by Laurel Aitken.

systems—such as Duke Reid, King Edwards or Clement "Coxsone" Dodds—became producers; they hired local musicians in order to record their own music without having to import it from the USA. Between 1960 and 1963, in Coxsone's *Studio One*, a new sound emerged: it was called *ska*, and was characterized by a rhythmic guitar that accentuates the beat, and a strong use of the brass section and piano, usually in a big-band formation.[9] Around 1965, ska gave way to *rock steady*, which had a slower rhythmic pulse and gave less importance to the brass section and more to the bass guitar and drums.[10] Rock steady was already a prefiguration of reggae, especially felt in the slower tempo; at the end of the sixties, reggae progressively emerged, with a slower rhythm, a back-beat guitar, and an all-important rhythmic structure; ska's big bands were replaced by small ensembles. In 1968, with the release of "Do the reggay," Toots & the Maytals were the first to use the term in a recording.[11]

The generic term *roots reggae* is used to designate the major part of reggae recordings between 1970 and 1981, characterized by a particular sound (the classical formation is rhythm guitar, bass guitar and drums, to which can be added solo guitar, piano, percussions, or a brass section) and a strong socio-political commitment, closely tied to Rastafari. Indeed, most artists, producers, or sound-engineers were also proclaimed rastafarians, or sympathizers. Roots reggae raises a large range of socio-political, religious, and identity issues, as well as the more traditional ones of love and sex. The seventies were characterized by the stabilization of reggae as a specific musical genre, a profusion of new artists and the recognition of older ones, the extension to an international audience, and a strong presence in Jamaican socio-political life. Additionally, "British" reggae emerged, with bands like Aswad in London or Steel Pulse in Birmingham.

---

[9] Recommended ska recordings: *Intensified: Original Ska 1962–1966* and *More Intensified: Original Ska, 1963–1967*, Island; *Ska Bonanza: The Studio One Ska Years*, Heartbeat; The Skatalites, *Ska Authentic*, Studio One.
[10] For rock steady: *Duke Reid's Treasure Chest*, Heartbeat; Bob Andy, *Song Book*, Coxsone; Ken Boothe, *A Man and his Hits*, Studio One; The Heptones, *On Top*, Studio One; Delroy Wilson, *Original Twelve*, Coxsone.
[11] For early reggae: *The Harder They Come*, original soundtrack, Island; Alton Ellis, *Sunday Coming*, Studio One; Dennis Brown, *No Man is an Island*, Studio One; Burning Spear, *Rocking Time*, Studio One; Toots & the Maytals, *Do the Reggae 1966–1970*, Attack; Dennis Alcapone, *My Voice is Insured for Half a Million*, Trojan.

Different styles can be distinguished within this period, beyond the difference that exists between the Jamaican and English sounds: they were linked to a specific period (for example *rockers* between 1975 and 1978), but also to the originality of each sound-engineer and producer (for example Augustus Pablo, King Tubby, Lee Perry, or Prince Jammy); additionally, a group of musicians was hired full-time by each studio (Channel One, Randy's Dynamic, Black Ark), and there is therefore a particular character to different artists' recordings.[12]

Dubbing is a must

Around 1965–1966, during the peak of rock steady, Coxsone and Studio One started releasing records without brass solos, which were called *riddim solos* because the rhythmic track completely replaced the solos. Clarke (1980) says that their release was due to the fact that the solo musician did not show up for the recording session, and that producers had decided to release the record as it was in order not to lose money. These riddim solos were very successful, and Duke Reid then released two recordings of "Girl I've got a date," which had a specific sound due to the guitar that "played a bass line."[13] Here can be found the beginnings of *dub*, which was originally a recording without solos. Hebdige, for his part, suggests that King Tubby created dub, almost inadvertently, while mixing songs for Coxsone:

> he began fading out the instrumental track, to make sure that the vocals sounded right. And he was excited by the effect produced when he brought the music back in. So instead of mixing ... in a usual way, he cut back and forth between the vocal and instrumental tracks and played with the bass and treble knobs until he changed the original tapes into something else entirely. These were the first ever dub records ... By the late 1960s, Bunny Lee was putting a dub "version" of the title track on the flip side of all his singles. (Hebdige 1987: 83)

---

12 In particular Robbie Shakespeare, Lloyd Parks or Aston Barrett (bass guitar), Sly Dunbar or Carlton Barrett (drums), Earl Smith (rhythmic guitar), Augustus Pablo (melodica), Vin Gordon (trombone), Tommy Mc Cook (tenor saxophone).
13 Jackie Mittoo, interview with S. Clarke, July 1978, in Clarke 1980.

Regardless which story is most accurate, the emergence of dub was tied to the development of sound systems, which combined the fading out of vocals with special effects (echo and reverberation) on the records they played; dub was born when sound-engineers started to reproduce these techniques in recording studios. In 1970, King Tubby recorded some combinations of bass and drums for Dodd's sound system, which could be played as *versions* for artists to talk over, as he says himself: "Dub mean raw riddim. Dub jus' mean raw music."[14] It is King Tubby again who mixed the first record to be composed of bass and drums only: "Psalms of Dub," with Lloyd Parks at the bass guitar. Lee Perry and Bunny Lee then started to work on dub mixing and to release dub versions as well as dub originals.

The birth of dub is also due to the existence, as early as in the mid-sixties, of an instrumental side, called *version*, on the B-side of single recordings, which became both a tradition and a necessity for sound systems.[15] Today, singles still have a vocal version on the A-side and an instrumental version on the B-side; on 12-inch records, the vocal version is usually extended ("extended version")— that is, followed by a dub version without any cut in between the two.[16] In the seventies, with technical progress in recording studios (especially when it comes to mixing tables), new manipulations became possible; the distinctive genius of sound-engineers—such as Lee Perry, King Tubby, Prince Jammy, or Errol Thompson—made dub possible: the "sound" that characterized each of them not only influenced roots reggae, but, as Veal's excellent and long overdue history of dub shows (Veal 2007), developed dub into a genre of its own, no longer limited to B-sides, that includes the production of both singles and albums.[17]

---

[14] King Tubby, quoted by Barrow on the jacket of "Dub gone crazy, 1975–1979," Blood & Fire 1994.
[15] Indeed, sound systems need versions to be "talked over," as well as vinyl records since they use turntables.
[16] For example the song "Love thy neighbour" by Vivian Jackson & the Defenders (on the album *Jesus Dread 1972–1977*, disc 1, song 1) and its dub version remixed by King Tubby (disc 2, song 22).
[17] For dub: King Tubby and Augustus Pablo, *King Tubby Meets Rockers Uptown*; Keith Hudson, *Pick a Dub*; Joe Gibbs & the Professionals, *Majestic Dub*; Lee Perry & the Upsetters, *Kung Fu Meets the Dragon*.

Reggae since 1980: The emergence of reggae dancehall
Originally, at the time of rhythm'n'blues, the selector's assistant "scatted" while records played, in order to encourage dancers. The term "scat" originated with Louis Armstrong, who vocally accompanied music as an instrument would. As time passed by—with the emergence of ska, rock steady and then reggae, the development of "riddims" (the musical versions recorded for sound systems) and finally of digital reggae in the 1980s—the function of the assistant who was "talking over" music expanded to the point of creating a specific style, and of having "dee-jays" enter the recording industry. Reggae dancehall then became "primordial within Jamaican music" (Stolzoff 2000: 100).[18] Talk over and then reggae dancehall therefore evolved in parallel with roots reggae, but both are linked and interdependent. The influence of Rastafari was less strong within reggae dancehall, especially during the eighties, as *slackness*[19] became dominant (Chude-Sokei 1994, Cooper 1995 and 2004, Stolzoff 2000, Hope 2006). Incidentally, the death of Bob Marley in 1981 coincided with a stylistic turn in reggae music: roots reggae was progressively replaced by digital reggae, characterized by the absence of instruments: electronic sounds replaced the instruments, and the rhythmic was created on "riddim boxes."[20] Simultaneously, reggae dancehall developed enormously; the lyrics echoed the increasing violence of Jamaican society, and reggae music refocused on pleasure and dance, instead of the socio-political message it had conveyed before.

At the time, some saw in this the end of the alliance between reggae music and the Rastafari movement. But this retreat from mass media attention, accompanied by an almost complete disappearance of socio-political content in reggae lyrics, began to weaken at the beginning of the nineties. Beyond the continuous success of "old" roots reggae bands, there has indeed been a revival of Rastafari among younger artists, especially within reggae dancehall.[21] If a

---

[18] For talk-over: Big Youth, *Dreadlocks Dread*, Virgin; U Roy, *Dread Inna Babylon*, Virgin. For reggae dancehall: the compilations *Strictly The Best* or *Jet Star Reggae Hits*.
[19] In reggae music, the term "slackness" (from "slack," obscene) is used for lyrics focused on sex and violence.
[20] The first digital reggae song was "Under me sleng teng," produced by King Jammy.
[21] This appears in the analysis of reggae charts, in a following chapter.

specific moment has to be found for this turn, it would probably be Buju Banton's song "Murderer," one of the hits of 1993, which appears to call for a return to Rastafari, expressed by the critique of violence and reference to the Bible.[22] This revival of Rastafari within reggae dancehall is particularly significant, because it is symptomatic of the vitality of the movement among youth (born during the seventies and the eighties), but also because reggae dancehall has always been, precisely, the musical space least attached to the sociopolitical and religious message of reggae music.

---

[22] To the Ten Commandments, and Psalm 23: "Murderer your inside must be hollow / how does it feel to take the life of another / why did you disobey the first commandment / walk through the valley I fear no pestilence / God is my witness and He is my evidence / lift up mine eyes from whence cometh help / you will never escape this judgement." Buju Banton, "Murderer," 1993.

2

Interpreting songs: Notes on methodology

Since the 1960s, popular music has developed enormously, largely due to technological progress in terms of musical delivery (vinyl records, cassettes, compact discs, minidisc, MP3 and so on) and to the proliferation of radio stations, television, and more recently personal computers (Jones 2000). Popular music gives a central importance to singing, and therefore to lyrics; from Otis Redding's love songs to The Police's "Roxanne" to the poetic texts of Bob Dylan to the seemingly innocuous blues of Muddy Waters, the vocal part is an essential component of popular songs—even when it is not particularly elaborated, poetic, politically engaged, or not very meaningful. In this chapter, I reflect on a very simple question: How do we, as sociologists of music, analyze songs and interpret lyrics? The analysis of lyrics is not a new phenomenon; Frith (1987: 77) reminds us that in the fifties and the sixties it was actually the principal activity of sociologists of popular music in the United States: they worked on the songs themselves, and were not concerned with the artists or their audiences. Because the great majority of popular songs have the general category of "love" as their main theme, popular music is often considered simple and banal, and even, at times, as a new "opium of the people." However, popular music has also often been the soundtrack of protest movements, if only because it represents the people as opposed to the elite: blues, rock, folk, soul, reggae, rap, and so on, are all musical styles which affirm a "different" identity, even when they do not maintain a strong tie with social or political movements nor transmit an ideological message through their lyrics. Even love songs can be regarded as

Interpreting songs: Notes on methodology

symptomatic of society and as reflecting its social and political conflicts and evolutions. As Mooney said in the fifties, "pop music reflects, as love songs always did, the currents of thought; because when values change, then the ideas and practices concerning love do as well" (1954: 226). In his view, popular music expresses the "emotional needs" of an epoch: he goes on to trace the evolution of American society through a content analysis of popular music. Between 1895 and 1925, patriotic and working-class songs reflect the construction of the young American nation; between 1930 and 1945, "negative and rather morbid" texts accompany the disenchantment provoked by the Great Depression and World War II; finally, in the fifties, pop music echoes the optimism of the baby boom. As Frith points out, Mooney's "general hypothesis is that songs can be *read as examples of popular ideology*" (1987: 79; emphasis added). While the idea that popular music expresses social attitudes, values, or even a "popular ideology" can seem obvious today, analyzing the content of songs remains the source of numerous methodological problems.

Is what they sing important?

One problem in the analysis of songs is the *a priori* correspondence asserted between a song and its audience, the latter being understood as fully agreeing with the content of the song, although this is not necessarily true: how could one prove that all the individuals who buy a given record agree, completely, with the content of the song? In the case of reggae music, can one say that all the people who buy a song by Sizzla are close to the beliefs not only of Rastafari but, more specifically, of the Bobo Shanti? Or can one say that all those who dance to a slackness song share the image of women conveyed by the song? The answer, of course, is no. Popular music is music before anything else, and in the case of reggae music it is also deeply rooted in dance: a song will be popular when it is able to make people dance, independently of its lyrical content. Moreover, while it is possible to specify a message conveyed by music, it remains difficult to infer the degree to which it is received and shared by the audience.

Love songs still form the majority of the music charts, and this is true for reggae as well. The analysis that I have made of Jamaican reggae charts shows this quantitative domination; and the distinction made by Peatman between three categories of love songs ("happy love," "unhappy love," and "love with sexual connotation," cited in Frith 1987: 78) remains valid today. The goal of my analysis of reggae charts is to observe the evolution of socio-political engagement within reggae, as well as the link with Rastafari. It would be easy to describe both as minimal, since there is almost always a majority of love songs, but one has to keep in mind that reggae makes up most of Jamaican popular music and that it would therefore be unimaginable that it did not produce love songs. Even without looking exclusively at the charts, reggae albums are rarely without a love song; this is true even for the most politically engaged artists, from Bob Marley to Black Uhuru to Buju Banton, who all sing about love and sex, simply because it is a major part of everybody's life, a traditional theme which has always been expressed in words and music, and which is likely to survive all styles and fashions.

Some of the main criticisms made of popular music concern its banality, its repetitiveness, and its extensive use of clichés. One good example is the contrast made between "popular" and "folk" music, the latter being often considered as a noble and authentic genre, in a way the "high end" of a popular music. This is well illustrated by the vocabulary used to speak of folk and popular music, respectively: within the former, the repetitive use of verbal forms and expressions does not constitute a cliché, but a *marker*, "the anonymous, spontaneous, communal process by which folk songs are created" (Frith 1987: 86), which Lloyd (1975) calls "lyrical floaters." I will not dwell on the reasons for the hierarchy made by some scholars between different forms of popular music, or within music itself. But Frith's comments concerning folk music are very interesting when it comes to reggae music, which seems to make extensive use of those markers or "lyrical floaters." They concern an ensemble of recurrent verbal forms, a way of speaking and singing, that constitute markers, of which three main categories can be distinguished: those which primarily come from reggae itself (from a sort of "reggae tradition of making music"), those which come from Rastafari, and those which come from Jamaican culture, in particular proverbs and sayings.

The first category is formed by reggae's specific vocabulary—that is, expressions such as "wheel up" (to play a song again from the beginning) or "killer" (a term used to claim the quality of an artist or song). The use of this vocabulary is characteristic of, and specific to, reggae music, and is often part of the technique used to record or play reggae music (for example see the intro to Paul Elliott's song

"Save me oh Jah," 1999). This first category also features a certain way of structuring the vocal part of the song, with repetition of the first verse at the end of the song: Intro / Chorus / Verse 1 / Chorus / Verse 2 / Chorus / ... / Verse 1 / Chorus. The presence of an intro is typical; usually spoken and sometimes sung, it introduces the song. For example, the intro to Anthony B's song "Raid di barn" (1996) is "Emperor Selassie I / Jah Jah is the only raid," in reference to the song itself, of which the chorus is "nobody waan to plant di corn / everybody waan to raid di barn." In Garnett Silk's "Lion heart" (1994), the song is introduced by "When the lion roars / oh jungle trembles / I know, jungle trembles." The lion here represents conscious reggae, as well as Garnett Silk himself (as opposed to "the dogs"), both being supposed to "rule"—that is, to be better. The intro can also be a dedication, which can be nominative or not; this practice is typical of reggae sound systems and concerts, in which it is used in the form of the call-and-response to install intimacy between the artist and the audience. Often, the intro is used to set up a distinction between "us" and "them," as a prerequisite to the song, for instance in "Hello mama Africa" (Anthony B, Buju Banton, and Garnett Silk, 1999). Countless examples could be given; the practice, now generalized to studio-recorded reggae, has come from the sound systems, in which the artist or the song was introduced as part of the communication between the audience and the artist. Indeed, sound systems work fundamentally through the approval or disapproval of the audience, which decides which songs must keep on or stop being played, or even be played again, and which artists must stay on or leave the stage; therefore, the sound system is above all an act of communication between the audience and the artist.

The second category features expressions that originated within the Rastafari movement: the *dread talk* vocabulary, for instance the use of terms like "overstanding" (instead of "understanding") or "downpressors" (instead of "oppressors") and of the "I-words" like Ital, Irie, Inity, etc., as well as the vocabulary linked to Rastafari religious beliefs, for instance terms like "Selassie I" or "Jah Rastafari." The use of this vocabulary is also often present with artists who are not rastas, which shows how strong the influence of Rastafari on reggae has been. One also finds borrowings from the biblical form of the English language, for instance "praise yeh Jah" (Sizzla), "He liveth over I and I" (Luciano), "Our father who art in Zion" (Buju Banton), etc. This use of the English of the Bible is a direct consequence of the centrality of the biblical text for the rastas, who read the Bible on a daily basis and often learn passages by heart. We will see later how not only the *form* but also the *content* of the Bible appears in reggae songs, through extensive quotes of the Bible, in particular from the Psalms (chapter 6).

Finally, another interesting marker is the frequent use of proverbs and sayings, which often come from the Bible as well, as shown in box 2.1.[1]

Box 2.1: Examples of proverbs used in reggae lyrics

- *The hotter the battle, the sweeter the victory*: in Vivian Jackson & the Prophets' "Run come rally" (1975: "The hotter the battle is, the sweeter Jah victory") or Bob Marley & the Wailers' "The heathen" (1977).

- *What comes around, goes around*: in Bob Marley & the Wailers' "So much trouble in the world" (1979: "now they sitting on a time bomb / now I know the time has come / what goes on up is coming on down / goes around and comes around") or Aswad's "Concrete slaveship" (1976: "what goes up must come down / what goes around always comes around").

- *The table is turning*: in Bob Marley & the Wailers' "Slave driver" (1973).

- *Who the cap fit, let them wear it*: in Bob Marley & the Wailers' "Who the cap fit" (1976) or Anthony B's "Cover your tracks" (1999: "nah call no fowl even though mi throw corn / seh who the cap fit tell dem put it on").

- *In the abundance of water, the fool is thirsty*: in Bob Marley & the Wailers' "Rat race" (1976: "don't forget your history, know your destiny / in the abundance of water the fool is thirsty").

- *Still waters run deep*: in Steel Pulse's "Tribute to the martyrs" (1979: "they are telling me silent waters run deep / so their knowledge I'll always seek").

- *As a man sow, so shall he reap*: In Bob Marley & the Wailers' "The heathen" (1977: "as a man sow, shall he reap / and I know that talk is cheap").

---

[1] These examples are taken from my corpus of songs. For a more extensive sample and analysis of proverbs in reggae music, see Prahlad 2001.

- *What is to be, must be*: In Bob Marley & the Wailers' "I shot the sheriff" (1976: "Reflexes had the better of me / and what is to be must be").
- *A wolf in sheep's clothing*: in Stevie Culture's "No more" (1998: "we don't want no more / no more / wolf inna sheep clothing") or Sizzla's "Hail Selassie" (1997).
- *He that fights and run away may live to fight another day*: In Bob Marley & the Wailers' "The heathen" (1977: "Rise up fallen fighters / rise and take your stands again / cause he who fight and run away / live to fight another day").
- *You never miss the water till the wells runs dry*: in Bob Marley & the Wailers' "Could you be loved" (1980), or Rod Taylor's "Look before you leap" (1979).
- *All that glitters is not gold / Looks is deceiving*: in The Gladiators' "Look is deceiving" (1976), Bob Marley & the Wailers' "Get up stand up" (1973), or Aswad's "Not guilty" (1979).
- *The big fish eat the small fish*: in Vivian Jackson & the Prophets' "Covetous men" (1975).

In his extensive study of proverbs in reggae music, Prahlad mentions several functions they assume; in particular, he speaks of "the power of proverbs in modern societies," especially "among societies in the African Diaspora" (2001: 205). Linked to Jamaican English and patois, these markers (from reggae itself, the Rastafari movement, and Jamaican proverbs) contribute in forging a language specific to reggae music, a way of speaking that traces boundaries between the inside and the outside. It is worth noting that Jamaican oral popular culture is present in reggae music through its extensive use of traditional sayings and references to Jamaican culture; it is not only *what* the lyrics say about society, it is also about *how* they say it. Additionally, this presence is an illustration of the function assumed by reggae music as a vehicle of reproduction, construction and maintenance of oral popular culture: a vehicle of transmission that, despite its internationalization, remains strongly attached to the culture from which it emerged. Edmonds' work on the cultural routinization of the Rastafari movement (2003) also points to the double penetration of Jamaican society by both reggae music and Rastafari. Moreover, reggae music is at the same time *product* and *producer* of Jamaican popular culture, and is considered and considers itself as representing Jamaica. This is an essential point: what appears here is a double movement functioning through identification and attribution, and through the existence of a cultural lineage: it is a matter both of tracing a cultural evolution (where reggae comes from and how it has evolved) and of observing the identifications and attributions of meaning, which work the other way around, from the audience (and the artists) towards the musical style. This basic hypothesis might appear simple; however, it has fundamental implications, in particular for the understanding of culture, not as an ensemble of distinct elements, but as a dynamic system which works by inheritance as much as by attribution. In the end, it is similar to a conception of memory as a double movement from the past to the present ("inheritance") and from the present to the past ("attribution"). More specifically in the case of reggae, it allows the analysis of reggae lyrics to be carried more thoroughly, by taking into account the dynamic movements that take place between music, global culture, Rastafari, and the audience. It allows an understanding of the complexity of these movements, of the different levels of their mutual influences, of the function of transmission assumed by reggae music towards the Rastafari movement, without being limited to it.

What they sing, or how they sing it?

One important issue in lyric analysis concerns the object of inquiry. Song lyrics are usually analyzed without taking into account their relationship with the vocal and musical performance (which can emphasize a word, or bring an emotional mark to a text otherwise neutral, etc). The issue here, of course, concerns both the pertinence of analyzing song lyrics independently of the musical content (i.e. as a text) and in the analysis of the text itself.

 Cooper notes how difficult it is to analyze reggae lyrics when they are detached from the music they accompany, or which accompanies them; however, she also argues that Bob Marley's very strength lies in the fact that, even when detached from the music, his texts retain their power of allusion (1995: 118). All lyrics, whatever the musical style, indeed make analysis difficult because they are written *to be sung*; this is in addition to the traditional issue of interpretation, as in any text. This matter is particularly relevant in reggae music because its lyrics hold multiple references—to the Bible, Rastafari,

Interpreting songs: Notes on methodology 43

the history of reggae, and so on—and these references are made through an extensive use of the techniques of allusion and metaphor. Bob Marley once remarked that his songs were interpreted in ways that surprised him, but he saw this as a good thing.[2] According to Cooper, interpretation is indeed particularly open in reggae music because it conveys the Jamaican paradox between the oral and the written; this openness of interpretation, shown by Bob Marley, is symptomatic of oral literature, for which the interpretation of the text possesses as much importance as the text itself (1995: 118).

King and Jensen (1995), by combining a semantic analysis with the acknowledgment that reggae becomes meaningful in the interaction between the verbal and the non-verbal, between the lyrics and the music, offer one way to answer the issue raised by Cooper. They analyzed forty songs, and found four main categories: God and Evil; Oppression and Freedom; War; and Unity. Each of these categories is metaphorically expressed through terms used by Marley, which are considered as semantic vehicles. According to King and Jensen, the second (Oppression/Freedom) and third (War) categories form the way in which Marley uses metaphors of social condition (1995: 27), which is combined with the first category (Jah/Babylon) to form an explanation of the suffering and oppression, enlightened by "a powerful force of redemption" (1995: 27). The metaphor of War implies that liberation will not come from God only, but will require human struggle; the metaphor of Freedom is the solution proposed by the Rastafari movement: the return, physical or spiritual, to Zion, where human beings will unite through the power of love (metaphor of Unity). This metaphorical organization constitutes what King and Jensen call Bob Marley's rhetoric of redemption. To be sure, King and Jensen's metaphorical categories are found within the ensemble of the corpus I have analyzed; semantic vehicles are sometimes different, and sometimes exactly similar. It is especially interesting to note the strong continuity that exists between the vocabulary used in the seventies, and the one used in the nineties: even if the texts of the nineties can be considered more violent, and perhaps less "universalistic," the vocabulary they use remains, to a great extent, the same. This is especially true concerning the category of Evil: terms such as "downpressor," "back-biter," "wicked," etc are used in a continuous way in the songs I have analyzed, from 1972 through 2000. Here is

---

[2] In *Everybody's Magazine*: 5, p. 24, 1981.

an example of the semantic vehicles used for each category in Buju Banton's album *Inna Heights* (1997):

Table 2.1: Examples of semantic vehicles in Buju Banton's *Inna Heights* (1997)

Categories	Examples of semantic vehicles
Jah	My Father who art in Zion; Ruler; Protector; King; Free the people; Give I strength; Greater than great; Shield; Give us the vision to differentiate; In all that we do he holds our fate; Jah is a stream constantly flow
Babylon	They, them, dem; The heathens; Pestilence; Plague; Tale-bearers; Back-biters; The rich; The oppressor; The minister; Dressed in monkey suit; The system; Come in all size, appear in different shape; Misleading the people
Oppression	It hard; Children crying; Hunger rampant; Pickney bawl; Never had a ball to play nor a cookie in the jar; Working so hard; Life ain't easy; Times get harder; Tears falling down cheeks; The pressure; Day and night we cry; The mass still suffer; Poor man mourn
Freedom	Zion; Jah free the people; My destination is homeward bound; Breaking chains; We waan go home a wi yard; We shall escape; We shall wear the crown in the end; One day things must get better; Free from the bondage
War	Fighting; They keep fighting me I'm not giving up; Fighting to attain our rights; Struggle; Have to get up; Be strong; Don't go down, keep your head above the water; Don't let them fool you; Keep our goals in sight
Unity	Thru that mystical communication we keep on coming together; Brothers and sisters looking out for one another; Stop tearing down each others; Put each man difference aside; Cease from tribal war and fights; No more shedding of blood; Let us learn to love

King and Jensen's semantic analysis could therefore be used for this album: the vocabulary that they have analyzed, like the categories they have defined, keep their validity. However, an analysis based on the distinction of levels of meaning seems to be at least as

Interpreting songs: Notes on methodology

pertinent: a socio-political level (rhetoric of oppression, problematic of resistance ideology or theology of liberation, and the sketching of revolution), a religious level (God, the categories of Good and Evil, religious redemption and eschatology), an identity level (collective boundaries, identification to a lineage and a tradition, construction of a diasporic identity that links Africa, the Americas, the Caribbean and Europe), and a level that could be termed "historical" (the past of slavery, the Twelve Tribes of Israel, struggle movements). Each of these levels indeed works through metaphors, and all function in an intermingled way and mutually influence each other. For instance, the religious level is present within the problematic of resistance and liberation, through the use of the concepts of Zion and Babylon, which are religiously rooted but also determine a specific conceptualization of oppression and of the struggle against oppression. The concepts of Zion and Babylon are also deeply influenced by the notion of Nature, and vice-versa. Similarly, history simultaneously plays on all four levels, since it implies a historical construction and a religious rooting, traces the boundaries between the groups and defines a lineage, and participates in the distinction between the Good and Evil.

In order to complement King and Jensen, I offer an analysis made in terms of meaning—without categorizing semantic vehicles—and based on a corpus of songs that includes, but goes beyond, Bob Marley. These are deliberate choices that call for more explanation. First, I have chosen to analyze the texts in their own terms, and to leave out their relationship to the music; I used a qualitative analysis of the texts, thereby acknowledging the multi-layered texture of interpretation. Given the extensive use of metaphor, it seemed difficult to make, for instance, a semantic analysis (e.g. to count the frequency of the occurrence of a given word, which would become an indicator), because the same word can take different meanings depending on the context of the song. For instance, while "revolution" can refer to the revolution within reggae music, it might also refer to spiritual, religious, armed, or ideological revolution, and that is precisely what is interesting in the meaningful content of reggae songs: I have chosen, in this book, to account for the complexity of meaning. Therefore, I have analyzed the texts one by one, trying to distinguish all the present references—for example, one song referring to another one, or one sentence being adapted from a biblical verse. When there was no official transcript available (that is, for most of the albums I have analyzed), I used personal transcriptions. This implies that there might be mistakes, since the transcription of a sung text is never easy. All transcriptions, and therefore the excerpts quoted, have been presented in their original version. The different levels of language used (British and Jamaican English, patois, dread talk, but also Amharic such as "satta amassa gana" in a song by the Abyssinians or Swahili such as the "uhuru" in Black Uhuru)[3] reflect the context of expression of the artists: the degree of use of each level of language is a major indicator of where the artists come from but also of whom they address. The high frequency of use of patois and dread talk characterizes artists that mainly address a Jamaican audience, while the use of a "less Jamaican" English, more normalized, is often considered as a sign of commercialization, because it makes the text accessible to a larger audience.

Hence, I have not taken into account, in my analysis, how the lyrics were sung, the performance, the instrumental part; and neither have I taken into account what the musical critics or the artists themselves said about the lyrics and their meaning. I have therefore treated reggae lyrics as texts. This approach, of course, is limited to the textual content and structure of the lyrics. Simon Frith once said that "it is not only what they sing, but how they sing it, which determines what a singer means to us and how we are placed, as audience, in relation to them" (Frith, 1987: 97); my analysis is about "what they sing," not because how they sing it is not important, but because what they sing also deserves consideration, and is susceptible to be analyzed on its own terms. And, indeed, my analysis is not about the reception of the lyrics, but about the lyrics themselves. Hence, I propose here a partial but nonetheless important analysis, which focuses on the words of the music.

---

[3] In the Anglophone Caribbean, spoken language can be analyzed along a continuum that stretches from Creole (called "patois" and usually spelled "patwa"; see Cassidy 1968, Lalla and D'Costa 1990, Sebba 1993 and 1996) to English. Alleyne (1988) shows how individuals use different levels of language, tending towards the "patwa" pole when the situation is familiar; moreover, within the same conversation and with the same interlocutor, they might use linguistic forms from every degrees of the continuum (Alleyne 1988: 169). The language used by the rastas, called *dread talk*, is positioned in opposition to the normative language, but it also uses all the available linguistic systems; on dread talk, see Pollard 1982, 1990 and 2000, Aly 1988, Pulis 1993, Homiak 1995.

What, in what they sing?

Whether the analysis is about what they sing or on how they sing it, a field of inquiry has to be defined and its relevance established: which songs do we work on? How representative are they? No matter the size of a popular musical style, it is never possible to provide an exhaustive analysis of its entirety. And, indeed, the constitution of a corpus of songs as a basis for analysis has repeatedly proved problematic in studies of popular music; Frith (1987) notes that, in the case of Mooney, "it seems that he chose the songs to support his thesis rather than the opposite."

This is an important issue in reggae scholarship: although reggae music has been the subject of an abundant literature, it has rarely been analyzed in a systematic way. Most works on reggae contain lyrical excerpts, accompanied by their interpretation, but their function is more one of illustration than a basis for analysis. Additionally, the constitution of the corpus (when corpus there is) often remains unexplained; the reader usually does not know how songs have been chosen, nor which criteria have been used for this choice, nor does there seem to be any rationale. Even in the case of King (1997), who works systematically on the texts and offers a content analysis of songs, thirty musical references are listed after the bibliography, but there is no explanation of the modes of selection of these rather than others. While he undoubtedly bases his analysis on the lyrics of a corpus of songs (he specifies "61 ska songs" for chapter 1, "81 rock steady songs" for chapter 2, and "95 early reggae songs" for chapter 3), he does not explain how the corpus was constituted. However, even if he does not inform us of his methodology, King's work is based on a systematic and exhaustive content analysis of the songs he has chosen. Additionally, the number of songs analyzed, in a quite short time period (early sixties until the early seventies), suggests that he did not "choose" the songs but has worked on a considerable part of the musical production of the time.

Another problem, often met in reggae scholarship, lies in the fact that the corpus favors the same artists, and among them usually Bob Marley. However, Marley alone does not represent roots reggae, and roots reggae itself is far from representing reggae music. Dancehall reggae is often absent from the studies on reggae music, with the exception of Chude-Sokei (1994), who offers an interesting analysis of the "ragga" of the eighties and nineties; of Cooper (1994 and

1995), whose book contains a chapter on slackness; and of Anglès (1995), who examined 41 songs from five reggae albums of the mid-80s (by Chalice, Half Pint, Freddie McGregor, Sugar Minott, and Frankie Paul—but the constitution of the corpus remains unexplained); more recently, however, scholars have produced a very interesting corpus of work that focuses on dancehall, in particular Stolzoff (2000), Cooper (2004), and Hope (2006). Nonetheless, to my knowledge, no academic work has offered a content analysis based on a unified corpus of both roots reggae and reggae dancehall songs. The present book is based on two main analyses: on one hand a content analysis that systematically covers a discography of approximately fifty albums, and on the other hand a quantitative analysis of reggae charts, which looks at the songs' content and the artists over a period of thirty years in Jamaica. The use of these presents different advantages: one is composed of artists linked to the Rastafari movement, but is not limited to the seventies and contains several dancehall artists; the other is based solely on the charts, and therefore gives due prominence to love songs and, since the mid-eighties, to reggae dancehall.

In order to constitute a corpus of songs for content analysis, I have tried to define what a "classic" was. In every musical style, some recordings stand the test of time and are considered as important by common consensus, both for their own quality and for the influence they have had on the musical style itself. These "classics" become musical symbols, able to describe a genre or an era; they are immediately recognized and named, and they are the recordings that a beginner would be advised to listen and buy. The status of "classic," and especially the way in which it is attributed, is fascinating from the point of view of collective memory. Indeed, if the attribution depends primarily on "objective" qualities (the inherent value of a recording), the status of classic is in a large part attributed for subjective and symbolic reasons: that is, for what it represents, or has represented, for the individuals and for the group. For example, in the case of Bob Marley (whose records have all, or almost all, become "classics"), individuals might give variable answers when asked to choose his most important album. Some would tend to answer *Survival*, because it is emblematic of African independences; others *Exodus*, because it is the best known, popular even beyond the world of reggae; and still others would answer *Catch a Fire* because it stands for a complete and authentic

Interpreting songs: Notes on methodology 49

engagement before commercial success. Hence, it seems obvious that the status of "classic" does not depend on (objective) history only, but also on (subjective) individual and collective memories: in short, an important point to keep in mind is that a "classic" is an album that makes sense for the group.

After thirty years of reggae music and the production of hundreds of albums, some are more famous, well known and widely distributed than others, and could therefore be considered as the common denominator among reggae fans around the world as well as across generations. Such albums are consensually recognized as valuable and of high quality, and they are numerous. If they stand the test of time it is likely to be because they are able, beyond their technical qualities, to touch people, express emotions with which they can identify and, as it was dear to Adorno, to represent and interpret social structure and conflicts. For instance, in the case of Bob Marley, it is clear that his success depended as much on his personal talents as a singer and poet as on his political engagement and social analysis, in close affinity with his time. In the end, I compiled a list of roughly fifty albums, by using five criteria on the basis of reviews contained in magazines and books on reggae music:

1. *Recognition within the history of reggae*: Each of these albums is consensually considered as important within the evolution of reggae music, and as having a high musical quality.

2. *Belonging to what is sometimes called "cultural" or "conscious" reggae*: Each album has strong ties to the Rastafari movement, and the texts echo socio-political and religious engagement. This criterion results from a methodological choice: the object of inquiry for content analysis, indeed, is the point of contact between Rastafari and reggae music (other recordings, however, appear in the analysis I have made of reggae charts).

3. *Popularity within reggae music*: All are widely known, beyond Jamaica. This criterion is essential because it allows the avoidance of the "strictly local."

4. *Two periods: 1973–1980 and 1995–2000*: It seemed impossible to analyze a longer period, which would have covered the entire history of reggae music and retraced its evolution from ska to dancehall. I have chosen these two periods because of their specific status: both are important moments in reggae history, and both represented an achievement and a passage: the first witnesses the establishment and

stabilization of roots reggae as a specific style, while the second covers an important change within reggae dancehall (which can be seen as having "gone back" to religious and/or socio-political commitment). Moreover, it was pertinent to adopt a comparative approach, based on the analysis of recordings separated by fifteen years, in that this allowed for the observation of stability, continuity, and change in a musical style.

5. *A predominantly Jamaican production*: Among the corpus, there is only a tiny minority of non-Jamaican artists. Indeed, Jamaica was, and still is today, prominent within the production of reggae music. Therefore, the only non-Jamaican recordings are those that seem widely known, across locations.

These five criteria combine to define the status of "classic" in reggae history, as seen by the specialists and critics of reggae as much as by those who make music or listen to it. Of course, because they are more recent, the status of "classic" among the albums in the second period is more difficult to confirm. Indeed, it is through its persistence over time that a "classic" is mostly, and permanently, defined: the corpus I have assembled therefore remains to be confirmed, and it will be interesting to see how many of the recent albums will still be considered as classics in the years to come. I suspect that many of them will not.

Box 2.2: Albums used in this study

Year	Artist	Album
1973	Bob Marley & the Wailers	*Burnin'*
	Bob Marley & the Wailers	*Catch a Fire*
1974	Bob Marley & the Wailers	*Natty Dread*
1975	Burning Spear	*Marcus Garvey*
1976	Bob Marley & the Wailers	*Rastaman Vibration*
	The Abyssinians	*Forward on to Zion*
	Aswad	*Showcase*
	The Gladiators	*Trench Town Mix Up*
	The Mighty Diamonds	*The Right Time*
	Johnny Clarke	*Rockers Time Now*
1977	Dennis Brown	*Wolves and Leopards*
	Burning Spear	*Dry and Heavy*
	Bob Marley & the Wailers	*Exodus*
	U Roy	*Rasta Ambassador*

1978	Black Uhuru	*Black Sounds of Freedom*
	Dennis Brown	*Visions*
	Burning Spear	*Social Living*
	Israel Vibration	*Same Song*
	Bob Marley & the Wailers	*Kaya*
	Hugh Mundell	*Africa Must be Free by 1983*
	Steel Pulse	*Handsworth Revolution*
	Culture	*Two Sevens Clash*
1979	Culture	*International Herb*
	Bob Marley & the Wailers	*Survival*
	Steel Pulse	*Tribute to the Martyrs*
	Barry Brown	*Superstar*
	Gregory Isaacs	*Soon Forward*
1980	Burning Spear	*Hail Him*
	Israel Vibration	*Survive*
	Bob Marley & the Wailers	*Uprising*
	Gregory Isaacs	*Lovers Rock*
	Dennis Brown	*Joseph's Coat of Many Colours*
1995	Buju Banton	*Til Shiloh*
	Burning Spear	*Rasta Business*
1996	Anthony B	*Real Revolutionary*
1997	Anthony B	*Universal Struggle*
	Buju Banton	*Inna Heights*
	Sizzla	*Black Woman and Child*
	Sizzla	*Praise Ye Jah*
	Luciano	*Messenger*
	Tony Rebel	*If Jah*
1998	Jahmali	*El Shaddai*
	Morgan Heritage	*Protect us Jah*
	Garnett Silk	*Collectors*
	Sizzla	*Freedom Cry*
1999	Anthony B	*Seven Seals*
	Bushman	*Total Commitment*
	Luciano	*Sweep Over my Soul*
	Paul Elliott	*Save me oh Jah*
Compilations		
	Yabby You & Friends	*Jesus Dread* (1972–1977)
	Junior Byles & Friends	*129 Beat Street* (1975–1978)
	Rod Taylor	*Ethiopian Kings* (1975–1980)

This corpus forms the basis of my analysis;[4] it is accompanied, however, by another set of data, which was analyzed quantitatively. As stated above, the politicization of reggae music experienced a weakening in the eighties, followed by a revival in the mid-nineties. This statement is a "general feeling" shared by reggae artists, fans, and critics, and it therefore had to be tested as a fact, which is why I took an interest in reggae charts. Indeed, the evolution of reggae music can be observed in different ways: by looking at commercial charts (based on record sales), at the playlists used by radio stations (e.g. all the songs played by reggae stations), or at the entire musical production (e.g. all the albums and singles recorded and distributed, independently of their success). Charts present the disadvantage of reflecting only legal sales, which might not be very pertinent when observing reggae music: they are not necessarily representative of what people actually listen to, because of the importance of radio stations, sound systems, and pirate recordings. Radio playlists raise the problem of the choice of the show: it is difficult to find a radio show that would exactly represent what people listen to, what reggae is at a given time, and had existed since the beginning of reggae. Finally, working on the entire production would have been impossible, and even choosing one or a few record labels would have been difficult. So in the end, specialized reggae charts were the most interesting; even if they concern only legal sales, they remain representative of a general tendency.[5] The choice of singles over album charts was prompted by different reasons: the importance of singles in reggae history, and the fact that they reflect a dynamic history in the making and allow to "take the pulse" of a given moment (since they are bought shortly after their release, while album sales depend less on a specific period). They are also more accessible to the audience in terms of cost, and are representative of an audience that tends to be "strictly reggae," while albums are also bought by individuals who would not define themselves as "reggae fans." These charts form the basis for a diachronic analysis that compares annual Jamaican

---

[4] This list is reproduced in Annex 2, along with the availability of each album and the ASIN number.
[5] Moreover, the only thing that can be observed by looking at reggae charts is what people buy, not what people necessarily like or adhere to. I also want to echo Grace Davie, who notes that quantitative analysis provides us with trends, not with explanations (Conference at NYU, New York, April 2, 2004).

Interpreting songs: Notes on methodology

charts between 1970 and 1999 (*The Star* charted hits) and tries to answer one principal question: How has reggae music evolved since 1970? This question is asked at the level of song content: what is the political, social, religious engagement of the songs' words? The construction of variables was not simple: how can content be defined, how can ideological engagement be measured? Additionally, while I had access to most of the songs present in the charts, some were missing: sometimes I did not know the song and could not find it, and therefore had to proceed by deduction from the artist and the title of the song. This analysis of the charts nonetheless allowed the testing of the "general feeling" shared by reggae artists, fans, and critics, which supports the hypothesis of a return to Rastafari within reggae music. In the next chapter, I will present the results of this analysis.

3

A diachronic analysis of Jamaican reggae charts, 1968–2000

Reggae charts mix different styles (roots reggae, dancehall reggae ...) as well as contents (love songs, slackness, religious or sociopolitical songs...). They are therefore representative of reggae music as a whole, in contrast to the data I am using throughout this book for a qualitative analysis of content, which pertain exclusively to reggae songs by artists more or less loosely linked to the Rastafari movement. The principal question underlying this chart analysis concerns the general evolution of reggae music since 1970. This is part of a more general issue, which my analysis aims to explore: the extent of the presence of the Rastafari movement within reggae music. The aim of this chapter is to legitimate my methodological choices concerning the elaboration of a corpus as a basis for the analysis of lyrics; in other words, I looked at reggae charts to verify the pertinence of analyzing reggae at its point of contact with Rastafari.

For this diachronic analysis, I have used Jamaican annual singles charts, which have existed since the beginning of the sixties and are based on weekly charts.[1] The available data were ranked charts until 1996 (23 or 26 best sales of the year, depending on the year), and charted hits after 1996 (e.g. all the singles that made it to the charts at least once during the year). Because of this disparity, I did not take into account the rank of each single—for example, the number one single was not given more importance than the last

---

[1] Weekly charts are published by *The Star*, a supplement of *The Daily Gleaner*, the main Jamaican daily newspaper.

ranked single. My analysis was carried out on the period of time between 1968—the year of emergence of reggae music—and 1999. I have reduced the charts to the 23 first ranked singles, in order to have a homogeneous data set. For the years 1997, 1998, and 1999, which were not ranked, I have selected 23 singles among all the charted hits, inferring on the basis of their popularity and comparing with the New York reggae charts; therefore, the charts for these three years are not necessarily accurate, as it is difficult to know which titles have had the biggest sales.[2] Charts were not available for the years 1974, 1975, 1976, and 1977; *The Star* indicates some of the songs which would have make it to the charts during this period, and I have included them in the corpus, although the charts are far from being complete.

Reggae charts reflect only what people buy and therefore listen to, but they do not reflect *all the music* that they listen to. This is especially true in the Caribbean, where a very large part of the audience does not buy records, but listens to music on the radio and in sound systems, and buys pirate recordings on tapes. Many people cannot afford to buy records or compact discs, and tapes also have the advantage that they require nothing but a tape deck to be played; so because people cannot buy records does not mean that they do not have access to music. Therefore, reggae charts have to be considered as only a small part of the music market. However, they remain an excellent indicator in terms of popularity: whether they are bought "officially" or in the street, the biggest hits are at the top of the charts, and dominate radio programs;[3] despite their limitations, reggae charts still represent a general tendency and correctly indicate the most popular tunes at a given time.

I have used two different variables: songs' content, and artists. This allowed me to examine simultaneously the presence of a sociopolitical and/or religious message in the charts, and the presence of artists linked to Rastafari, even when they sing love songs.

---

[2] The "big hits" always make it in the top 15; but it gets more complicated for the top 15 to 23 and I assume that errors might have appeared at this level.

[3] One indicator of the popularity of songs and albums comes from what is played most on the radio, but also in bars, collective taxis, etc. This is hard to test, but nonetheless gives a "feel" of what people listen to.

First variable: An analysis of the content of the songs

Each song has been placed into one category, depending on its lyrical content: (A) explicit reference to the Rastafari faith; (B) socio-political content without reference to Rastafari; (C) none of the above (mainly love songs, gun lyrics and slackness lyrics). This category system is based on the song itself, independently of the artist who sings it. For example, Buju Banton's "Love sponge" (1997) is placed in category C: the song is about love and sex, although Buju Banton is a proclaimed rastaman, and although the album from which the single is taken can be considered as religiously and politically engaged; similarly, a song like Zebra's "Selassie warning" (1998) is placed in category A, although the artist is not a rastaman. It is essential to distinguish the songs with socio-political content, even if they do not refer to the Rastafari movement, because they indicate the socio-political commitment of reggae music (or its lack) although they do not speak for its religious commitment. For example, Horace Andy's "Skylarking" (1972) and Bounty Killer's "Anytime" (1999) are both placed in category B, because of their social content. This is also the case for a song like Baby Cham's "Desperate measures" (1999), which has a strong political content.

It is sometimes difficult to distinguish the songs with socio-political content that contain reference to Rastafari from those which do not—especially because, even when the artists do not embrace the faith, Rastafari has considerably influenced the Jamaican political and artistic scene as a whole. So the way of treating a social issue is often more revealing than the topic itself. A good example of this distinction is found with the issue of homosexuality, which is strongly rejected by the Rastafari movement, in global Jamaican society, and in Caribbean culture in general. For instance, Bounty Killer's "Caan believe mi eye" and Capleton's "Pure sodom," both in the 1998 charts, cover this topic in two very different ways:

> Mi caan believe some name mi a hear say a men
> Mi caan believe say tight pants comin again
> Mi caan believe say gunman an battyman a fren
> ... Mi caan believe di gal dem a guh the other way
> Mi never know Jamaica woulda have so much gay

> Mi caan believe di government dem inna foul play
> Mi caan believe mi eye, mi caan believe mi eye.
>
> Bounty Killer, "Caan believe mi eye," 1998

> Yuh nuh seh a battyman dem, a sodomite dem
> ... Dem nuh like me and mi nuh like dem
> ... Weh mi guh caught dem all
> Which part wi caught dem? Inna di dancehall
> None a dem can't escape this judgment ball
> From mi found dem guilty after all
> ... Nuff seh dem a Moses but mi see seh dem a Saul
> Nuff seh dem a David but mi see seh dem a Saul
> Weh dem a guh do all ina di roll call
> Judgement gwaan tek dem ina di Judgment ball.
>
> Capleton, "Pure sodom," 1998

Both Bounty Killer and Capleton strongly oppose and criticize homosexuality, but Capleton calls on divine judgment; Bounty Killer's song therefore belongs to category B, while Capleton's is placed in category A.

It is also difficult to distinguish traditional love songs from slackness songs, not only because I did not always have access to the totality of the lyrics, but also because a qualitative classification did not seem completely pertinent from a methodological point of view: it would have lead to a normative distinction. Why would talking about sex be less important than talking about love, for example? Where do we exactly draw the limit between "love," "sex," and "slackness"? Moreover, as Cooper (1995: 136–173) pointed out, slackness can also be considered as a pertinent description of Jamaican society. For example, female answers to male sexual auto-glorification, although they are as crude, are an interesting observation of gender relations in Jamaica, as in Tanya Stephens' song "Yuh nuh ready fi this" (1997), in which she answers male artists ("Mr Mention" refers to a song by Buju Banton) and presents the female point of view on sex and sexual performance:

> O Mr Mention
> Ask yuhself this question
> Unno say unno a don man
> An a unno run the program, the program
> But have yuh ever stop to think wha mek a gal cheat

> Yuh need fi check yuhself before yuh start kiss yuh teeth
> Caw yuh nuh ready fi this yet bwoy
> Have yuh ever wonder what mek a girl cum
> A woman fus fi satisfy before yuh say yuh done
> Yuh caan say a thing if yuh end up a get bun
> Caw yuh nuh ready fi this yet bwoy.
> Tanya Stephens, "Yuh nuh ready fi this," 1997

While the difference between traditional love songs and slackness songs can seem obvious, this is mostly a difference in terms of the vocabulary used by the artist, or in terms of some "general attitude" that he adopts towards women; in order to avoid any judgmental position, I have therefore chosen not to distinguish between love songs and slackness songs. However, it does seem that slackness lyrics are dominant between 1988 and 1994—for example Admiral Bailey's "Punany" (1987); as for gun lyrics, which literally speak of shotguns and shootings, they appear at the same time; an example is found with Tiger's "Yu dead now" (1992).

Second variable: An analysis of the artists and their link with Rastafari

The second variable is based on the artists only, and depends on their relationship with Rastafari. This distinction is once again complicated because the vast majority of reggae artists, whether they are rastamen or not, remain influenced by Rastafari. I have therefore distinguished three categories: (A) rasta artists; (B) non-rasta artists who refer to Rastafari on a regular basis, or who use vocabulary, language, or symbols that come from the Rastafari movement; (C) artists who are not linked to Rastafari. In category A are found reggae artists such as Bob Marley, Dennis Brown, Sizzla, or Buju Banton, who clearly are rastamen (and usually explicitly claim to belong to the faith), and constantly refer to Rastafari in their songs. In category B is placed someone like Beenie Man who, although not a rastaman, is influenced by Rastafari as shown in his lyrics and interviews (e.g. references made to Rastafari's ideology and theology, vocabulary taken from the rasta talk...). In category C are found artists like Bounty Killer or Baby Cham, who are neither rastamen nor refer to Rastafari on a regular basis (although they might of course mention the movement in some songs, but in an external,

Analysis of Jamaican reggae charts, 1968–2000

Figure 3.1: Evolution of the content of the songs

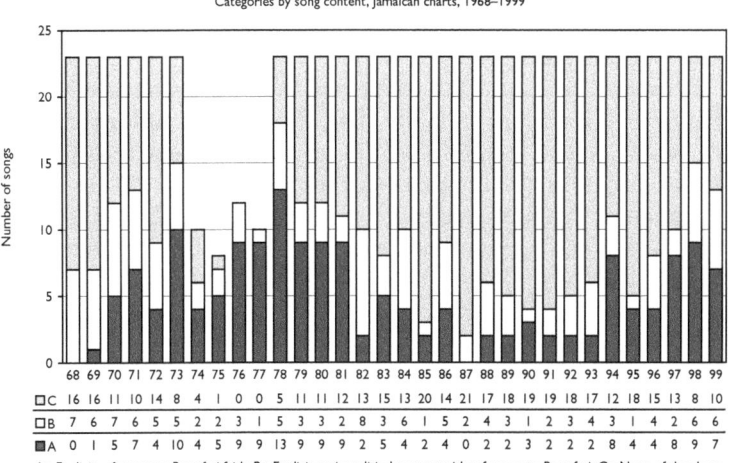

A= Explicit reference to Rastafari faith; B= Explicit socio-political content with reference to Rastafari; C= None of the above

observational way). This second variable is important, because it allows the identification of the presence of rasta artists even when they are in the charts with a love song, for example, which would not appear if using the content variable alone (Figure 3.1).

A first period in the development of the space occupied by Rastafari within the reggae charts, in terms of content, takes place in the seventies. This fast progression (as there was not a single song with an explicit reference to Rastafari in 1968) seems to stabilize at its highest level between 1975 and 1978, although the curve is stopped by a quasi-absence of material in 1974, 1975, 1976 and 1977 (there were no available complete charts for this period). In 1973, 10 songs out of 23 contain explicit references to Rastafari (among them Dennis Brown's number 1, "Westbound train"). In 1978, this number increases to 13, which represents 56% of the best-selling songs (among them "Zion gate" by the band Culture and "Jah Jah give us life" by The Wailing Souls). It seems reasonable to infer that between 1973 and 1978 the influence of Rastafari remained at the same level, if it did not increase; in 1976, for example, 9 songs out of the 13 available were interpreted by rasta artists and strongly refer to Rastafari (Mighty Diamonds' "I need a roof," Max Romeo's "War ina Babylon," Bob Marley & the Wailers' "One love"...). So between 1974 and 1979 roots reggae indeed "exploded," as is reflected in the charts: numerous bands, all having a direct link with Rastafari, gained success in Jamaica and beyond, among them Bob Marley & the Wailers, Culture, Black Uhuru, Inner Circle, and Mighty Diamonds.

Between 1980 and 1982, there is a significant decrease in songs that refer to Rastafari; from this date, the influence of Rastafari over the songs' content seems to be at its lowest level from 1982 to 1991. Without completely disappearing from the charts (with the notable exception of 1987), its presence remains extremely limited. Between 1982 and 1992, only a few songs have lyrics directly linked with Rastafari, among which are Dennis Brown's "Revolution" (number 2 in 1983), Bob Marley & the Wailers' "Buffalo soldier" (number 7 in 1983), Black Uhuru's "Solidarity" (number 12 in 1985), Junior Reid's "One blood" (number 4 in 1989), and Tony Rebel's "Fresh vegetable" (number 12 in 1991).

This decade (1982–1992) simultaneously sees a decrease in the influence of Rastafari over the songs' content and the appearance of slackness lyrics, such as dancehall songs with explicit content centered around sex and violence (for example, Yellowman's "Belly move," number 3 in 1984; Supercat's "Boops," number 4 in 1986; Admiral Bailey's "Punany," number 1 in 1987; Shabba Ranks' "Trailer load of girls," number 1 in 1991; or Tiger's "Yu dead now," number 13 in 1992). This important change within reggae music, which takes place during the first half of the eighties, originates in the musical evolution of reggae itself—with the apparition of digital reggae, which gives less importance to instruments, and the growing success of dancehall dee-jays—but also in the Jamaican global situation, at a social and political level. The eighties began with the election of Edward Seaga, leader of the conservative party (JLP), following the most violent political campaign in Jamaican history, during which hundreds of people were killed. Seaga's government (nicknamed "CIA-ga" in reference to the support he found with the United States) implemented a policy of budgetary restriction and entered the IMF program. Throughout the eighties, unemployment increased, salaries stagnated, and urban violence exploded. Reggae music followed this evolution in a striking way: according to Barrow and Dalton (1997: 231), a "conservative and self-centered" music developed that used already tested "riddims" while the lyrics stayed away from social, political and historical topics. Emphasis was placed on traditional dancehall characteristics: dance moves and steps, slackness lyrics, sound clashes (which are a sort of competition between two sound systems). Barrow and Dalton explain the extensive use of already existing "riddims" by the economic situation: by using them over and over again, producers were taking fewer financial risks. Without going as far as saying that the techniques of music itself were grounded in the socio-political context of the time, it remains that the growing lyrical violence observed in the reggae charts during the late eighties paralleled the increasing harshness of life faced by the greatest part of the Jamaican population.

However, after ten years of quasi-absence, a new growth in the influence of Rastafari over the content of songs took place after 1993, a year during which new artists with direct links with Rastafari appear in the charts—such as Garnett Silk (with "Hello Mama Africa," number 13 in 1993), Capleton (with "Tour," number 4 in 1994), Luciano (with "One way ticket," number 6 in 1994) or Tony Rebel (with "Fresh vegetable," number 12 in 1991, and "Teach the children," number 12 in 1994). Reversing the trends of the previous decade, the songs placed in category C ("Rastafari") after 1992 have what could be called a "strong" Rastafari content, which makes an important qualitative difference: during the seventies, and after 1992, category C is considered as "full," while between 1982 and 1992 it mostly contains short references. Therefore, not only did Rastafari-linked songs increase numerically in the charts after 1992, the qualitative texture of this category also became stronger. After 1992, many songs with a very religious or strongly socio-political content made a come-back in the reggae charts, such as the following:

- *Strong religious content*: Buju Banton's "God of my salvation" (1994), Luciano's "It's me against Jah" and Garnett Silk's "Lord watch over our shoulder" (1995), Tony Rebel's "Jah by my side" and Sizzla's "Praise yeh Jah" (1997), Glen Washington's "Jah glory" and Luciano's "Sweep over my soul" (1998), Luciano's "Jah blessing" and Buju Banton's "23d Psalm" (1999).

- *Strong socio-political content with reference to Rastafari*: Buju Banton's "Murderer" and Tony Rebel's "Teach the children" (1994), Buju Banton's "Untold stories" (1995 and 1996), Everton Blender's "Lift up your head" (1996), Sizzla's "Black woman and child" and "One away" (1997), Capleton's "Pure sodom" (1998).

Most are reggae dancehall songs, performed by artists who were not active in the seventies, mostly because they were children at the

Figure 3.2: Evolution in terms of the artists and their link with the Rastafari

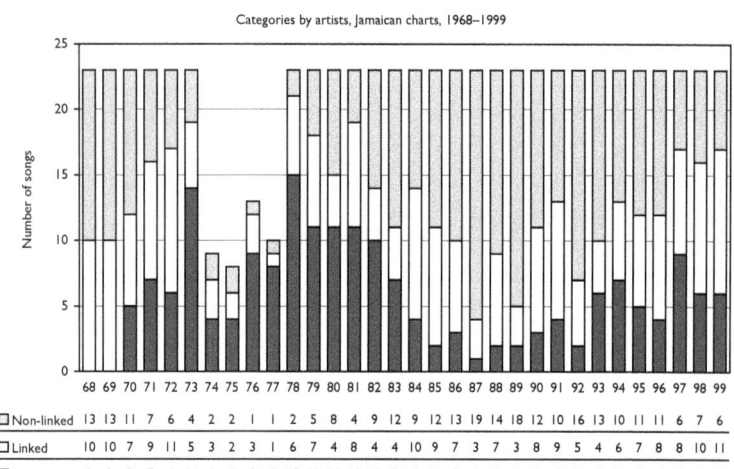

time. So the reappearance of Rastafari in the charts after 1992 is not due to a "come-back" of seventies reggae artists, although many are still active today (for example Israel Vibration, Black Uhuru, Gladiators, or Burning Spear), sometimes reaching the Jamaican charts, and are very popular in terms of album sales, especially in Western countries. On the contrary, this new growth of songs with Rastafari-linked content shows the penetration of Rastafari into dancehall reggae, which was, until then, almost exclusively centered on slackness. It is also visible in terms of the artists themselves, as shown by the analysis of the second variable, based on the relationship that artists maintain with the Rastafari movement.

The first impression given by Figure 3.2 is that rasta artists were absent from the charts in 1968 and 1969, although some of them were linked to Rastafari, such as the members of the bands The Heptones or The Ethiopians. Second, the overall pattern follows almost exactly the evolution in terms of songs content (as seen in Figure 3.1), with the same peaks (1970–1982, and after 1992) and the same quasi-disappearance between 1985 and 1992. However, it is noticeable that the presence of Rastafari in terms of artists is stronger than in terms of content, due to the fact that rasta artists also perform love songs, while the vast majority of the songs with Rastafarian content

Figure 3.3: Cumulated categories A and B (rasta artists and artists linked to Rastafari)

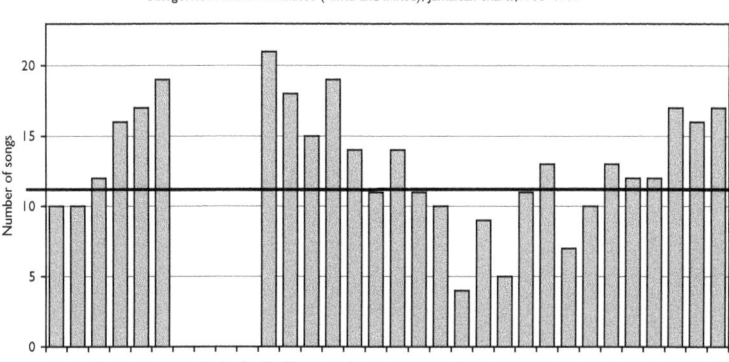

are sung by rasta artists.[4] Love songs performed by rasta artists and present in the charts included Dennis Brown's "Ain't that loving you" (number 4 in 1979), Mighty Diamonds' "Pretty Woman" (number 21 in 1982), Dennis Brown's "Your Love got a hold on me" (number 1 in 1983), Gregory Isaacs' "Night nurse" (number 4 in 1983),[5] and Buju Banton's "Love sponge" (1997).

It is interesting to bring categories A and B together. When considering rasta artists and artists who are linked to Rastafari altogether, both groups then represent more than half of all the artists, as appears in Figure 3.3.

The horizontal black line shown on the table refers to the median of each sample (gradation goes from 0 to 23, which is the size of each sample). It appears that the percentage of rasta artists and

---

[4] In other words, when a song is sung by a Rastafarian artist, its content might or might not be linked with the Rastafari movement, whereas when a song has a content linked with the Rastafari movement, it is almost always sung by a Rastafarian artist.

[5] Although this song has an ambiguous content, some saying that it refers to cocaine. Depending on the period, Gregory Isaacs himself can sometimes be considered as a rasta artist, sometimes as an artist linked to Rastafari. His long career and the shifts in his involvement within Rastafari make him difficult to classify. However, at the time of the *Night Nurse* album, he was clearly referring to Rastafari in most of his lyrics.

artists linked to Rastafari, when brought together, goes above half the sample in seventeen years. I have not shown incomplete samples (1974 through 1977), but they contain between 70% and 90% of artists in cumulated categories A and B, which could indicate that, on a complete sample, a majority would be attained, especially when we know that those years are at the heart of Rastafari's influence on reggae (1972–1982). During eleven of the thirty years, cumulative figures for categories A and B were under the 50% level, especially in 1987, 1988, 1989, and 1992, when they represent fewer than 10 artists out of 23. Besides, between 1984 and 1992, the percentage of strictly rasta artists within the cumulated categories A and B is extremely limited.

Therefore, the tendency observed in terms of song content is very similar to the evolution observed in terms of the artists: two peaks (1973–1982 and 1993–1999), and a weak period in between, during which the influence of Rastafari seems to have been extremely limited, at least when it comes to the charts. It is worth noting that the two peaks in the influence of Rastafari are qualitatively different: there is a vast majority of roots reggae bands during the seventies peak, while most of the rasta artists during the nineties peak are individuals coming from sound systems and dancehall reggae, as shown by Tables 3.1 and 3.2.

Table 3.1: Rasta artists with more than one charted hit during the two peaks of Rastafari influence, in decreasing order

Artist	Number of charted hits
Seventies peak (1973–1982)	
Dennis Brown	14
Bob Marley & the Wailers	11
Big Youth	6
Mighty Diamonds	5
Gregory Isaacs	5
Jacob Miller	5
Culture	4
Max Romeo	4
Junior Byles	3

Artist	Number of charted hits
Judy Mowatt	3
Bunny Wailer	3
Brent Dowe	3
Nineties peak (1993–1999)	
Buju Banton	14
Capleton	6
Luciano	5
Sizzla	3
Junior Reid	3
Garnett Silk	2
Tony Rebel	2
Morgan Heritage	2
Cocoa Tea	2

Table 3.2: Artists linked to Rastafari with more than one charted hit during the two peaks of Rastafari influence, in decreasing order

Artist	Number of charted hits
Seventies peak (1973–1982)	
Toots & the Maytals	5
Beres Hammond	4
Barrington Levy	3
Ken Boothe	2
Sugar Minott	2
Johnny Osbourne	2
Jimmy Cliff	2
Nineties peak (1993–1999)	
Beenie Man	25
Sanchez	5
Beres Hammond	5
Anthony Red Rose	1
Ini Kamoze	1

Concluding remarks on the analysis of the charts

The analysis presented here must not be considered as an exact and complete expression of reality. To start with, it is not a statistical analysis but only an observation of the evolution over time; and the corpus itself can be contested, as it represents the sales of singles while, as already mentioned, reggae is a musical style that gives an important place to pirate recordings and in which sound systems and radio stations play an essential role. Additionally, charts are traditionally dominated by love songs or "neutral content" songs (non-religious, non-ideological), as is the case for other musical genres; it is therefore important to keep in mind that, when one third of the artists are rastamen, this represents a strong influence on the musical life of that time (just try to imagine one-third of the American charts occupied by Christian rock'n'roll, for instance). If we take two years as an example (1978 and 1999), we obtain the following results by considering both the content and artists variables:

Table 3.3: Categories for the year 1978, Jamaican charts

	A: Rastafari	B: Socio-political	C: Neither
Content	13 (56%)	5 (22%)	5 (22%)
	A: Rastas	B: Linked to Rastafari	C: Not linked
Artists	15 (65%)	6 (26%)	2 (9%)

Table 3.4: Categories for the year 1999, Jamaican charts

	A: Rastafari	B: Socio-political	C: None
Content	7 (30%)	6 (26%)	10 (44%)
	A: Rastas	B: Linked to Rastafari	C: Not linked
Artists	6 (26%)	11 (48%)	6 (26%)

In 1978, the year during which the percentage of songs with content linked to Rastafari is the highest (56%), 65% of all the artists are rastamen, and 26% are linked to Rastafari. In fact, only 2 artists out of 23 are not rastas nor linked to Rastafari.

The important percentage of songs with Rastafari-linked content is therefore reinforced by a massive presence of Rastafari among the artists, even though their songs can be love songs without any socio-political or religious content (for example "How could I leave" by Dennis Brown). A few songs have a socio-political content without explicitly referring to Rastafari; this is the case for the song "Tribal war" by George Knooks.

The 1999 reggae chart is very different from the 1978 one. First, the percentage of songs with Rastafari content as well as rasta artists is less significant (respectively 56% in 1978 as opposed to 30% in 1999, and 65% in 1978 as opposed to 26% in 1999). Besides, the percentage of songs with content in category C (not rasta, not socio-political) is much more important in 1999. Second, there are more songs with Rastafari content than there are rasta artists in 1999, while the situation was reversed in 1978. This is due to the presence of songs like "Better Learn" by Beenie Man or "Selassie Warning" by Zebra, which content is in category A, with a performer in category B; with the exception of Buju Banton's "Di women dem phat," all the songs performed by rasta artists have a content in category A, sometimes very religious (for example Buju Banton's "23d Psalm"). However, in terms of content, the songs in category B represent about one-quarter, which is slightly more than in 1978; and, in terms of artists, the percentage of artists linked to Rastafari is very high (almost half the songs), which strongly reinforces the percentage of rasta artists. Cumulated categories A and B reach a percentage of 75%, which indicates a strong presence of Rastafari in the 1999 chart.

While reggae charts only represent the sales of single records, with all the limitations it implies in terms of representation, it remains interesting to see that they confirm a "general feeling" expressed by reggae fans, artists and critics (such as John Masouri, for example): after ten years of quasi-absence, Rastafari made a reappearance within reggae music, including in terms of commercial sales. The 2001 reggae charts in London, Kingston and New York also confirm this tendency, the presence of Rastafari, both in terms of content and artists, being comparable to its presence in the 1999 reggae charts (and even, in the case of New York, more important). By taking into account the diverse limitations evoked earlier, the diachronic observation of reggae charts can lead to a few concluding remarks that describe general tendencies. The question "What is the evolution of reggae music since 1970?" in terms of the influence of Rastafari was at the center of this diachronic analysis. An evolution in three stages can be observed: a peak in between 1973 and 1982; a regression and quasi-disappearance between 1983 and 1992; and finally a revival since 1993. In other words, although they reflect the most popular songs and are therefore largely dominated by songs without any socio-political or religious content, reggae charts show the existence of the interrelation that exists between reggae and Rastafari: in the very space of the most commercialized music, there is still a presence of rasta artists and of songs with a Rastafari-influenced content; and it is worth noting that, although it varies greatly in degree, this presence never completely disappears over the years.

4

The construction of a musical memory

The history of reggae music is long and complex and, in reference to a common expression within reggae and the Rastafari movement, "half the story has never been told." In opposition to other scholars who describe it in terms of a linear evolution stemming from one source, and hence consider each new development as the extension or direct product of the preceding one, Bilby argues that Jamaican music "has evolved in a considerably more disorderly manner than this and has always been stylistically more heterogeneous and complex than such a view would suggest" (Manuel and Bilby 1995: 158). Two main elements can be seen as crucial to this disorderly evolution. First, reggae developed on the basis of numerous and diverse influences, and all of them continued to influence reggae throughout its evolution, but to different degrees depending on the moment. Bilby takes the example of Kumina, which according to him influenced reggae dancehall of the late eighties more than it had influenced roots reggae of the seventies—but is nonetheless present from the beginning and throughout the history of reggae music. He argues that reggae "represents nothing less than a synthesis of many diverse stylistic influences, ... the balance of which has continued to shift over time" (Manuel and Bilby 1995: 158). Second, reggae has usually remained what amounts to "at-home production," and this is still mostly true today, despite the commercial success of artists like Bob Marley, Aswad or Beenie Man. This implies that the production of reggae music is seldom centralized, commercial and official. Record labels are numerous and generally of a small size; in Jamaica, they are sometimes nothing more than a studio and backyard; in the seventies, records were then sold in the street, while stocks lasted. Many recordings were therefore pressed only once, and their distribution was hazardous, using more or less informal networks. Even today, many compact discs have an erratic presence within the mainstream distribution networks, while vinyl records (whether albums or singles) are usually only available in reggae shops. This point is important, because one of the characteristics of reggae music is the importance of singles, for technical as well as economic reasons. Single records (7-inch or 12-inch) are numerous; among them, many do not leave the island, and most remain limited to an audience of aficionados. There might be an interesting point to argue here, about a multiform "island" which would geographically include Jamaica as well as specific, closed networks of distribution beyond the borders of Jamaica. In relation to other musical styles—in particular hip hop and house, two genres in which vinyl records occupy a major space—new recordings are extremely important in reggae music, especially singles. Mthembu-Salter and Dalton (2000: 449) say "Jamaican music is totally singles oriented ... Most singles are pressed on 7-inch once, and then deleted. Hits usually make it to the 12-inch, and last longer, but even then you have to move fast. The only way to follow it is to go to the dances, or listen to pirate radio, or buy reggae magazines"; or, it could be added, to listen to the latest recordings in reggae shops. And the knowledge concerning what was just released, who recorded what, or what has just been recorded, is a marker for the definition of boundaries between the fans and the others: to know is to belong. Radio shows are, in this sense, producers of identity: they weave ties within the community, inform individuals of what is going on, produce and share a sense of unity and belonging.

Beyond this unconditional love for new recordings, reggae fans also listen to old recordings. While thirty years separate them, Buju Banton and Bob Marley usually are part of the same record collections, as well as of the same history, memory and family. Rare are reggae fans who listen to one specific sub-style only—only dancehall, or only seventies roots reggae, for instance. The rejection of reggae dancehall and the almost exclusive preference for pre-eighties recordings are mostly characteristic of Western fans; when Bilby talks about Kumina and late-eighties dancehall, he notes that only the latter perceive digital and dancehall reggae as being "less authentic" than roots reggae; in fact, according to the dub

The construction of a musical memory

poet Linton Kwesi Johnson, dancehall reggae has become "more roots" because the rhythms are "more Jamaican," and more heavily influenced by Afro-Jamaican religious cults.[1]

This coexistence of the old and new clearly appears by simply listening to reggae shows on the radio. Some are devoted to new releases, while others play recordings that range from the ska of the sixties to the latest album of Anthony B. Reggae stations (such as Irie FM in Jamaica) play the whole range of the musical production, from the early sixties until today. This combination of the old and new, in individuals' musical taste and preferences as well as in their view of "what reggae is," confirms Bilby's argument. If one observes reggae music through its historical evolution only, then this paradox might be missed, because reggae will probably be considered as a linear evolution containing distinct styles and periods. But if one takes the angle of collective memory, through the attributions and identifications made by individuals themselves, this paradox then clearly appears, giving back to reggae music its unity in diversity. The presence of both old and new recordings in people's records collection is not only a question of taste or persistence: in reggae music; *the new itself also conveys the old*, through a process that is characteristic of reggae: the importance of the "riddim."

The riddim: Persistence and musical creation

One of the consequences of the sound-system tradition and of its prominence within the reggae scene is a massive production of single recordings; another is the existence of the "versions"—that is, recordings without the vocal part—which are usually found on the B-side of singles. Versions are used in sound system because dee-jays and singers can "talk over" them; sound systems used to "work" the versions by using sound effects such as echo or reverberation. At the beginning of the 1970s, these versions began to be remixed in recording studios; since then, the sound-engineer has become

---

[1] LKJ, 1993: Introduction in the booklet of the four-CD set *Tougher than Tough: The Story of Jamaican Music*, Island Records. Of course, arguments about the "blackness" of music are linked with claims of authenticity and the conflictual relationship between a musical style considered "black" and its success with a Western audience, in a way similar to the case of jazz musicians in the United States.

as important as the artist, and the version an essential tradition and characteristic of reggae music. One of the most interesting consequences of the central importance of versions is the persistence of the "riddims," the rhythmic line of a recording (its rhythm). The basis of the riddim is the bass line, accompanied by a drum line and sometimes by a melody; the riddim is usually born out of a hit ("Cherry oh baby," "Night nurse," "Under me sleng teng"...), and is then extensively used and re-used, sometimes for years: the most famous riddims survive the succession of fashions and styles.[2] For instance, the riddim of the song "Satta amassa gana" by the Abyssinians (1976), known as the "Satta riddim," has been remixed and used a good hundred times, a recent version being Sizzla's "One away" (1997); similarly, the riddim of Gregory Isaacs' "Night nurse" (1982) has been used by Anthony B in 1997, on "Waan back."[3] We can take an early example to illustrate the multiple uses of one riddim, which comes from "Stop that train" (The Spanishtonians, 1965):

- Keith and Tex, 1967: "Stop that train."
- Ike Bennett & the Crystalites, 1969: "Stop that man."
- Scotty, 1971: "Draw your brakes."
- Big Youth, 1973: "Cool breeze."
- Clint Eastwood & General Saint, 1983: "Stop that train."
- Ernest Ranglin, 1998: "Stop that train."

Steve Barrow, of the reggae label Blood & Fire, argues that the use of riddims became so important that, by 1983, almost no Jamaican recording had a completely original rhythmic track. If riddims can be used this way, it is because copyright laws have been, and remain, non-existent in Jamaica. As Dermott Hussey says, "You can copyright a song, but you can't copyright a rhythm" (in Hebdige 1987: 82). Moreover, the use of the riddim has become an essential component of reggae music, a tradition that very few artists would contest, even those who have contracts with major labels

---

[2] As reggae artist I Roy said, "It is easier for a camel to go through the eye of a needle than for a version to die" (in Davis 1992: 99).
[3] Other famous riddims are the Bam-Bam, the Sleng-Teng, the Bogle, or the Bada-Bada.

The construction of a musical memory

in the USA or Europe. Any restriction on the use of the riddims would prevent artists from giving their own version of somebody else's song, and therefore would endanger the very existence of the sound systems.

Some might say, especially if they are not familiar with reggae music, that the permanent and repetitive use of riddims lacks musical creativity. But this persistence is in itself a creation: of the artist who sings, of the sound-engineer who remixes. And the speed with which styles, fashions, and artists succeed each other is such that originality is actually a necessary condition to success, especially in reggae dancehall. This originality of course implies an important creativity, even if it is achieved by using an already existing version. And their continuous use, as a sign of recognition of their quality by the artists as well as by the audience, is also a way of paying homage to them: indeed, for a reggae artist to have his or her own song re-used all over again is something like a consecration. By using and re-using a riddim, respect is shown to the artist who created it; at the same time, it makes the riddim persist over time, and therefore keeps it alive because it keeps being played in the dancehalls.

The texts make the history of music

If the continuous use of riddims show how much there exists a continuity throughout the thirty years of existence of reggae music, and how much recordings are able to persist, this continuity is also reinforced by the lyrics themselves, which often refer to other artists or other songs. In 1976, for instance, the Mighty Diamonds evoke "the days of Johnny too bad," referring to a 1972 song by the Slickers:

> What you gonna do when the voice is gone
> 'Member in the days of Johnny too bad
> Pick up your guns and you go to town
> See your black brother and you shoot him down
> That's wrong.
> The Mighty Diamonds,
"Why me black brother why," 1976

> Walking down the road with a pistol in your waist, Johnny you're too bad

> Walking down the road with a ratchet in your waist, Johnny you're too bad
> You're just robbing and stabbing and looting and shooting, now you're too bad.
>
> The Slickers, "Johnny too bad," 1972

But the lyrics sometimes contain more than simple references, and literally "make" the history of reggae music, for instance in "DJ's choice" (1973) by Dennis Alcapone, in which he "lines up the competition" by mentioning other dee-jays, along with references to their famous songs of the time (for instance "Draw your brakes" for Scotty), and tell people to make their choice. There is a similar process in Morgan Heritage's "Liberation" (1998), which remembers artists who have passed away (Jacob Miller in 1980, Bob Marley in 1981, Peter Tosh in 1987, and Garnett Silk in 1994) and establishes a continuity with today's artists (Morgan Heritage, Sizzla, Luciano, Stephen, Ziggy and Kymani Marley, Capleton, and Buju Banton).[4] The song pays homage to both dead and living artists; it also introduces a temporal continuity and succession, by linking artists from the past to young artists who are emerging in the present. Anthony B does the same in his song "Cut out that" (1999):

> Dem did use Ninjaman and go compete Shabba
> and dem use Beenie Man compete Bounty Killa
> and dem use Bob Marley compete Jacob Miller
> and dem use Derrick Morgan compete Prince Buster
> and dem use Garnett Silk compete Luciano
> now dem wah compete Anthony B and Sizzla
> but member say we a Rasta, King Selassie I we chant for.

In fact, Anthony B retraces the history of reggae decade after decade: Derrick Morgan and Prince Buster in the 1960s, Bob Marley and Jacob Miller (with his band Culture) in the 1970s, Ninjaman and Shabba Ranks in the 1980s, Beenie Man and Bounty Killer in the

---

[4] "Bob Marley rise and gone and dem think we done / Peter Tosh rise and gone and dem think we done / Jacob Miller rise and gone dem think we done / Garnett Silk him rise and gone but look out / Morgan Family come rise and many rise thru our uprising / Sizzla rise and many rise thru his uprising / Luciano rise and many rise thru his uprising … Marley children rise and many rise thru their uprising / Capleton rise and many rise thru his uprising / Buju rise and many rise thru his uprising." Morgan Heritage, "Liberation," 1998.

1990s, and finally the young, "cultural" dee-jays of reggae dancehall, who emerged in the mid-90s: Garnett Silk, Luciano, Sizzla, and Anthony B. In 1996, Anthony B already had a song about dancehall artists ("Repentance time"): Bounty Killer, Buju Banton, Professor Nut, Sanchez, Everton Blender. The song contains many references that cannot be understood by an outsider (for example a reference to Sanchez's 1994 hit "Brown eye girl").

Through the persistence of the riddims and their permanent use, and through the references made to other artists, whether they are from the past or from the present, reggae thereby continually makes its own history. Whatever their favorite song is, one will hear it in the dancehall sooner or later: one only has to wait long enough. This permanent "self-history" is a powerful identity marker: first because it immediately sets aside the outsiders, who will neither be able to locate the references nor, most importantly, to understand them. Second, because it allows the group to build its own history, in its own terms, and establishes a strong and immediate sense of continuity through the construction of a musical genealogy. Therefore, this self-history traces and maintains boundaries between insiders and outsiders, and also consolidates a sense of belonging within the group itself, by narrating its own history. It chants the artists, past and present, and the evolution of reggae music.

The remembrance of the dead: The case of Bob Marley and Garnett Silk

A social group is based on the interaction that exists, within it, among its members, as well as the interaction between the group and the outside; it considers itself as forming a group, and is recognized by others as forming a group; its members have the feeling, the consciousness of forming a group. This essential importance of interaction has been emphasized in relation to ethnic groups (Barth 1969): boundaries are dynamically defined in interaction, both by the group itself and by the others. This collective feeling is based on a common past (which can be historical or mythical), and, usually, on the contemplation of a shared future. Memory therefore plays a central role in group formation, since it is the principal component for the construction and maintenance of a continuity in time, and for the transmission of the past. Memory is here considered as a narrative of the past, as the point of view of the people on the past, which explains why the past does not need to be real—or, in other words, historical. What matters is identification, individual and collective, with a (chosen) past that makes sense for the individual and the group. Collective memory works in numerous and diverse ways. The sense of belonging and definition of collective boundaries are built and maintained through the establishment of a collective memory, which gives the group a constructed past upon which an imagined future can be built. One of the most powerful tools used by collective memory concerns the remembrance of the dead, because it unites the group through a shared sense of belonging, through the memory and emotion linked to the disappearance of their own people. Among others, two examples are especially significant in the case of reggae music: Bob Marley and Garnett Silk.

Bob Marley died in 1981 at the age of 41, of complications linked to cancer. He is the emblematic figure of reggae music, and is largely considered the "father" of reggae. At the time of his death, he was at the peak of his musical career, and internationally famous. Countless books, articles, and films concern him; he is on postcards, calendars, shirts, and posters. Of course, this presence is linked to commercial interests, for example his use by the Jamaican government, which is obviously a way of serving political or economic interests (Waters 1989). What remains interesting though, beyond his persistent and continuous commercial success, is the fact that he remains present within reggae music, twenty-five years after his death and with a strength that seems always renewed. He remains today the best-selling reggae artist; for example, in May 2000, his album *Exodus* (1977) was in the Jamaican albums top 10, twenty-five years after its initial release.

Other facts, less obvious but perhaps more interesting from the point of view of collective memory, show the continuous presence of Bob Marley in reggae music. First, there is the homage paid to him by other artists by recording their own version of his songs. There are countless examples of this. Sometimes these songs are grouped in one commemorative album, usually entitled *Tribute to Bob Marley*. It is worth noting that this phenomenon is not limited to reggae music, from the version of "I shot the sheriff" by Eric Clapton, who actually opened the North American market to Bob Marley himself, to the house remix of "Sun is shining," which was number one in the UK charts in 1999. Second, multiple references are made to Bob Marley in other artists' songs, for instance in Sizzla: "I see Bob Marley rise and unnuh kill mi prophet / why yuh don't kill those standing on yuh pulpits?" ("Praise Yeh Jah," 1997). Sometimes, songs use his own lyrics; this kind of tribute is more discreet, and not accessible to everyone: only the fans know that a given sentence comes from this or that Marley song. For example, Anthony B tells that "Bob Marley shot the sheriff and mi go shoot the deputy" ("Who shoot first," 1999), referring to Bob Marley's "I shot the sheriff / but I didn't shoot no deputy" ("I shot the sheriff," 1973). Bob Marley shot the sheriff, Anthony B will shoot the deputy: the latter echoes a radicalization; and beyond the homage to Marley, Anthony B also claims to be his heir, the one who continues what Marley has started.[5] Sizzla also mentions "I shot the sheriff" in his song about violence, police, and guns: "di cowboy dem still ah hype cause Bob him shot di sheriff" ("Cowboy," 1997). This mode of belonging is linked to what I have already mentioned about the singles: to know is to belong. The understanding of references that outsiders do not understand (or even the simple fact of knowing that there is a reference) is a powerful tool for establishing the boundaries between "us" and "them." And it is essential in reggae music, because a large part of the lyrics are in fact references, which might be made to other songs or artists, to events, to the Bible, to history, and so forth. An outsider, foreign to the group's memory, will be able to understand the texts, but this comprehension will remain literal, without the complete meaning conveyed by the words. In reggae music, everything is linked to everything else, nothing is wasted, and the history of the musical style is made through music, which refers to the music that was played before: other songs, other lyrics, other riddims. This is partly due to the sound system tradition, based on competition and mutual defiance among dee-jays: many songs are in fact answers to songs that preceded them. It implies that one who does not know the preceding songs cannot really pick up the reference or appreciate its meaning. Third, another way in which Bob Marley is remembered in reggae music is as a model to whom artists are compared. Some even complain about his omnipresence; Buju Banton for instance, who has often been considered as the possible and long-awaited "new Bob Marley," has said on numerous occasions that he was tired of this perpetual comparison. But it remains true that Bob Marley is as

---

5   Another citation of Bob Marley's "I shot the sheriff" is found in Sizzla: "di cowboy dem still ah hype cause Bob him shot di sheriff" ("Cowboy," 1997).

present in reggae as he was before his death, if not more. As has been the case for Haile Selassie, physical death does not imply spiritual disappearance, and absence can even reinforce presence.

Garnett Silk, born Garnett Smith, owed his music name to his voice, which was said to be "as smooth as silk." He emerged in reggae dancehall at the very beginning of the 1990s, performed with the Killamanjaro sound system, and recorded with many artists such as Tony Rebel, Buju Banton, or Anthony B. Garnett Silk was famous for his engagement within the Rastafari movement and its opposition to slackness reggae (of which he said "it a go soft like porridge"). He died in December 1994, during a fire at his home in Mandeville, Jamaica. The circumstances of his death remain unclear: the police declared that gunshots provoked the explosion of a gas tank, while others said that his house had been attacked with explosive devices. Thousands attended Garnett Silk's funeral; his death provoked deep emotion within reggae music, because he was greatly respected and admired, and opposed "gangsta dee-jays." Soon after his death, two major albums were released: the first is a compilation of some of his recordings (the *Collectors* compilation), and the second is a selection of dubplates recorded with his sound system, Killamanjaro (*Killamanjaro Remembers Garnett Silk: The Dubplates*). Both have a clear and explicit goal: they are an homage to Garnett Silk, murdered at the age of 28. In the *Collectors* compilation, the dee-jay Tony Rebel introduces the album with an a-cappella song:

> In our hearts always
> that's where he will stay
> for days and days and extra days ...
> a lot of pain, a lot of strain but we nah complain
> cause we don't want to fly outta Jah faith
> first thing we start to cry and water rolled from our eye
> but then the twinkle of our eye things were rectified
> cause every human has to suffer and die
> we continue to love our brother even if he's not here
>   physically
> who is wise then will see, please set your heart free cause
>   what is to be got to be.
>   Tony Rebel, intro in *Garnett Silk Collectors*, 1998

Clearly this song is in homage to Garnett Silk; it is also, more generally, a reflection on life and death ("every human has to suffer and die") as well as on religious faith ("we don't want to fly outta Jah faith," despite a death that seems unjust, and "who is wise then will see ... what is to be got to be," in reference to the will of God, who always has his reasons, as well as in reference to redemption). The song that follows this Intro by Tony Rebel is Garnett Silk's song "A man is just a man," which refers to the fact that, whether it is felt just or unjust, deserved or undeserved, death is a part of life and the will of God. In the other album, *Killamanjaro Remembers Garnett Silk*, the spoken introduction of the album is again a memorial that expresses everlasting remembrance, as well as a strong sense of belonging between the people who appreciated Garnett Silk, who all remember him like the members of Killamanjaro sound system.[6]

The example of Garnett Silk is interesting because it is very different from the case of Bob Marley. The process of remembrance is both less intense, because he was not as famous as Marley, and more intense, because his death belongs to the recent past: many listeners were only children when Bob Marley died, while Garnett Silk was part of their adult life. In both cases, the importance of commemoration and homage is obvious. From a "technical" point of view, the remembrance of deceased artists contributes to the establishment of continuity in the history and collective memory of reggae music, by building a progression and defining epochs and generations that follow one another. From an emotional point of view, it participates in the continuous affirmation of the solidity of the ties that exist within the group, and contributes to the maintenance of a sense of unity and belonging. The remembrance of the dead, through collective commemoration, must therefore be considered as a factor of continuous reinforcement of the identity of the group, which owes its efficacy to the intense emotion that it brings forth. And here the remembrance of the dead has to be understood as a continuation of, or succession to, mourning itself; it is a piacular rite, as defined by Durkheim: "rites that are conducted under conditions of uncertainty or sadness" (Durkheim 1912: 393). But the function of piacular rites is the same as for positive rites: through sharing the loss of one of the members of the group, mourning produces collective effervescence and reinforces the unity of the group (Durkheim 1912: 402–403). The function of piacular rites, therefore, is above all a cohesive one;

---

[6] "To all the Garnett fans in the world / Killamanjaro remembers Garnett Silk." Intro in *Killamanjaro Remembers Garnett Silk*, 1999.

indeed for Durkheim, it is not individual, but collective pain and sadness that is expressed in mourning:

> The basis of mourning is the impression of enfeeblement that is felt by the group when it loses a member. But this very impression has the effect of bringing the individuals close to one another, putting them into closer touch, and inducing in them the same state of soul. And from all this comes a sensation of renewed strength, which counteracts the original enfeeblement. People cry together because they continue to be precious to one another and because, regardless of the blow that has fallen upon it, the collectivity is not breached. To be sure, in that case they only share sad emotions in common; but to commune in sadness is still to commune, and every communion of consciousnesses increases social vitality, in whatever form it is done. (Durkheim 1912: 405)

Hence the effect of piacular rites is that they transform individual and collective *negative* emotions into a *positive* effect for the group. What is of interest here, beyond the mourning phase, is the resilience of collective mourning through commemoration: loss is repeated over time, reenacting the original mourning and revitalizing the bonds of the group. Collective memory proceeds both from historical facts and the life of the individuals themselves, and works through a process of symbolization. It is, in a way, the manner in which people build a collective past, and with it an identity and unity, cemented by the a past believed to be shared. But collective memory also plays a fundamental role in the elaboration of a common imagined future. This function is acutely expressed in the commemoration and remembrance of the dead: by remembering its deceased, the group builds solid ties between its members in the present (since they share the pain together, and celebrate their common belonging while celebrating the disappearance of one of them) and establishes a continuity between the times. Indeed, by remembering the dead, the group also *remembers a common past* ("we celebrate the memory of one of our kin, absent today"), *acknowledges a shared present* ("if we come together to celebrate today, it is because we belong to the same group"), and *builds a collective future* (since "others will remember me tomorrow just like I remember ours today"). Concerning the familial group, Déchaux (1997: 305) said that, through the remembrance of the dead, the succession of generations allows a consolidation of individuals' sense of permanence and conscience of their existence, as well as a confirmation of the strength of the lineage. It is the same with groups: the remembrance of the dead participates in the elaboration of a past, present, and future as well as the continuity that links them. It also contributes to the construction of boundaries of identity and a sense of belonging. In other words, the remembrance of the dead participates in the construction and reinforcement of the unity and solidity of the group, and of its collective identity.

Reggae therefore offers, through its texts and practices (especially sound systems), a construction and transmission of its own musical memory. This memory participates in the definition of the boundaries that determine collective belonging, in particular through the references present in the lyrics, which trace immediate limits between "those who understand" and "those who do not"—that is, between the inside and the outside. It also does so through the use of communal markers (the "lyrical floaters" mentioned in chapter 1). Moreover, through repetition, re-use and commemoration, reggae music succeeds in building a strong temporal continuity that plays an essential role in the maintenance of collective identity (which, too, defines the inside and the outside) and builds homogeneity, within the group as much as in the eyes of the rest of the world.

Part II

Remembering the past

5

Slavery and the diaspora: Temporal and spatial articulations

Our relationship to the past is not a simple process; it mixes, in a complex way, a linear history-time with a memory-time that makes the past an experience lived in the present. Events that produce meaning, in particular when they have not been "resolved," never stop "surviving"; in the case of the African diaspora, the past of slavery still makes sense today, as if the slaveships were still crossing the Atlantic each day, over and over again. Indeed, memory is not a linear phenomenon. It uses symbols and proceeds by circular and back-and-forth movements, from the past to the present and from the present to the past, and even projects itself into the future. While the past influences the present, memory also—and maybe above all—functions in the reverse direction: individuals and groups identify with a past that makes sense *to them*, they interpret history and even organize it, by taking from the past but also leaving some of it behind. Collective memory, through the collective and individual identifications it sets up, produces identity; it allows people to know where they come from (whether this origin is "real" or not), and therefore where they are going; it establishes a continuity, a succession, whether it is at the level of the family, the group or the nation. When people identify with a common past or origin, or with a shared path throughout time, they recognize each other as belonging to the same group. As Max Weber pointed out, indeed, the ethnic group is based on a "subjective belief in ... common descent," which might be linked to physical or cultural similarities or to "memories of colonization or migration" (Weber 1978: 389); this belief, in turn, facilitates political formation.

The question of common origin and history becomes acutely important in situations of displacement. Because people in exile do not have any territorial anchorage, because their land does not belong to them anymore, the land becomes less of a given and still increasingly charged at the symbolic and emotional levels. The construction of the diaspora as such, and the emergence of a sense of collective belonging, are then increasingly based on the transmission of memory—because the land is not here to transmit its history and presence spontaneously, through the marks it bears and the history of the people who inhabit it. A little like a city destroyed by bombing or an earthquake has lost the concrete traces of its history, people in exile have to rebuild a historical topography in order to keep alive what has happened before and is not built, written, nor present "before one's eyes." Moreover, in the case of the African diaspora, one could read the slave trade as an explicit attempt to cut a group from its past; indeed, one of the central processes within the slavery system, particularly in the British colonies and in the American South, was the purposeful destruction of kinship ties and cultural transmission;[1] in other words, the destruction of collective memory. For the slaves and their descendants, the transmission of memory therefore became an essential project, because it had been endangered in an extreme way, but also because they had to face a quasi-artificial "diaspora-ization" and to build themselves again as a people.

  But what is a diaspora? The term is now widely used, within and without academia. This development can be considered as a success story, as evidenced by the wide use of the term for situations that were not, before, considered as "diasporic" (such as migrant workers, political refugees, or transnational groups with or without an existing homeland). Although the widespread use of the term diaspora is quite recent, it is in fact part of the investigation of cultural movement and contact, which can be traced back to the emergence of the "anthropology of cultural contact" in the works of Melville Herskovits and Roger Bastide, in the first half of the twentieth century. Both were interested in a simple question: What

---

[1] See Meillassoux 1992 and Patterson 1982, who both argue, in different ways, for the desocialization and depersonalization of the slave. The severing of kinship ties, in particular through the intentional dispersal of relatives by the slavemasters, was counter-balanced by attempts to preserve kinship, for instance through the naming of children by their parents (Cody 1982).

happens to culture when cultures meet? And both emphasized "the Americas" as societies born not of a simple juxtaposition of cultures, but of their intermixing, giving way to a new construction. The creolization model, derived from linguistics and applied to "culture making" by anthropologists like Hannerz (1987), is grounded in this questioning; just as Herskovits insisted on seeing North American society as being, itself, a syncretic society, the creolization model insists on the necessity of seeing Western societies as being the product of a Creole process. In other words, creolization is considered a part of the very process of culture making, at least in modernity: to a certain extent, all societies are Creole, and all cultures the product of a creolization process. This aim to weaken the borders between "the West" and "the rest" (Hall 1996) has to be seen in relation to the need to overcome the traditional distinction between a sociology of industrialized societies and an anthropology of exotic (or primitive) societies, as well as to the desire to denounce the colonial discourse on the value of culture. If I mention these models here, it is for two reasons. First, because both recognized the Africans in the Americas as forming a *diaspora*, although they did not use the term, and because their work proved seminal to its latter conceptualization. Second, to point out that there has been an evolution of vocabulary rather than a change of object of inquiry. Do we speak of diaspora today because reality has changed, or is it simply a new term for an old reality? The negative side of the success of the term is, indeed, that it is now used broadly to speak about "people in movement" (and cultures, social systems, symbolic systems, in movement). And its main consequence is that, oftentimes, there seems to be no need to define the term anymore; as Anthias states, diaspora is "an over-used but under-theorized term" (1998: 557). In the most basic way, the term refers to the dispersal of people from their homeland. Within the last two decades, two positions have appeared as central within the conceptualization of diaspora: the first emphasizes the relationship of the diaspora to the homeland, while the second emphasizes the transverse relationships that exist within the diaspora outside of the homeland. Interestingly enough, the first position, represented by scholars like Safran or Cohen, centers on the descriptive definition of a category and the need for typological comparison, while the second, represented by Hall, Gilroy, or Clifford, centers on a condition or process derived from the notion of movement.

The first position can be called a "centered model." In 1991, in the first volume of the journal *Diaspora*, Safran published a seminal article in which he aimed to define the notion of diaspora. He takes the Jewish Diaspora as the model; although he speaks of it as being an "idealtype," there seems to be a confusion between his model and the ideal type in the Weberian sense of the term. It might seem to be a minor problem, but nevertheless it has important consequences, common to several typologies of diasporas: groups themselves are taken as an ideal-type, thereby reversing the methodological movement; reality becomes the ideal-type instead of being explained by it. From this methodological problem stems one of the difficulties in applying and using the typologies: there is an endless list of types, since each new group one looks at is susceptible to "become" a new type. Moreover, groups are considered within a static and unifying frame, which does not allow one to grasp the diversity found within the groups themselves: in reality, no diasporic group is homogeneous, whether synchronically or diachronically. Hence the types become difficult to use as analytical tools.[2] The issue of the elaboration of ideal-types is not the only problem in Safran's model. According to him, the term diaspora should be applied to "expatriate minority communities" whose members share several of the following characteristics (1991: 83–84):

1. They have been dispersed from one original 'center' to two or more 'peripheral' regions;
2. They retain a collective memory, vision, or myth about their original homeland;

---

[2] Ideal-types are built in order to make reality intelligible; they are a methodological tool that Weber considers as necessary for a sociological understanding and explanation of reality, but they are not a *description* of reality; they are a rational construction used to explain an irrational reality (Weber 1978: 6, 20). They are, in Weber's words, a utopia; they do not exist in reality in their pure form: "an ideal-type is formed by the one-sided accentuation of one or more points of view and by the synthesis of a great many diffuse, discrete, more or less present and occasionally absent concrete individual phenomena, which are arranged according to those one-sidedly emphasized viewpoints into a unified analytical construct. In its conceptual purity, this mental construct ... cannot be found empirically anywhere in reality. It is a utopia" (1949: 90).

Slavery and the diaspora 89

3. They believe that they are not—and perhaps cannot be—fully accepted by their host society and therefore feel partly alienated and insulated from it;

4. They regard their ancestral homeland as their true, ideal home and as the place to which they or their descendants would (or should) eventually return;

5. They believe that they should, collectively, be committed to the maintenance or restoration of their original homeland and to its safety and prosperity;

6. They continue to relate ... to that homeland in one way or another, and their ethnocommunal consciousness and solidarity are importantly defined by the existence of such a relationship.

Here, the essential element in the typology is the homeland, and therefore the notion of origin. An ongoing relationship to the homeland (and furthermore a faithful relationship, expressed by both the impossibility of full acceptance by the host country and the contemplation of return) defines the diaspora. One problem lies in the unification of homeland and diaspora: there is here an underlying assumption that we are in presence of, first, a unified community that shares a common sense of belonging, consciousness, and experience *because* its members are in diaspora; and, second, of a homeland that is a unified, original center. If indeed there is a unified center, is it not to be found in the *dynamic construction* of the center as being unified, rather than in its inherent character? In other words, the very centrality of a unified homeland might be a construct that was elaborated during the process of becoming a diaspora. Similarly, the unified, communal character of the group in diaspora might itself be a construct—and even a dynamic consequence of being in diaspora, as opposed to an inherent character of the group. In Safran's model, there is an *assumption of unity*: the origin makes the group, whereas in fact it might be more pertinent to see the group as making the origin.

One difficulty in applying the typology is revealed by the fact that several groups are qualified as diasporas *at a more or less high degree*. In other words, some diasporas are "more" diasporic than others. This is well illustrated by the case of the African diaspora which, when confronted with Safran's typology, can hardly be considered a diaspora because most points are highly problematic. First, the center is geographically multiple, unless we consider the African continent as a single, unified, and homogenous place. Indeed, Africa has been constructed as such: the African origin as being the common denominator of the group was progressively elaborated after, and not prior to, enslavement. The oneness of the center, therefore, is questionable: perhaps what characterizes diasporas is their ability to invent or reinvent the center *a posteriori*, and their insistence on referring to this imagined center. Second, lack of acceptance and feelings of alienation are complex matters, usually linked to the colonial and post-colonial situation. As Stuart Hall mentions, in the Caribbean "everybody is from somewhere else," which creates a situation that is slightly different from the displacement of a group to an established nation-state, since until the second half of the twentieth century most Caribbean countries were colonies. Therefore the host country is not really a free nation-state, and alienation is experienced more in terms of slavery than in terms of nationhood. Third, return is sometimes contemplated, but not always. On a concrete level, return has been unusual, although it has happened and still does. Even the symbolic importance of an idealized return cannot be considered as characteristic of the African diaspora: it is sometimes essential, sometimes absent. Finally, the very category of people to which Safran's typology applies to is problematic. Both the "minority" and "community" terms might not really fit the case of the African diaspora: we find situations of numerical minority and majority, and situations of symbolic minority and majority. Does this mean, then, that the African diaspora is not a diaspora, or is a weak one, or is less of a diaspora than the Jewish Diaspora? The main point here is the primacy given to the notion of center (and to the notion of diaspora as being "what is outside of the center") and the assumption made about its inherent and given character. Through the primacy of the center, there is the underlying assumption of a communal unity between the homeland and the diaspora. The case of the African diaspora clearly resists the idea of the primacy of the center as well as the assumption of a unified community.

The multi-centered model tries to answer the problems raised by the assumptions of the centered model. It is concerned with the multiform character of the center; as Clifford notes (1997: 250), "a shared, ongoing history of displacement, suffering, adaptation, or resistance may be as important as the projection of a specific origin." Indeed, the center does not necessarily have to be a land or a country; it can be a reinvented tradition, a book, a "portable eschatology." In other words, the center can be purely symbolic. In the case of slave descendants, it is also a shared experience of the slave trade; what matters is not geographical origin *per se*, but the idea of a "before" and of an "elsewhere," associated with a shared history, a common memory, a path of exile characterized by the same suffering. Return—like the relationship maintained with the homeland—does not need to be concretely enacted, nor even really contemplated; and it does not need to be the same for everyone. For the rastas, the homeland is Ethiopia: it is indeed a reconstructed, reinvented, imagined center. As Homiak (1994b: 958) points out, "those in the African diaspora have traced their links to a homeland through the trauma of slavery and a welter of invented traditions. The maps they have imagined of Africa are made meaningful in ideologies of struggle and resistance forged in a crucible of exile." Hence the idea of the return might work as a symbolic structure, without any need for actual realization.

The multi-centered model is, secondly, concerned with the equal importance of multiple relationships and movements within the diaspora, as opposed to the primacy of the relationship to the center. Gilroy (1993) argues that what matters in diasporic consciousness are *both* the roots of the group—that is, its origin—and the routes it has taken—that is, its shared history subsequent to dispersal; both, in a dynamic interplay, shape the positioning of the diasporic group. In other words, what happened *after* the original dispersal matters as much as what happened before: to a vertical and unidimensional relationship to the homeland is added a fundamental, multidimensional relationship both within and outside the diasporic group; Clifford (1994) speaks of the "lateral" movements and relationships, which coexist with the centrality of the origin—and it could even be added that it is *precisely* the history of displacement, traced after the founding event of exile, that gives the homeland its essential symbolic importance as a center.

I propose to enter the problematic of the diaspora at the level of symbolic processes. The diasporic process can be considered as involving, on one hand, some sort of relationship, sometimes concrete but always imagined, with some sort of land, sometimes real but always idealized, and on the other hand a set of transverse relationships within the diaspora; it is characterized by the simultaneity of being *from one place and of another*. This approach allows for an understanding of the coexistence of homogeneity and heterogeneity within diasporic groups. In the case of the African diaspora, there is a strong identification with African origins, considered as a center that acts as a unifying identity, and so as a producer of homogeneity; simultaneously, there is a multitude of identifications that produce differentiated identities, for instance Jamaican, Colombian, or African-American. If we exclusively emphasize the relationship to the center, then we miss the multidimensional character of the diaspora, by ignoring the history shared after its occurrence; this produces the assumption that the diasporic group is a community, and is therefore unable to account for its multidimensional form. On the contrary, taking the historical context—a context processed through memory—into account, both within and between groups, allows for an understanding of the variations found within and between them, while acknowledging the elements of homogeneity. Additionally, characterizing the diasporic process as the articulation between being *from* one place and *of* another helps us to understand the dialectic of return. Indeed, while being based on the idea of return (whether it is possible or impossible, soon to come or very far in the future, towards an existing country or one that has disappeared), most diasporas indefinitely postpone this contemplated return. This articulation between the necessary idea of the return and its simultaneous impossibility seems to be characteristic of diasporic consciousness, and echoes the dialectic between failure and success developed by Desroche (1979) concerning messianic religious movements, or by Weber (1978) concerning the routinization of charismatic authority: in both cases, failure is needed for, or produced by, success—since charismatic authority can survive only by transforming into something else. One question that might arise, then, is whether the impossibility of the return is not in fact dynamically set up by the diaspora itself, in order to precisely survive as diaspora.

By focusing on a symbolic process, on a diaspora that is imagined and, further, imagined through the construction of memory, my argument is therefore situated within—or close to—a theoretical frame that owes as much to the Durkheimian school as to Max Weber. Indeed, what I am looking at is a process of meaning attribution: in the end, what matters is what the homeland means to the group in the present, not what the homeland is or was. In other words, the homeland does not matter in itself, as a fixed entity and within an inherent relationship, *it matters because individuals and groups make it meaningful in the way they identify and act.* As Weber pointed out,

Slavery and the diaspora

"ethnic groups" can be formed on the basis of any form of similarity or dissimilarity, be it physical or imagined; and his definition of the ethnic group emphasizes both belief and memory:

> We shall call "ethnic groups" those human groups that entertain a subjective belief in their common descent because of similarities of physical type or of customs or both, or because of memories of colonization and migration; this belief must be important for the propagation of group formation; conversely, it does not matter whether or not an objective blood relationship exists. (Weber 1978: 389)

By imagining their homeland and making it matter in their present identifications, as well as by inserting themselves in the history that they share outside of this same homeland, diasporas create a continuity in time: they rely on a past that matters in their present and allows for a representation of the future. However, the process at work here is not one of static conservation, but rather of dynamic interpretation: the past is not a trace, but a narrative. This is not, of course, a specificity of diasporas alone, but it matters most in this case: the diasporic process provides a beautiful example of how the past is made to matter, rather than how it matters inherently. The importance of the center is relative, not inherent; it is born out of the present, not out of the past; it is a part of an inscription in tradition, not of tradition itself. Again, it is part of the construction of a temporality that is made for and from the present, and links the past to the future because it matters in the present, not because it is the order of things.

Let's now turn to the case of reggae music, and more specifically to the object of inquiry in this study—that is, the corpus of songs used for analysis.[3] It can be argued that here it is not just one, but two centers, which are constructed and produce a sense of unity for the group. On the one hand, slavery appears as a temporal center; on the other hand, Africa constitutes a spatial center; both have to do not only with the origin, but with the subsequent history of the group. Hence there is a foundational land (Africa) and a foundational historical event (the Middle Passage); both are multi-textured, and articulated in a non-linear way.

---

[3] Which, I remind the reader, accounts for the point of meeting between reggae music and Rastafari.

Remembering slavery

The past of slavery is one of the most prominent themes in reggae music. Insistently, reggae remembers where its people came from and what they have lived through. References to the trade and the time spent in slavery are numerous, using the symbol of the slaveship and telling the story of the Middle Passage, for instance in "African race" by the Abyssinians (1976):

> Our forefathers were taken away
> taken away, taken away
> they were bound in ships and taken all away
> that boat just brought them to the West.

The history of the slave trade is told by emphasizing a strong continuity between today's Jamaicans and the slaves of yesterday ("our forefathers"). Indeed, while Gordon (1998: 96–101) notes that, in the case of the Black Creoles of Nicaragua's Mosquito Coast, the tie with the past of slavery is ambiguous and does not constitute, for individuals, a proof of African origin, the situation is completely reversed in reggae music: slavery and the slave trade are a part of the history of their people, and even constitute the essential events of this history.

Moreover, an undeniable, clear, and direct lineage is traced between the slaves and their descendants, themselves considered to be Africans. Hence for the Abyssinians,

> We are the slave descendants from the African race
> the African race, the African race
> we are the slave descendants from the African race
> we're proud, it's no disgrace.
>
> "African race," 1976

This clear lineage is not only accepted, but proclaimed ("we're proud"). Often singers use the first person of the plural, "we," because the African slaves captured in Africa by the Europeans and their actual descendants are considered as one single people, tied by a blood lineage. This is the case of the band Culture: "We've been too long, too long, too long in slavery … put us on a big ship they stole us away and took us away from Africa" ("Too long in slavery," 1979). The history of the slaves and the history of their descendants is the same, and the group that they form together, through the succession of generations, remains united by their sharing a past, which installs a permanence of "we," as well as "they"—that is, the slave masters. For the Abyssinians, "Look how long they brought us down there … they took us away from civilization / brought us to slavery in dis a big plantation" ("Declaration of rights," 1976). In this excerpt there is a reference to civilization, a notion that is essential to Rastafari: civilization is opposed to slavery, and implies the recognition of pre-colonial African civilization, but also a "lost paradise." Another illustration of the consideration of a united history is a song by Dennis Brown that tells about the crossing of the Atlantic:

> Have you read about the days of slavery
> when some of our brothers' life goes away
> they die each and every step of the way …
> could you imagine on their journey
> from Africa to Jamaica
> some went over board alive
> and some of them survived.
>
> "Jah can do it," 1978

There is here both a temporal separation between the trade and the present ("have you read," "could you imagine"), and an extreme proximity between the slaves who lived at the time of the trade and their descendants who live today ("some of our brothers," not fathers nor forefathers, which induces a generational closeness that tends towards superimposition). For Dennis Brown, it is a question of remembering a past that might be far away from the present (with intimacy, "imagine"), but that still touches the present very strongly, since it is about "our brothers."

As in this song by Dennis Brown, reggae texts sometimes go beyond a simple proximity or continuity of generations. In "Slave market" (1979), for instance, Gregory Isaacs sings that

> I saw you with your cargo
> in the midst of the Atlantic
> with my brothers and my sisters
> heading towards the Western slave market
> you killed so many slaves.

as if he had really lived through these historical facts, and using the first person singular: "I saw you." Bob Marley sings about the slave trade, *as if he had lived it*:

> Old pirates yes they rob I
> sold I to the merchant ships
> minutes after they took I
> from the bottomless pit.
>
> "Redemption song," 1980

The continuity between the slaves and their descendants also appear in the same song when he says, "We forward in this generation / triumphantly." The simultaneous use of the first person singular when telling about the Middle Passage and the first person plural when referring to the slaves and their descendants strongly suggests first a unity and a continuity in time (the succession of generations that are linked to each other), and second the intimate proximity of the experience of slavery (the past makes sense not only for past generations but also for present ones and, implicitly, for the ones to come). In "Slave driver" (1977), Marley for instance tells us that

> Every time I hear the crack of the whip
> my blood runs cold
> I remember on the slaveship
> how they brutalize my very soul

although he was not alive during the time of slavery.

Therefore, slavery is not a history lesson that one learns, but a history that is told and, moreover, felt in one's flesh and experienced in one's mind. It is part of a history, of course, but it is above all part of a memory, a memory strongly charged in emotions and intensely linked to the *symbolic*—that is, which operates through symbols that can express a feeling, a relationship, a sense of belonging, or even the "essence of a group," as Déchaux put it (1997: 18). In the case of reggae, many symbols are at work, and slavery constitutes one of the most essential. In "Crazy baldheads" (1976), Marley again establishes a strong continuity between the past and the present—that is, between the slaves and their descendants on the one hand, and between the slave masters and their descendants on the other hand: "didn't my people before me / slaved for this country." There has been no recognition of the work of the slaves and their descendants, although they have worked in the fields, houses and cities, and contributed to the riches of the Europeans. And history is repeating itself: just like during the time of slavery, the oppressors ("you") reap the fruits of the work of the oppressed ("I and I" and "we"): "I and

Slavery and the diaspora

I build a cabin, I and I plant the corn ... now you look at me with scorn / then you eat up all my corn." The same parable is used on a collective level: "Build your penitentiaries, we build your schools / brainwash education to make us the fools / hate is the reward for our love."

What Marley expresses, in the end, are two essential points: the constitutive quality of the past of slavery, which unites generations and individuals, and the way in which this past influences the present. It is fascinating to see how history can shape mentalities and behaviors, from familial history to the history of a people or a nation; in the case of the African diaspora, it seems obvious that the slave trade and slavery have marked the present. For Rastafari, slavery is an essential past, in the sense that it is an extremely strong symbolic referent, which produces meaning and from which many identifications are elaborated. It is also the object of a *devoir de mémoire*. Africa, the slave trade and slavery must not be forgotten:

> Do you remember the past of slavery?
> and how they beat us
> and how they worked us so hard
> and they use us til they refuse us
> do you remember the time of slavery?
> it's we time recall, it's we time recall the days of slavery
> oh slavery days
> do you remember?
> please remember.
>
> Burning Spear, "Slavery days," 1975

The past of slavery is considered as a constitutive memory, which should never be forgotten. That is why texts often take the form of a direct call ("I remember, do you remember?") and use the first person. Slavery is not simply a historical fact: it has a lived dimension and becomes a collective experience. As descendants of slaves, the rastas assert a shared emotional experience of slavery and hold a mission of remembrance:

> If I didn't seek for my culture, what would happen to my future
> maybe I would be under the earth
> maybe I would be in shackles and chains.
>
> Black Uhuru, "Time to unite," 1978

Forgetting is hence a synonym of death or mental slavery; on the contrary, remembering is a source of life and freedom, both physically and mentally. In "This man," Burning Spear quotes Marcus Garvey: "Any nation without their roots / is like a tree without their roots" ("This man," 1995); the slave trade, in between a before (Africa) and an after (slavery), must be remembered in order for the people to exist today, but also to project a vision of the future and, therefore, make a future possible: the history of the people must be alive, known, told, and transmitted, in all its reality and truth. If this is the case for slavery, it is also the case for a complex category formed around the African origin.

Africa reinvented

Slavery implies two essential notions, those of deracination and domination, which call forth two "elsewheres": one is spatial, referring to a mythical land, across the ocean, which is the place of origin, and a way of life, language and world that are now far away; the other is temporal, in reference to a sweeter past ("before") and to a better future to come ("after"). According to Chude-Sokei (1994: 80), reggae of the generation of Bob Marley is characterized by "nostalgia and longing for elsewhere."[4] Indeed, Africa, the land of origin, is omnipresent in reggae lyrics (under a diversified vocabulary: Africa, Ethiopia, Abyssinia, mother, mama …). It has a strong maternal character and is considered somewhat as the feminine counterpart of a masculine God (Jah). But it is not *simply* the land of origin: Africa also symbolizes an elsewhere, both spatial and temporal, a space of several levels of identifications which permanently mix and are superimposed: simultaneously land of the forefathers, contemporary Africa, and promised land, Africa is idealized, imagined, thought. The Africa of which Rastafari speaks, the Africa evoked in reggae music, is a "reinvented Africa"[5] that confronts three tenses (past, present, future) and three places (Africa,

---

[4] According to him, "Instead of dwelling psychically 'elsewhere,' the narratives of dancehall feature an exploration and celebration of the microrealities … what DJs … describe as strictly reality" (1994: 80–81). Unfortunately, Sokei's analysis does not take into account dancehall production after 1993.

[5] Capone (1999) uses the same term about Brazil, and Chude-Sokei (1994) about Jamaican reggae.

Europe, and the diaspora). Africa represents what could be called an "archetypical elsewhere" that is articulated by the experience of slavery. Indeed, the African diaspora is characterized by an intense tie to a homeland that has remained out of reach. Collective memory was forged within this material impossibility of the return, at least during the time of slavery, deep in the nineteenth century. But in the twentieth century, the material impossibility of returning to Africa has considerably decreased—which does not imply that return was concretely contemplated or implemented: while some return to Africa, they remain a tiny minority, even among the Rastafari movement. The notion of Africa therefore takes on different but simultaneous dimensions, articulated around the idea of a spatial and temporal elsewhere.

First of all, Africa represents *a spatial elsewhere and a temporal before from which slaves have been forced away*. It constitutes a lost paradise in the sense of Mircea Eliade (1954), which has been idealized in order that one might endure the pain of slavery and deracination, in the face of the harshness of the present, or finally simply because it is out of reach. For example, for Anthony B, Buju Banton, and Garnett Silk:

> the sweetest things are there to be found
> the golden sunshine
> the wind blows around
> the fresh vegetation which comes from the earth
> oh mama Africa you make me know what life is worth.
> "Hello mama Africa," 1999

It is a natural and ideal Africa, as God created it in the beginning; it is a maternal, original, fertile figure, the source of all life. Moreover, Rastafari associates this maternal figure with Ethiopia, considered as the place of religious origin and redemption, which reinforces its symbolic intensity. Africa therefore represents both the land of origin and the land of God; in this sense, it is symbolic location of the Good, heaven, and liberation—and therefore also an archetype of freedom.

Second, Africa is *the center of origin, from which the diaspora was scattered*. It is fundamentally considered as "home," the land where the forefathers were born, and hence the only place where slave descendants do not feel like foreigners. This dimension appears in many songs, for example in Burning Spear's "Old timer" (1995):

we all come from Africa
during the days of slavery
some of us were sent to the East
some to the West
some to the North
some to the South.

This center from which scattering took place is as spatial as it is temporal: it represents both a "before" (before the trade and forced exile) and an "elsewhere" (in opposition with the land of slavery). Luciano thus links the trade, slavery and the homeland:

Sweet African sunshine
I know you're mine all the time ...
most of the time, when I contemplate, reminiscing
I know I'm an African king
though they carry I and I abroad
and dem work black people so hard
and dem nah gave us no regard
still we waan go back a we yard
sometimes I wonder when we'll be home again.
"When will I be home," 1999

Here Luciano expresses the desire for return, but also the fact that return is still out of reach, or at least uncertain.

Third, Africa also symbolizes *an alternative to the West*, sometimes its complete antithesis; it is simultaneously the kernel of "civilization," the authentic culture of the slave descendants, and a better way to live and "be in the world." There is the idea here that culture is indeed linked to blood: to be African and to be European are two social belongings that imply fundamental cultural differences and are transmitted from one generation to the next through blood as much as through learning and symbolic inheritance. Africa and the West are therefore considered as inherently holding two cultures, two opposed ways of life. For instance, slavery might be considered as "a white thing" that was imported to Africa by the Europeans.[6] The existence of characteristic traits comprising African culture is

---

[6] I would like to add, at this point, an important comment: the only "truth" that I consider is the meaning that representations have for a given group at a given time. Here, therefore, the possible origins of slavery in Europe or elsewhere will not be discussed at all.

closely tied to the problematic of authenticity. Africa represents the authentic, original, and only culture, as opposed to an imposed and superficial European culture. Whether they are from a strict African lineage or not, and whatever the place they live in, rastas consider themselves Africans, as is explicitly stated in U Roy's "True born African" (1991):

> So we a true born Africans
> say natty a true born African
> living inna Jamaica
> sometimes you live in America
> sometimes you live inna London.

It is also what rastas assert when they quote Marcus Garvey's words ("Africa for the Africans, at home and abroad"). People must transmit and conserve their own culture, which implies that slave descendants must preserve their African roots. Within the Rastafari movement, numerous practices are directly justified by their "Africaness": what matters is not *real* but *attributed* Africaness, the fact that some practices symbolize Africa in the eyes of the people. As Wade (1999: 457) points out about Afro-Colombians, "it was not a collage made of anything ... some elements only were historically pertinent in relationship to their local and personal situations." There is therefore a logic of symbolic investment (what makes sense for the individuals, in light of their own situation), which might exclude some elements although they are historically "true," but which always obeys a pertinent logic.

Finally, Africa represents *the promised land, redemption and liberation*—in other words a temporal elsewhere which promises the end of oppression. As the counterpart to a paradise lost through slavery, Africa symbolizes the promised land (with or without a religious content) to which slave descendants will eventually return. As Chude-Sokei (1994: 80) says, "Zion, the promised land of Ethiopia, was both pre-colonial utopia and the imminent future of black people." Africa is then also a "temporal elsewhere" simultaneously articulated to the past and to the future; it is a complex spatial and temporal construct where one is from and where one is headed: a better, idealized world from before slavery, as well as a better world to come, within a problematic of expectation, longing and hope, these two temporal "elsewhere" being tightly tied to each other.

As a symbol of a temporal and spatial elsewhere, Africa is therefore a representation that has to do with *utopia*. The term comes from the Greek *ou*, "no," and *topos*, "place," and originally means "in no place." In no place, or in no time: Africa is a distant past as well as an ideal future that is not yet reached; it is also a place from which people have been taken away and of which they preserve memories. Therefore, it is not completely a "no-place" or a "no-time," but rather a "not-here" and "not-yet" (I borrow the expression from Bloch 1995): Africa is a place and time that remain out of reach at this moment—or which, as emphasized by Desroche (1960, 1969) *must* remain out of reach for the sake of the dynamics of the group. Simultaneously, Africa is also the place of symbolization for a religious and socio-political utopia, which can be realized through repatriation to Africa. It is a simultaneously unrealizable and realized utopia, which conjugates tenses that are both distinct and superimposed (in particular through the articulation between a future redemption and the contemporaneousness of eschatological time) as well as places articulated by the notion of diaspora.

Diaspora and diasporic functioning

In the case of the Rastafari movement, then, Africa is not only the land of origin or the center of dispersion: it is also a spatial elsewhere (across the ocean "reddened by the slave trade") and a temporal elsewhere (which calls not only to the past, but into the future as well). While Africa is a central place, the slave trade must also be considered an essential event for the diaspora, and slavery an essential collective experience. There is therefore a diaspora spatially scattered from a geographic center (Africa), which has a history that was also organized on the basis of a historical center (the slave trade). While Africa is the place where one is from, slavery is the founding event of the diasporic construction; it also is a shared experience, a path walked together, which not only commands the construction of the diaspora (since it provoked exile, and therefore forced the diasporization of a people), but also determines the diasporic identity it creates, by opposing slaves and slavemasters in a fundamental way (Figure 5.1).

The analytic model proposed by Safran (1991) gives an essential place to the notion of center. While this remains pertinent in the case of the African diaspora, the prominence given to Africa as the

Figure 5.1: Representations of Africa

Promised Land / Liberation / Redemption

Temporal Elsewhere / Future

Original Culture   AFRICA   Center of Origin

Cultural Elsewhere   Spatial Elsewhere

"Before Slavery"

Temporal Elsewhere / Past

center is also a limitation. Indeed, Africa does not only symbolize a center; by focusing on the notion of center, slavery (and its role in the construction of the diaspora) is greatly neglected. The centrality of Africa is not simply due to its quality as a homeland: it is also, and maybe above all, required by history and memory. The relationship to Africa and its essential importance as a center was indeed also shaped by the experience of slavery and by a history of European attempts to erase African history and culture (and the slaves' attempts to maintain it or go back to it). As Clifford says (1997: 247), diaspora is indeed, at the same time and with the same significance, both a history of dispersion and a memory of the homeland; moreover, it is a memory of the shared experience of slavery and a memory of the homeland. In other words, the history of displacement, traced after deracination, gives the latter an essential importance as center: what comes *afterward* participates in the construction of a diasporic memory as much as the center does. The common origin is hence not more important than the shared experienced that, after exile, follows it. Moreover, the common African origin is not a concrete reality, but a social construction. While slaves all came from Africa, the latter was not culturally uniform. The prominence of an "African" identity over, for instance, Fon, Ashanti, or Yoruba was progressively built into a shared history that starts with the slave trade and the Middle Passage, and in a fundamental opposition between the slaves/Africans and the slavemasters/Europeans, which was the consequence of the system of slavery.[7]

There is therefore a multitude of back-and-forth movements between an original center (Africa) and a shared history, the latter varying according to location. If the slave descendants are considered only as a diaspora essentially centered around a homeland, it becomes difficult to understand how the belonging to a group determined solely by African origin comes to be in tension with the history that followed the slave trade: this tension lies between unity and diversity, between an African center (that was built and not given) and a shared history, and between this shared history and a diverse history depending on a multiplicity of individual experiences as well as cultural differences (for instance, between the Portuguese, Spanish, Anglo-Saxon, and French systems of slavery). The diaspora was therefore constructed, and continues to be, not only with reference to an original center, but also through the displacements that line its history. Africa is not only an origin; the *multiple relation* between the center of origin and shared experience is the basis for the diaspora—superimposed melodic lines that have their own independence but to which is added a new dimension that is born of their combination.

---

[7] A consequence that might have been voluntary: slave masters indeed did their best to erase cultural belongings, by separating families or individuals who came from the same region, in order to make it impossible for them to speak African languages with each other. One might say that the slavery system privileged a homogeneous African/slave group over a multitude of prior belongings. See Meillassoux 1992.

6

The construction of a religious chain of memory

J'ai plus de souvenirs que si j'avais mille ans.
Baudelaire, "Spleen"

Ancient memories come on in thru my door
Rastafari is so true and so pure.
Sizzla, "Ancient memories," 1998

Reggae music and the Rastafari movement transmit a memory of slavery and a memory of Africa, which can be characterized as diasporic, in relation to an original center as much as to the shared experience that followed a founding event: the forced exile provoked by the slave trade. This collective memory is reinforced by a strong identification with the history of the Bible, especially the story of the Twelve Tribes of Israel: a people without a land, and gods in exile who, in Desroche's words (1973: 210–211), "are not dead" but participate in the transmission of a memory that is alive and in the construction of a collective identity. The Rastafari movement transmits a religious memory as well as a religious construction of the origin; like Afro-American Baptist Churches before it (Jenkins 1975; Raboteau 1980; West 1982), it proposes a fundamental re-reading of the Bible, with as its essential goal the *revelation* of a fact that, it argues, had been voluntarily hidden: the presence of the black people in biblical history. According to Rastafari, European Churches have falsified and modified the Bible in order to serve the representations that suited them. In other words, history has been adapted to the requirements of the Western nations, as well as europeanized and whitened in order to transform Europe into the sole bearer of civilization. This criticism occurs within the broader notion of a Christian lie, essential within many Afro-American, as well as African or Caribbean, religious movements: the falsified Christian representation of God and of biblical characters has been a means to affirm white superiority and therefore to dominate other people, through colonization or slavery. According to the Rastafari movement, not only is Africa present in the Bible, it is omnipresent. One of the justifications it advances is the geographical location of the events described in the Bible:[1] how could the Queen of Sheba be white, if her kingdom was in Axum? How could the Hebrews and Egyptians, from Jerusalem onto the Nile valley, have blonde hair and blue eyes? This re-reading of the Bible is strongly expressed in reggae music, for example in Rod Taylor's "Ethiopian kings" (1978): "King David, he was a black man / King Solomon, he was a black man / King Moses, he was a black man / from Africa" or in Sizzla's "Praise Yeh Jah" (1997), twenty years later: "Jesus and his disciples were all black / and so were the ancient of days hey Sizzla say dat." In "Buss up barriers" (1999), Morgan Heritage tells how history has been falsified by the Europeans:

> Society teach us Joshua to say he was a white man
> They teach us Jesus Christ to say he was a white man
> But hear this truth
> I never heard of no white man with hair like lamb's wool
> I never heard of no white man with feet like pure brass
> It's only a conspiracy
> To take away and change our history
> ... rastaman come to release the truth
> Black is the beginning of creation
>
> Morgan Heritage, "Buss up barriers," 1999

Hair like wool and feet like brass are the attributes of Jesus as he is described in the Book of Revelation: "His head and his hair were white as white wool, white as snow; his eyes were like a flame of fire; his feet were like burnished bronze, refined as in a furnace" (Revelation 1: 14).[2] This verse also constitutes the major argument

---

[1] Also supported by other movements, including various currents within African-American Islam and Christianity.
[2] It is the only description of Jesus found in the Bible. See also Sizzla, "Praise yeh Jah," 1997: "I did behold, until the throne was casted down yeah /and

advanced by the rastas to prove that Jesus was not a white man: if he is described in the Bible as having hair "like white wool" and feet "like burnished bronze," it is because indeed his hair was frizzy and his skin black. Reggae music participates in Rastafari's re-reading of the Bible, which is present in its texts at the levels of the constitution of a lineage as well as of a literal transmission of the biblical text, through the identification with the Twelve Tribes of Israel.

Children of Israel: The identification to the Twelve Tribes

For the rastas, the members of the African diaspora, exiled across the ocean, are the descendants of the biblical Twelve Tribes of Israel, scattered around the world. That is why they call themselves "children of Israel" or "Israelites," as it appears in Dennis Brown's song "Children of Israel" (1978) and as shown by the names of some reggae bands, for instance Israel Vibration or The Israelites. Through the identification with the people of Israel, the rastas read their own history in the Bible, by giving an essential importance to the benedictions and maledictions of the Patriarchs and to some strongly symbolic events in the history of Israel such as slavery in Egypt or the exodus. Israel Vibration, for instance, draws a parallel between the biblical exodus and the current situation:

> We gonna walk the streets of glory
> Babylonian gonna run and try to get there before us
> it's like the time in Egypt, when Egypt chased after Israel
>   through the Red Sea
> then it's like right now dem a chase after Israel through the
>   bloody sea
>   "Walk the streets of glory," 1978

"Babylonians" are assimilated to Pharaoh and his army, and the "rastas" to the people of Israel guided by Moses; chased across the Red Sea as they escaped to Canaan in the past, the children of Israel are chased again today as they escape to the new Promised Land (the New Jerusalem), this time across another sea that is still red ("the bloody sea") from the blood shed by the slave trade. In its very simplicity, the parable is powerful: it establishes a correspondence

---

the ancient of days King Haile Selassie Jah?/ you know with His garment as white as snow?/ His hair as pure as wool."

between the past and the present, and refers to the categories of Good and Evil (the Pharoah-Babylonians-Oppressors bloc facing the Israel-Rastafari-Oppressed bloc), to the history of slavery (through the correspondences between slavery in Egypt and the slave trade, and between the Red Sea and the Atlantic Ocean reddened by the Middle Passage), and to redemption (through the correspondences made between the past exodus to Canaan and the present, or future, exodus to Zion).

According to Raboteau (1980: 311), "slave Christianity" is characterized by an identification of the history of Exodus, which functions as an archetypical event through which the present of slavery could be interpreted. The same process is at work in the Rastafari movement: because the people of Israel were enslaved, identification operates perfectly; just as the Hebrews, slaves of Pharaoh, followed Moses to the Promised Land, the rastas walk towards liberation through the teachings of Marcus Garvey, who was actually nicknamed "the Black Moses." Hence, Rastafari sets up a correspondence between its own history and the history of Israel as narrated in the Bible. According to Levine (cited in Pratt 1990: 50), Black Spirituals contain a "compelling sense of identification with the children of Israel" and a "tendency to dwell incessantly upon and to relive the stories of the Old Testament." This analysis can easily be applied to reggae music, which cannot be considered a religious music but nonetheless transmits an intense identification with the people of Israel as well as a narrative of the Old Testament.

Among the Twelve Tribes,[3] the Tribe of Judah has a special status: it is seen as the most important and noble, in conformity with what is said of it in the Old Testament: "Judah, your brothers shall praise you; your hand shall be on the neck of your enemies; your father's sons shall bow down before you. Judah is a lion's whelp; from the prey, my son, you have gone up. He crouches down, he stretches out like a lion, like a lioness—who dares rouse him up? The scepter shall not depart from Judah, nor the ruler's staff from between his feet, until tributes comes to him" (Genesis 49: 8–10). Judah, fourth son of Jacob and Leah, who often plays the role of moderator (especially in the quarrels between Joseph and his other

---

[3] The Twelve Tribes were founded by the twelve sons of Jacob: Reuben, Simeon, Levi, Judah, Zabulon, Issachar, Dan, Gad, Asher, Nephtali, Joseph, and Benjamin. See Genesis 49.

brothers), is hence blessed among his brothers; it is within his tribe that leaders will be born, and other tribes will obey him. This special blessing of Judah is reiterated in the Book of Psalms: "He rejected the tent of Joseph, he did not choose the tribe of Ephraim; but he chose the tribe of Judah, Mount Zion, which he loves" (Psalm 78: 67–68). The tribe of Judah is also, in the history of Israel, the most populous. Haile Selassie comes from the line of Solomon, son of David, himself from the tribe of Judah; Jesus is also from the line of Judah (Hebrews 7: 14). For all these reasons, Rastafari's preference for the tribe of Judah is not surprising.

The prestigious status of the tribe of Levi appears less evident. Levi was the third son of Jacob with Leah. During his benedictions, Jacob said of Levi and Simeon: "Simeon and Levi are brothers; weapons of violence are their swords. May I never come into their council; may I not be joined to their company—for in their anger they killed men, and at their whim they hamstrung oxen. Cursed be their anger, for it is fierce, and their wrath, for it is cruel! I will divide them in Jacob, and scatter them in Israel" (Genesis 49: 5–7). In the Book of Deuteronomy, Moses gives to the Levites the function of priesthood; the tribe's mission is to serve God, and above all to conserve and transmit His word: the Levites carry and take care of the Ark of the Covenant, in which are kept the Ten Commandments: "At that time the Lord set apart the tribe of Levi to carry the ark of the covenant of the Lord, to stand before the Lord to minister to him, and to bless in his name, to this day. Therefore Levi has no allotment or inheritance with his kindred; the Lord is his inheritance, as the Lord your God promised him" (Deuteronomy 10: 8–9). On his deathbed, Moses speaks of Levi in the following words: "For they observed your word, and kept your covenant. They teach Jacob your ordinances, and Israel your law; they place incense before you, and whole burnt offerings on your altar. Bless, O Lord, his substance, and accept the work of his hands; crush the loins of his adversaries, of those that hate him, so that they do not rise again" (Deuteronomy 33: 9–11). Finally, in the book of Joshua, as the land is distributed by God among the Twelve Tribes, the Levites receive God as their only inheritance: "To the tribe of Levi alone Moses gave no inheritance; the offerings by fire to the Lord God of Israel are their inheritance, as he said to them." As priests, the Levites possess nothing but the word and law of God. Their prestige within Rastafari is undeniably linked to their status of priests, to the fact that they are the ones charged by God with keeping his word and transmitting his law. But it could be speculated that their prestige might also be linked to the fact that they are, among the Twelve Tribes, the only one without a land, the one that gets for sole inheritance what can be kept in heart and soul, as it is the case for the rastas, who are in exile far away from their homeland.

The identification to the people of Israel: Psalms in reggae music

Reggae thus transmits a religious message that concerns the history of Israel as it is told in the Bible, and echoes an identification with the people of Israel and the construction of a lineage. Moreover, reggae also conveys the biblical text itself: not only does it *refer* to the text, it also *preaches* it, literally, by reproducing it in the lyrics. These excerpts come from the Old Testament and the Book of Revelation, in particular the Book of Psalms, to which I now turn. Within reggae lyrics are found three types of "Psalm borrowings": simple *references* to the original Psalm, *adaptations* (the original text being reproduced with some terms being modified, for instance "God" being replaced by "Jah"), and literal *quotations* that conform to the original.

> The Lord is my shepherd; I shall not want
> He maketh me to lie down in green pastures:
> He leadeth me beside the still waters
> He restoreth my soul:
> He leadeth me in the paths of righteousness for His name's sake
> Yea, though I walk through the valley of the shadow of death, I will fear no evil
> For thou art with me; thy rod and thy staff they comfort me.
> Anthony B, "Burn down Sodom," 1996
> (quotation, Psalm 23: 1–5)

> The Lord's my shepherd, I'll not want
> He make me down to lie in pastures green
> Jah leadeth me the quiet waters by
> My soul thou hath restored again and me to walk thou made
> Thy rod and staff they are with me, they surely comfort still
> My table thou hath furnished in the presence of my foes
> My head thou hath anoint with oil, my cup it overflow

Construction of a religious chain of memory

> Goodness and mercy all my life shall surely follow me
> And in Jah's house forever more my dwelling place must be.
> > Buju Banton and Morgan Heritage,
> > "23rd Psalm," 2000
> > (adaptation, Psalm 23: 1–6)[4]

> You know I walk thru the valley of the shadow of death; I fear no evil
> Selassie I is my shield and my guide
> And He will always be on my side.
> > Anthony B, "Rumour," 1996 (adaptation, Psalm 23: 4)

Psalm 23 is among the most referenced psalms in reggae music, especially recently, as shown by the dates of the three songs given here as examples. It is a psalm of faith, of trust, and of protection: God provides his people with everything they need, and protects them. In the context of the Rastafari movement, this psalm also takes on both the colour of war (God offering protection against earthly enemies) and of the apocalypse ("the valley of the shadow of death"), which is ascribed within the opposition between the Righteous and the pagans, the oppressed and the oppressors, the slaves and the enslavers.

> Deliver me from me enemies, oh Jah
> Fight against those who rise up against me.
> > Paul Elliott, "Save me Oh Jah," 1999
> > (quotation, Psalm 59: 1)[5]

This verse of Psalm 59 is used extensively in reggae songs (here by Paul Elliott in 1999, but countless examples can be found since the emergence of reggae music). The importance of the notion of adversity within the Rastafari movement explains the wide use of

---

[4] Psalm 23: "The Lord is my shepherd; I shall not want. He maketh me lie down in green pastures: he leadeth me beside still waters. He restoreth my soul: he leadeth me in the paths of righteousness for his name's sake. Yea, though I walk through the valley of the shadow of death, I will fear no evil: for thou art with me; thy rod and thy staff they comfort me. Thou preparest a table before me: thou anointest my head with oil: my cup runneth over. Surely goodness and mercy shall follow me all the days of my life: and I will dwell in the house of the Lord forever."

[5] Psalm 59: 1: "Deliver me from my enemies, O my God, protect me from those who rise up against me."

this verse: one essential belief of Rastafari indeed lies in God's action of deliverance from the enemies, which are considered as countless and vicious. Millennial expectation is articulated by the notions of hope in deliverance and in the victory of Good over Evil.

> The Lord is my light and my salvation
> So when asking these questions I shall not fear no
> I know when asking these questions, war shall rise up against me
> But in Jah I put my trust and confidence, he'll protect me.
> Morgan Heritage, "What man can cry," 1998
> (adaptation, Psalm 27: 1–3)[6]

> Let Jah be praised, and the wicked man be scattered
> … Let Jah rise and the heathen scatter
> Have to give thanks and praise no matter
> Even if the flames a getting hotter and hotter.
> Buju Banton and Garnett Silk, "Complaint," 1995
> (adaptation, Psalm 68: 1)[7]

> Let Jah arise and let his enemies be scattered away.
> Barry Brown, "Enter the Kingdom of Zion," 1979
> (adapatation, Psalm 68: 1)

> Let Jah arise, and his enemies all scatter.
> Bob Marley & the Wailers, "Jah live," 1976
> (adaptation, Psalm 68: 1)

> As I reread the book of history
> I read song 68, the songs of victory
> It says let Jah arise and his enemies are scattered.
> Morgan Heritage, "Exalt Jah," 1998
> (adaptation, Psalm 68: 1)

---

[6] Psalm 27: 1–3: "The Lord is my light and my salvation; whom shall I fear? The Lord is the strength of my life; of whom shall I be afraid? When the wicked, even mine enemies and my foes, came upon me to eat up my flesh, they stumbled and fell. Though an host should encamp against me, my heart shall not fear: though war should rise against me, in this will I be confident."

[7] Psalm 68: 1–2: "Let God arise, les his enemies be scattered: let them also that hate him flee before him. As smoke is driven away, so drive them away; as wax melteth before the fire, so let the wicked perish at the presence of God."

> Jerusalem is calling, Ithiopia stretch forth her hands in valley
> Jerusalem is calling, on its shore I saw my ancestors waiting.
>
> Anthony B, "Jerusalem," 1997
(quotation, Psalm 68: 31)[8]

Psalm 68 is an essential psalm for the Rastafari movement, although it is not the most often cited in reggae music. It tells the great events of the history of Israel and sings its victory (which is why Morgan Heritage calls it the Psalm of the "songs of victory"). The beginning of the psalm is almost a war song that glorifies the power of God and exalts his victory against his enemies. Additionally, in this psalm is found a major reference used by Rastafari to legitimate the importance of Ethiopia as well as the messianic quality of Haile Selassie: "Princes shall come out of Egypt; Ethiopia shall soon stretch out her hands unto God" (Psalm 68: 31, here in Anthony B's "Jerusalem").

> Save me oh Jah, cause the vipers are coming after my soul
> Save me oh Jah, cause the vipers they're trying to take counsel
> And I sink in deep mire, where there is no standing
> I have come into deep waters where the floods overflow me
> I don't bury off my crying, my throat is dry
> My eyes fail me while I wait for my Lord.
>
> Paul Elliott, "Save me Oh Jah," 1999
(adaptation, Psalm 69: 1–3)[9]

Paul Elliott refers to the murders of his two brothers, which took place in real life, therefore using Psalm 69 as a prayer to God; the song can also be interpreted as a larger lament that complains about the "enemies" in general—that is, the enemies of the believers, here referred to as "the vipers."

---

[8] Psalm 68: 31: "Princes shall come out of Egypt; Ethiopia shall soon stretch out her hands unto God."

[9] Psalm 69: 1–3: "Save me. O God, for the waters have come up to my neck. I sink in deep mire, where there is no foothold; I have come into deep waters, and the flood sweeps over me. I am weary with my crying; my throat is parched. My eyes grow dim with waiting for my God."

> Inna Psalm 87 that's where we see clear
> His foundation is in the holy mountains.
>> Anthony B, "Rumour," 1996
>> (quotation, Psalm 87: 1)[10]

Psalm 87 evokes Zion, the Holy city of God which will become the spiritual capital and "mother of all the people." It is inspired by the Books of Isaie and Zacharias, which indeed give a strong maternal character to Zion: the feminine counterpart and fertile spouse of God. Here, the beginning of the psalm is evoked by Anthony B to illustration the holy character of Zion.

> He that dwelleth in the secret place of the most High
> Shall abide under the shadow of the Almighty High
> King Selassie I the first, blessing you'll never get no curse
> I will say of the Lord Jah Rastafari
> He is my refuge and my fortress: Jah, in Him I will trust.
>> Anthony B, "Burn down Sodom," 1996
>> (adaptation, Psalm 91: 1–2)[11]

> He that dwelleth in the secret place of the most High shall abide under the shadow of the Almighty.
> I will say of the Lord, God Jah Rastafari, He is I refuge and I fortress, He is I God; in Him will I trust.
> Surely He shall deliver me from the snare of the fowler and from the noisome pestilence.
> He shall cover me with his feathers and under His wings shalt thou trust; His truth shall be thy shield and buckler.
> Thou shalt not be afraid for the terror that falleth at night, nor from the arrow that wasteth at noon.

---

[10] Psalm 87: 1: "His foundation is in the holy mountains."
[11] Psalm 91: 1–8: "He that dwelleth in the secret place of the most High shall abide under the shadow of the Almighty. I will say of the Lord, He's my refuge and my fortress: my God, in him will I trust. Surely he shall deliver thee from the snare of the fowler, and from the noisome pestilence. He shall cover thee with his feathers, and under his wings shall thou trust: his truth shall be thy shield and buckler. Thou shalt not be afraid for the terror by night; nor for the arrow that fleth by day; Nor for the pestilence that walketh in darkness; nor for the destruction that wasteth at noonday. A thousand shall fall at thy side, and ten thousands at thy right hand; but it shall not come nigh thee. Only with thine eyes shalt thou behold and see the reward of the wicked."

> A thousand shall fall at thy side and ten thousand at thy right hand; but it shall not come nigh thee.
> Until every one just stand and see the reward of the wicked.
> Big Youth, "Jah Jah shall guide," 1985
> (adaptation, Psalm 91: 1–8)

> If Jah is standing by my side
> Then why should I be afraid of the pestilence that crawleth by night.
> Tony Rebel, "Jah by my side," 1997
> (reference, Psalm 27: 1–3 and Psalm 91: 1–8)

Psalm 91 is, with Psalm 23, among the more frequently referenced psalms in reggae music, and it is also one of the most central psalms for the Rastafari movement. It is a psalm of protection that sings the almighty power of God ("he is my refuge and my fortress," "He shall deliver me," "thy shield and buckler"...). It also uses war-like vocabulary, within the evocation of a battle: "Thou shalt not be afraid for the terror by night; nor for the arrow that flieth by day; Nor for the pestilence that walketh in darkness; nor for the destruction that wasteth at noonday. A thousand shall fall at thy side, and ten thousands at thy right hand; but it shall not come nigh thee" (Psalm 91: 6–7). This battle is a parable that evokes the earthly and daily struggle between Good and Evil, but it is also, for the rastas, the evocation of the final battle between the forces of Good and the forces of Evil. Thus this psalm describes both the spiritual battle that each individual leads against evil throughout his or her life, as well as the apocalyptic battle that will take place between God and Satan.

> How good and how pleasant it is for I and I to dwell together in the light of Jah Jah.
> Barry Brown, "Enter the Kingdom of Zion," 1979
> (adaptation, Psalm 133: 1)

> How good and how pleasant it would be, before God and man
> To see the unification of all Africans.
> Bob Marley & the Wailers, "Africa Unite," 1979
> (reference, Psalm 133: 1)

These excerpts by Barry Brown and Bob Marley refer to Psalm 133: "Behold, how good and how pleasant it is for brethren to dwell together in unity!" The fraternity evoked in the psalm is, in the second excerpt, transposed into the question of the unity "of all Africans" (which includes Africans "from Africa and from abroad"). Finally, in Bob Marley's "Small axe," references are multiple, to Proverbs (26) and Psalms (7, 52, 94):

> Whosoever diggeth a pit
> Shall fall in it, fall in it
> Why boastest thyself o evil man?
> Working iniquity to achieve vanity
> The goodness of Jah Jah I-dureth for I-ver.
> Bob Marley & the Wailers, "Small axe," 1973

These excerpts—which do not, of course, form an exhaustive list—show how the biblical text is used in reggae music, sometimes in complete conformity to the original and most of the time with only minimal modifications (for example in Big Youth's song, the only change is the appearance of "God Jah Rastafari"; the rest of the text is strictly similar to the original psalm). Reggae songs, however, do not simply borrow from the Bible: they not only transmit the sacred text on which Rastafari bases its message, but also bring about an identification with the people of Israel that enables the rastas to *read their own history in the Bible*, since the psalms are, in general, the songs of hope and faith of the people of Israel.

In between past and present, or how to re-read one's history in the Bible

Beyond literal borrowings from the Book of Psalms, the Bible is present within reggae lyrics with textual consistency, if only because artists often use Biblical English (this is especially visible in the past tense: in -eth such as "crawleth," instead of "crawled," and in personal forms such as "thee" and "thou" instead of "you"), as well as numerous expressions that are found in the Bible. The use of the Bible in reggae lyrics is well illustrated by Bob Marley, whose songs contain numerous references to the Scriptures, as shown in Table 6.1.

For instance, in "Ride natty ride" (1979) Bob Marley uses an expression found in the Psalms (118: 22) and Matthew (21: 42): "The stone that the builder refuse / shall be the head corner stone" is used to express the idea that the oppressed will not remain so forever.

Table 6.1: References to the Bible in Bob Marley & the Wailers

1961	Judge not: Matthew 7: 1–2
1964–1965	Wings of a dove: Psalms 55: 6
1973	Pass it on: Luke 12: 3; 1 Corinthians 4: 5
	Rastaman chant: Revelation 5: 1–2
	Small axe: Proverbs 26–27; Psalms 52: 1; Psalms 94: 4
1974	So Jah seh: Psalms 95: 7; Psalms 100: 3; Jeremiah 23: 1
1976	Night shift: Psalms 121: 6
	Want more: Joel 3: 14
1977	The heathen: Job 4: 8; Psalms 126: 5
1979	Ride natty ride: Psalms 118: 22; Matthew 21: 42
	Survival: Daniel 3: 26; Daniel 6: 16–23
1980	Forever loving Jah: Matthew 11: 25; Luke 1n0: 21; Psalms 1: 1–3
	Zion train: Mark 8: 36
1981	Rastaman live up: 1 Samuel 17: 50, Judges 15: 15–16

First present in Psalm 118, this expression then takes, in the New Testament, a millenarian character, since it is a parable used by Jesus to evoke the Kingdom of God:

> Jesus said to them, "Have you never read in the Scriptures: 'The stone that the builders rejected has become the cornerstone; this was the Lord's doing, and it is amazing in your eyes'? Therefore I tell you, the Kingdom of God will be taken away from you and given to a people that produces the fruits of the Kingdom." (Matthew 21: 42–43)

Those who are weak today will be strong tomorrow—"tomorrow" relating to a long-awaited time to come that mixes earthly future and Kingdom of God. In "Destiny" (1997), Buju Banton cites two of the Proverbs of Solomon (28: 11 and 18: 11), insisting on the opposition between the rich and the poor, the exploitation of the latter by the former, but also the ephemeral and fake character of material fortune. And Bushman adds, "why sell your soul for money / now you're living in misery" ("Live your life right", 1999).[12]

---

[12] "The rich is wise in his own conceit / but the poor that hath overstanding

This use of biblical vocabulary and expressions is typical of the Rastafari movement. The Bible is used as a model, as a corpus of references that can be applied to daily life, from the smallest things to great ethical and moral issues. It constitutes an ensemble of rules that rastas follow more than anything else; for them, the law of the Bible prevails over the laws of men. This permanent reference to the Bible seems close to what can be observed in other fields, for instance pentecostalism in Latin America: the Bible is considered as a practical book, almost as a manual of reference, and is able to provide each daily problem with an answer; moreover, it is sometimes the only book that people own, and therefore represents one's access to education.[13] The Bible is considered as the book of revelation and therefore of knowledge. Hence in "Children of Israel" (1977), when Dennis Brown sings that "There is the book of knowledge / for those who want to learn truth and right", he is referring to the Bible. In reggae songs or in everyday life, the Bible is used as the ultimate and main reference; indeed the Bible is not a legend, nor just one explanation among others: it is reality, it is the truth. In reggae songs, the Bible is the "Book of Knowledge" (Dennis Brown, "Children of Israel," 1977), the "Book of Life" (The Abyssinians, "Satta a massagana," 1976; Anthony B, "Our Father," 1999—linked with the Book of Life that will be opened for the Judgment: Revelation 20: 12), or the "Book of History" (Morgan Heritage, "Exalt Jah," 1998). This is deeply linked to the fact that, considering themselves as the descendants of Israel, the rastas read their own history in the Bible.

Lineage is hence expressed both through blood (a genetic lineage that goes back to the Twelve Tribes) and through spirit (a truth transmitted by the Bible, which remains actual forever). For Luciano, several messengers were sent by God: "Jah send I as a messenger / to teach the youth about roots and culture / and tell di massive fi

---

searcheth him out." Buju Banton, "Destiny," 1997. "Understanding" becomes "overstanding" in order to express the positive meaning of the word. "The rich man's wealth is his city / destruction of the poor is his poverty / destruction of your soul his vanity." Buju Banton, "Destiny," 1997. "Why sell your souls for money / now you're living in misery / I heard the rich man's wealth is his city / But what a pity, what a pity." Bushman, "Live your life right," 1999.

[13] An interesting literary example, in the North American context, can be found with William Styron's novel *The Confessions of Nat Turner* (1992, originally published 1967).

remember Jah / that's all I deal with Iyah / you remember how Jah send Jonah / and Elijah, Moses and Noah / Martin Luther King and Marcus [Garvey] too / dem never falter, di man dem duh dem works and move on" (Luciano, "Messenger," 1997). A spiritual lineage (or tradition) is built through a continuous movement from Moses to Martin Luther King: all are messengers sent by God in order to guide his people and show the way. And Luciano, like any other believer, must carry on this mission: "so I nuh deh yah fi look / I and I must carry on Jah works." While we have seen that rastas identify most strongly with the Hebrews' history of slavery and their escape from Egypt, they do not limit themselves to it. The ensemble of the biblical text is just as revealing—simply because, as the people of God, the Bible is a book that is addressed to them. Each time the people goes through difficult times, when it is persecuted, dominated, or in pain, identification is not only possible but intense: for instance, with Daniel in the lion's den (Daniel 6) or with Shadrach, Meschach, and Abendigo in the furnace (Daniel 3), in Bob Marley's "Survival" (1979):

> We're the survivors, yes the black survival
> yes we're the survivors
> like Daniel out of the lion's den ...
> we're the survivors, like Shadrach, Meschach and Abendigo
> thrown in the fire but never get burn.

The parable is clear: black people have faced numerous tests (the trade, slavery, exile), but like Daniel they will survive through their courage and the will of God. The same reference is present elsewhere in reggae music (Abyssinians, "Abendigo," 1976; Anthony B, "Dem a question," 1999; Buju Banton and Luciano, "We'll be alright," 2000). Similarly, Bob Marley identifies his dominated people with David who, although he seemed small and weak, defeated Goliath with a slingshot (1 Samuel 17: 50), and with Samson, who fought the Philistines with a donkey jaw-bone (Judges 15: 15).[14] In "Strength and hope" by Sizzla (2000), Israelites are opposed to the Pharisees:

> Be not like them old pharisees and scribes

---

[14] "David slew Goliath with a sling and a stone / and Samson slew the Philistines with a donkey jaw-bone." Bob Marley & the Wailers, "Rastaman live up," 1983.

be not like them who always fuss and fight
just live in love and protect your life, Israelites.

Here again the reference to the Bible is explicit: the Israelites, people of God, are opposed to the pharisees and scribes, who were responsible for the crucifixion of Jesus.

The Bible is frequently quoted and, above all, it tells both one's past history and one's future. Hence the story of Jonah is read as a parable of the almighty protection of God, of the believer's duty of faith, and of liberation, for instance in "Not an easy road" (1995) where Buju Banton directly addresses the listener:

> From the scribes and pharisees you've got to stay wide
> hold up your head glancing at both side
> waiting anticipating praying fi your slide
> righteousness prevails with Jah by my side
> deliver Jonah from the whale
> never leave him to die.

The pharisees and scribes have betrayed Jesus, and therefore represent the category of Evil (as in Sizzla's "Strength and hope," 2000); but as God delivered Jonah from the belly of the whale, he will deliver his people from the yoke of oppression and will protect it. In the song "Jonah" (1998) by Luciano, it is another part of the story of Jonah that is emphasized, his God-given mission to warn the people of Nineveh:

> Now Jonah, go down to Nineveh and tell the people that if
>   they repent from their pagan ways, they will be saved ...
> time to go to Nineveh, Jonah
> tell the likkle youth dem what a gwaan, Jonah ... just like
>   those days in the wilderness
> when Moses leads all his children
> now the time has come back again
> you must play your role, Jonah.

Niniveh, the pagan city, represents the non-believers as well as those who believe but do not respect the law of God. As in the time of Jonah, when people had forgotten God, and as in the time of Moses, when in the desert the Hebrew lost their trust in God and adored the golden calf, the contemporary world renounces God. Both exaltation and menace of punishment, this song also contains a strong prophetic and messianic feeling: a new Jonah must rise and stand again, and guide his people along the right path.

Moses of course remains the main reference for liberation. In a song about Apartheid, Steel Pulse asks God to send a "new Moses" to liberate his people:

> Oh, oh Jah Jah
> take them where life sweeter
> send a Moses to set them free
> Pharaoh's army won't let them be.
> "Biko's kindred lament," 1979

The intensely messianic use of the Bible is essential to reggae music; the identification with biblical stories concerns the establishment of an opposition between the oppressed and the oppressors, and parables tend to express the resistance and final victory of the oppressed, for instance in the song "Wicked people" by Anthony B (1999):

> A no me say so, a no me say so
> a just the bible say so, a just the bible say so
> all wicked people shall be burning on the rock hotter fire
>   bun
> all wicked people shall be burning on the rock my lawd.

The Bible, from Genesis to the Apocalypse, is nothing but the long history of their people; it provides *parables of hope and redemption* that tell their *past* and reveal their *future*. The pain, obstacles and domination do not really matter, nor the fact that the oppressed are weak and the oppressors strong, because in the end what has been revealed will be:

> none of them can stop the time
> how long shall they kill our prophets
> while we stand aside and look
> some say it's just a part of it
> we've got to fulfil the Book
>   Bob Marley & the Wailers, "Redemption song," 1980

The key of the parable is always the almighty power of God: while the oppressors might appear impossible to fight, while the game might seem already played and lost, the Bible is here to remind the oppressed that God exists, and that he is more powerful than any man will ever be. The Bible tells the children of Israel about their past history, but it also contains the revelation of their future, with the Book of Revelation. So, for Israel Vibration, "We've been travelling from Genesis down to Revelation" ("So much youths," 1998). Pharaoh was engulfed in the waters, Babylon was destroyed, Nineveh repented, the whale threw Jonah back on the shore: God always came to the help of this people, even when men believed he had given up on them. What appears in reggae music, through the Bible, is that the righteous can be overwhelmed with despair and powerlessness—from the wilderness of the desert to the wilderness of today's world—but that, just as Moses guided his people from slavery to the Promised Land, they will be again guided towards a sweeter land. The Bible tells at the same time the history of the world, from its creation to its destruction, and the history of the people of God, from its birth to its redemption. And this history also functions as a parable for each individual life: from birth to death, a path paved with obstacles, similar to the long road walked by Israel.[15]

---

[15] "It's not an easy road / many see the glamour and the glitter and think it's a bed of rose / who feels it knows / Lord help me sustain these blows / from the minute of birth you enter this earth / obstacles in your way to overcome first / throughout every day they seem to get worse / oh my God cast away this curse." Buju Banton, "Not an easy road," 1995.

Part III

Revealing the future

7

Messianism, between past and future

Through a rereading of the Bible and the identification to the Twelve Tribes of Israel, Rastafari therefore sets up a religious construction of the origin, accompanied by a transmission of the past of slavery. This construction enables individuals to situate themselves within a lineage, both recent and ancient. It works in a double movement: on the one hand, from the past to the present, since the rastas accept and even claim their past as slaves and explain the present as being inherited from the system of slavery, therefore recognizing the weight of the past on the present; on the other hand, from the present to the past, since the Rastafari movement rebuild a lineage on the basis of identification to a past history, which operates from the present to the past. This religious construction of the origin, associated with the recognition of the past of slavery, is for the rastas an essential act, necessary for people to live the present, but also to build their future; in that sense, it is thought to be constitutive of the group. This restitution of history is made both at the level of reappropriation (by accepting the past of slavery and tracing the lineage) and at the level of the revelation of hidden facts, in response to the devaluation of general African history (through the recognition of the presence of black people in the Bible, their participation to Egyptian civilization, or the resistance of the slaves). As Roudinesco puts it, "it is true for people too: if their historical truth is masked, they are alienated. The secrets of their past make them blind to their future ... A people that ignores its past and its secrets is a subordinate people."[1] In the case of the slaves' descendants, there exists a forced rupture in

---

[1] In *Le Nouvel Observateur*, March 2, 1995, page 28. Personal translation.

kinship systems caused by the trade (and the constant efforts of the slavemasters) and a devaluation of African history by Europeans. As Garvey said, a people without a past is like a tree without its roots: it always ends up dying. Therefore, these roots are what Rastafari is trying to recover and keep alive, and from this found past depends the life of its people, and therefore its future. The millenarian and messianic aspects of the Rastafari movement play an essential role in this process.

Messianism is defined as the religious belief in the coming of a redeemer who will end the current order of things, either in a universal manner or for a specific group, and who will install a new order of justice and happiness (Kohn in Desroche 1969: 7). It may therefore be characterized as a state of expectation of a messiah, whose arrival will provoke a considerable change that can be immediate or only announced by the messianic presence. Millenarianism refers to the belief in and expectation of the establishment of a divine kingdom, usually after a struggle between the forces of Good and Evil; this kingdom is often conceived on the model of a lost paradise (Eliade 1949) or of an ideal world. Millenarianism thus is about the hope for earthly, collective happiness, taken as an object of history. But this collective happiness is also elitist: it is always reserved for only a part of mankind, defined by various modalities: the righteous, the believers, the penitents, the members of a given group, and so on.

Desroche (1969) points out that messianism and millenarianism are often linked, since the messiah announces a new order of things, which usually takes a millenarian dimension; according to him, millenarianism is the socio-religious movement of which the messiah is the central character. Messianism and millenarianism are among the most fertile expressions of religious belief, expressed through the articulation of the fundamental categories of *expectation* and *hope*; and they take on a particular density and intensity in situations of colonization, slavery or oppression, where they mix religious beliefs, social revolt, identity affirmation, or even national liberation (Lanternari 1960, Mülhmann 1968). Desroche (1969: 9) thus notes that

> from one end of the world to the other, social revolts or protests appear as both being started and masked by a religious claim: claims of men who postulate a God who would be theirs, and this operates either through the appearance of God within a character (messianism), either in his imminent announcement by a messenger

(prophetism), or in the advent of a reign or a kingdom (millenarianism) antecedent or subsequent to such an appearance (post- or pre-millenarianism).

The Rastafari movement, as noted by most of the works that concern it, has a pronounced messianistic and millenarian character: Selassie is indeed the messiah who announces the end of the world as described in the Book of Revelation, and which will be followed by the establishment of an earthly kingdom of perfect happiness, during which God will "dwell with them" (Revelation 21: 3). The death of Haile Selassie, in 1975, allows for the observation of the messianistic foundation and of the millenarian expectation, followed by the disappearance of the messiah, and therefore, in Desroche's words, for the observation of a "failed messianism."

The coronation of Haile Selassie and the foundation of Rastafari messianism

On November 2, 1930, in Addis Ababa in Ethiopia, the 225th Emperor of the dynasty of King Solomon was crowned; his name was Ras Tafari Makonnen, and he took the title of Haile Selassie I, Emperor of Ethiopia, King of Kings and Lord of Lords, Conquering Lion of the Tribe of Judah, from the line of Solomon son of David, as mentioned by Sizzla.[2] In Jamaica, the newspaper *Daily Gleaner* covered the event, and those who were to become the rastamen made the link with the prophecies of Alexander Bedward in the nineteenth century, and especially with Marcus Garvey's 1916 prophecy: "Look to Africa when a black king shall be crowned, for the day of deliverance is near." For them, this black king could only be Haile Selassie, who reigned over the only non-colonized African country: Ethiopia, mother of the nations, biblical Africa and supposedly the place where the Ark of the Covenant is kept. Selassie therefore became the long-awaited messiah, and the symbol of a soon-to-come liberation. For the rastas, his coronation signified the fulfillment of the prophecy announced by the Bible as well as by Garvey:

> Marcus Garvey words a fulfill now
> and Jah Jah words a fulfill too ...

---

[2] "I know He is a Nazarite, the offspring of King David." Sizzla, "Praise ye Jah," 1997.

> Marcus Garvey says that the blood want run
> and Jah Jah says him a go bring down fire.
> Johnny Clarke, "Be holy my brothers and sisters," 1976

This implies that the present is the time of the proximity of the Apocalypse, announced by the presence of the messiah. The rastas demonstrate the messianic quality of Haile Selassie by two means: first, a reconstitution of his *lineage* in the Bible (that is, the search for proofs in the historical past told by the biblical text), and second the *biblical confirmation* brought forth by the Book of Revelation (that is, the search for clear signs, within the prophecy itself, that prove the messianity of Haile Selassie).

First, by retracing the lineage of Haile Selassie back to the house of David and the throne of Solomon, his authority is legitimated in the present; moreover, this gives back to black people their place within the Bible; the evidence of a blood lineage thereby plays a double role of legitimacy in the present and of revelation of a presence in the past, which is accompanied by a major consequence: the confirmation of the prophecy, the proof that the Bible tells not only what has happened before, but also what is going to happen in the future; the link of Selassie with the house of David legitimates his status as a messiah as well as the prophecy itself. As Sizzla sings, both Jesus and Haile Selassie are linked to the house of David:

> yuh talk bout Jesus a who dat?
> I know him as di Nazarite, the offspring of King David
> nuh condemn Selassie, yuh a idiot
> Earth Rightful Ruler, He's from di same lineage.
> Sizzla, "Praise yeh Jah," 1997

Second, by reading the Bible, the rastas look for, and find, the proof that Haile Selassie is the messiah, announcer of the Apocalypse and Last Judgment; these justifications are found in the Books of Genesis (49: 10) and Revelation (5: 1–5, 17: 14 and 19: 16). In Genesis, they use the messianic oracle that concerns Judah, within a general oracle pronounced by the Patriarch (here Jacob) about his sons:

> The scepter shall not depart from Judah, nor the ruler's staff from between his feet, until tributes comes to him. (Genesis 49: 10)

The expression "until tribute comes to him" can also be translated by "until Shiloh comes," "to whom obedience is due," "to whom hope is due"; in the translation made from Hebrew to French by Lemaitre de Sacy in the seventeenth century, it becomes "until the one who has been sent has come; and he will be the expectation of the nations."[3] The messianic character of the verse is therefore very clear: the benediction of Judah by Jacob is a barely veiled announcement of a king from within Judah, who will dominate the nations. In Christianity and Judaism, this messianic oracle is traditionally reported to David, understood as the type of the messiah; for the rastas, it refers to Haile Selassie, from the tribe of Judah and the house of David: he is the sent messiah, the expectation of the nations. The rastas also invoke the Revelation according to Saint John, which they say proves that Haile Selassie is the messiah:

> Then I saw in the right hand of the one seated on the throne a scroll written on the inside and on the back, sealed with seven seals; and I saw a mighty angel proclaiming with a loud voice, "Who is worthy to open the scroll and break his seals?" And no one in heaven or on earth or under the earth was able to open the scroll or to look into it. And I began to weep bitterly because no one was found worthy to open the scroll or to look into it. Then one of the elders said to me, "Do not weep. See, the Lion of the tribe of Judah, the Root of David, has conquered, so that he can open the scroll and its seven seals. (Revelation 5: 1–5)

> These shall make war with the Lamb, and the Lamb shall overcome them: for he is Lord of lords, and King of kings: and they that are with him are called, and chosen, and faithful. (Revelation 17: 14)

> And he hath on his vesture and on his thigh a name written: King of kings and Lord of lords. (Revelation 19: 16)

The terms used to describe the Lamb, the messiah of the Book of Revelation, are similar to the ones given to Haile Selassie by his crowning: "King of kings" and "Lord of lords." The first verse (17: 14) evokes the fight raised against the Lamb, and rastas often link it to the Italian invasion of Ethiopia at the end of the 1930s. For them, these passages therefore prove that Haile Selassie is the

---

[3] "Le sceptre ne sera point ôté de Juda, ni le prince de sa postérité, jusqu'à ce que celui qui doit être envoyé soit venu; et c'est lui qui sera l'attente des nations" (Lemaitre de Sacy, 1998).

long-awaited Messiah: the scepter, "the Lion of the tribe of Judah, the Root of David," "King of kings and Lord of lords," all are irrefutable proofs, since they are found in the Bible, word of God. Indeed for the rastas, the Bible is not simply a dogmatic religious text: it is *the history, truth and prophecy*, in the fullest meaning of the terms; they consider that all past and present events are narrated in the Bible, and also that it announces future events.

Failed and successful messianism: How to survive the messiah's disappearance

Today, what is left of these beliefs? On August 27, 1975, the Ethiopian Emperor passed away; but how can a messiah die? What happens to a messianic religious movement when the prophecy is not fulfilled, when the messiah disappears, or when the prophet fails? In the case of Rastafari, the movement has not disappeared in the aftermath of the death of Haile Selassie, nor has it weakened; as a matter of fact, its greatest and most rapid expansion took place in the late 1970s. Nonetheless, the death of Selassie has lead to a redefinition of beliefs.

For the rastas, the death of Selassie is a *mystery*, in the mystical sense of the term, and this mystery is doubled by a *conspiracy*. Most agree on the biological death of the Emperor, although some argue that it is only an illusion, a trick of either Selassie himself, or of Babylon, which would have orchestrated the rumor of his death in order to weaken the Rastafari movement and black struggle. The doubts concerning Selassie's death are reinforced by the fuzzy circumstances of his disappearance, one year after communists came into power in Ethiopia, as well as by the hiding of his body until 2000, when its interment finally took place in the Cathedral of Addis Ababa. For some rastas, even the latter is not a firm proof of Selassie's death, since no certainty has been offered concerning his body. For Bob Marley indeed, in a 1976 song, "Fools say in their heart, rasta, your god is dead / but I and I know ... Jah live" ("Jah live," 1976); similarly for Burning Spear in 1978:

> They try to fool the black population
> by saying Jah Jah dead
> and they try to fool the black population
> by telling that Jah Jah dead

> I and I know that Jah no dead
> Jah no dead
> "Marcus say Jah no dead," 1978

Whether they speak of the biological death of Haile Selassie or of his spiritual disappearance is not really important because, in any case, the biological death of Haile Selassie only implies that his body has disappeared, not that he is not the messiah, nor that the prophecy is not fulfilled. Bob Marley and Burning Spear here express the fact that whatever "they" say, the disappearance of the prophet does not endanger the prophecy, as well as the fact that biological death only means the loss of physical presence. Anthony B, twenty years after Bob Marley and Burning Spear, sings that

> Rumours dem a spread seh Selassie dead
> how di body fi function without him
> said Marcus Garvey and Emmanuel gone
> without the Trinity seh life couldn't gwaan.
> Anthony B, "Rumour," 1996

The best proof that Selassie did not "simply die" is that life has not stopped; for the rastas indeed, biological death or not, Selassie simply switched from a spatio-temporal dimension to a spiritual one; they then speak of "the mystic exile of Rastafari." Instead of being a loss, as it would be if following a biological view of death, Selassie's death is a gain, because he is even more accessible to the believers than before, as Barrett (1988: 109) argues: "the rastas considered Haile Selassie as a true messiah incarnated in flesh until August 1975 [date of his death], and incarnated in a spiritual body since his death. His spiritual presence is within them in all they do." For the rastas indeed, Jah is a living God: "Almighty God is a living man / don't you overstand" (Anthony B, "Hurt di heart," 1996), which implies that each rastaman and rastawoman is God. Morgan Heritage adds,

> What man can say they've seen the face of Jah (no man)
> what man can say that Jah is not alive (no man)
> what man can say that Jah is not the guiding light (no man)
> for Jah is the unseen that dwells within I and I.
> Morgan Heritage, "What man can cry," 1998

Haile Selassie, as the incarnation of God on earth, is therefore present within each human being, but also in each part of the creation. This conception of God strongly influences many beliefs and practices, especially the concept of nature and practices linked to the body: if God inhabits each element of the creation, then this creation itself is sacred. This is expressed in the respect for environment, the quest for harmony with nature, and the vegetarian diet, all typical of the Rastafari movement. Moreover, this conception of God explains why dread talk, that is, the language specifically developed by Rastafari, uses the term "I and I" instead of "I," "you" and "we": duplicity is avoided and the language itself conveys a strong sense of unity, between God, mankind, and nature, as well as within mankind. Therefore, whether rastas accept or deny the physical death of Haile Selassie, what matters is the omnipresence of the messiah in each and every part of creation.

The presence of the divine within all also implies that Jah is seen as almighty, omnipresent, omnipotent, and omniscient. As in Christianity, there is a strong sense of God as knowing and seeing everything:

> Jah see and know
> your heart desire
> your meditation
> your thinking
> your doings
> Jah see and know.
>   Burning Spear, "Jah see and know," 1980

Human beings cannot escape the gaze of God, even in their thoughts. The notions of Good and Evil (and the actions linked to them) are of extreme importance, leading respectively to reward or punishment: "Lift up the name of Jah in abundance / every single thing we do, we are liable to a sentence" (Buju Banton and Garnett Silk, "Complaint," 1995). God's omniscience provides him with a knowledge of all the acts of men, as well as of their thoughts and most intimate intentions, which cannot be hidden to him. Acts are not enough; intentions must be good as well:

> Some say they walking your holy way
> but in their hearts lies the blood and violence, help them oh
>   God I pray
> some say calling on your name is not the way

but he that exalted themselves oh Jah, I know you shall make obey.
Morgan Heritage and Tony Rebel, "People are fighting," 1998

The belief that those who have sinned will pay sooner or later is essential; God does not forget the victims, he knows the pain endured by his people, and his punishment will come. This trust in God is expressed relentlessly in reggae lyrics, for instance in Morgan Heritage's "Let them talk" (1998):

> Fight war with the wicked no more, for in fire shall they burn
> let them talk, let them talk
> let them say what they wanna say
> let heathen talk, let them talk
> Jah will make a brighter day
> children of Jah
> fight war with the wicked no more, for in fire shall they burn.

It is in fact a message of hope: the words and acts of the "wicked," their apparent domination does not entail their victory. In the end, those who seem weak are strong, and vice versa:

> Let the news men write
> what they wanna write
> let the wicked believe
> what they wanna believe
> Jah Jah bring forth honey
> Jah Jah bring forth milk and honey
> let the sufferers
> be alway strong
> and give dread natty the power
> to be true and strong
> Jah Jah bring forth milk and honey.
> Dennis Brown, "Milk and honey," 1978

Only God, not what the pagans believe, matters: He who will "bring forth milk and honey"—that is, a parable for the Promised Land, for the final redemption of the righteous notwithstanding the suffering they endure in the present. Trust in God therefore has no limits:

> If Jah is standing by my side
> then why should I be afraid
> of the pestilence that crawleth by night
> the gates of hell can never prevail
> for I know Jah he never fail
> what you think I'm gonna do, give up now?
> no no nah go bow
> my foes intact and I just smile
> they don't seem to understand my style
> my confidence is so high, high in Abbabajoni.
>
> Tony Rebel, "Jah by my side," 1997)

This excerpt refers to the Psalms 27 and 91, which sing a protective and almighty God. And it is the same for Aswad:

> I and I know that Jah is on I side
> what you gonna do when the Judgment Day come
> where you gonna run, where you gonna hide.
>
> Aswad, "Judgment Day," 1979

By trusting God, the rastas *know* that the righteous will be protected by their God, while the heathen will face the divine judgment and will neither be able to hide from it nor escape it. This emphasis on *knowing* as opposed to *believing* is crucial (Owens 1976: 90); it involves a specific way to conceive of religious beliefs, which stresses their certainty but also their truthful character, in opposition to the false beliefs of colonial Christianity. Prahlad (2001: 13) mentions that *"One should know and not believe,* the Rasta proverb goes. To believe implies a false knowledge." As Sizzla sings, "wi have di knowledge, inno? wi done perceive" ("Praise yeh Jah," 1997); Rastafari brings forth knowledge as opposed to belief or perception, as opposed to a false knowledge, which slaves were led to believe was true and which concerns both religion and history, as I will analyze in details in the fourth part of this book.

Alluding to Bastide's idea of "successful" and "failed" messianisms (1958), Desroche asks the following question: "Is it not the essence of every messianism to be, more or less, a failed messianism? And if messianism ... is a fundamental religious category, is this category not also, fundamentally, a category of failure?" (1960: 61). According to him, because messianism sets up the expectation of an ideal and the hope in a perfect world, "its very success would be its failure"

(1969: 33): in order to maintain messianic hope and millenarian awaiting, their intensity must be reactivated and reactualized on a regular basis, while their ultimate goal is, at the same time, constantly postponed. As Durkheim says, the moment of intensity "can never last because the exaltation cannot maintain itself at such a pitch; it is too exhausting" (Durkheim 1974: 92). Once emotional intensity has come down, it becomes thought

> in the form of ideals ... Nevertheless these ideals could not survive if they were not periodically revived. This revivification is the function of religious or secular feasts and ceremonies, all public addresses in churches or schools, plays and exhibitions ... These moments are, as it were, minor versions of the great creative movement. But these means have a temporary effect. (Durkheim 1974: 92).

Hence the appearance of the messiah constitutes the moment of intensity, which announces the proximity of the establishment of the kingdom of God and therefore reinforces both the expectation and hope present in the religious movement. This is the case of the Rastafari movement: the messiah has come, and the apocalyptic cycle, therefore, has started. However, the messiah disappears: the religious movement, instead of falling apart, reinforces its certitudes (by insisting on the change of dimension, in particular) and finds in the earthly world more and more pressing signs of the apocalyptic cycle. At the same time, the disappearance of the messiah coincides with a subtle displacement from a purely mystical hope that concerns a distant ideal (in our case, repatriation towards an Africa that is idealized and associated with the New Jerusalem) to an earthly hope that concerns a reachable ideal, for which men have to fight actively. Not that this displacement will take place entirely, which would completely evacuate a religious eschatology conjugated in the future tense to the benefit of a socio-political engagement conjugated in the present tense: on the contrary, this displacement is in fact an association, millenarian hope being complexified in order to form an articulation between a celestial ideal and an earthly ideal, between a "here" and an "elsewhere" that take a double spatio-temporal dimension, between the proximity of the Apocalypse and its distant character, between the present accomplishment of the prophecy (since the Messiah has come) and its extension in the future (the time of the prophecy has started, but there is no certainty about the moment at which it will end).

In the end, it is difficult to say to what degree the disappearance of the messiah has, in the case of Rastafari, provoked the birth of a complex coexistence between the religious expectation of the New Jerusalem and socio-political engagement, here and now, although they coincided in time. In the late sixties, an important event occurred in the history of Rastafari: the meeting with reggae music accompanied, in the aftermath of the independence of Jamaica, by the growing issue of political engagement. However, the premature disappearance of the messiah also represented an opportunity, for the religious movement, to depict him in the desired image, and greatly facilitated, instead of compromising, the validation and legitimation of beliefs—since Haile Selassie, once absent, could neither oppose Rastafari nor refute its beliefs nor deny his own status of messiah. And, as will appear later in this book, the articulation between the origin and the future, simultaneously conjugated in different tenses and modes and associated with the present situation, produces an actualization of the millenarian expectation, which takes the form of a struggle in the present for a better life on earth, necessarily linked to the establishment of an ideal celestial kingdom in the future.

The disappearance of the messiah has also modified the way in which he is considered, although these modifications remain limited. The conceptions of God, called Jah, do not vary much within the Rastafari movement. In general, there is no major distinction made between Jah and Selassie, since the latter is the emanation, the earthly incarnation of the former. The Emanuelites have their own conception of the Trinity, as mentioned by Anthony B: God ("the King," Jah/Selassie), Marcus Garvey, and Prince Emanuel:

> Rumours dem a spread seh Selassie dead
> how di body fi function without him
> said Marcus Garvey and Emmanuel gone
> without the Trinity seh life couldn't gwaan.
> Anthony B, "Rumour," 1996

Hepner (1998) notes that, since his death, Prince Emanuel is considered less as a spiritual guide, and is increasingly associated, like Selassie, with God. The most common conception considers Haile Selassie as being both the messiah and the incarnation of God on earth, which implies that he remains distinct from God, although this distinction is not always clear: for the rastas, Selassie and Jah are inextricably associated, which is not surprising since

God is also considered as living in each human being. Within historically present messiahs, Desroche (1979: 88–89) distinguished the *claiming* messiahs (who self-proclaim themselves messiahs) and *claimed* messiahs (to whom the status of messiah is given). Haile Selassie is indeed a pretended messiah, since he has never confirmed the beliefs of the rastas.[4] The distinction traced by Desroche between the historically present messiahs and the historically absent messiahs is interesting in the case of Rastafari because Haile Selassie is present early on in the movement, but absent later on. After his death, he becomes a physically absent messiah but remains spiritually present, and throughout the existence of the religious movement he is also a messiah who is here but whose presence is recognized by the believers only, by the chosen, by those who know: that is, the rastas (he is even a messiah who does not recognize himself as such).

A vetero-testimentary messianism?

Through the reference to the biblical history, the identification to the Twelve Tribes of Israel, and the conceptions that concern God and the prophetic and messianic characters, it seems obvious that Rastafari, and with it reggae music, refers essentially to the Old Testament and the Book of Revelation of Saint John. The Pentateuch is especially symbolic, and contains the books most quoted: those books tell the history of the world and of mankind, the narrative of the origin of the people of Israel, its enslavement in Egypt, its escape and the crossing of the desert, the establishment of the alliance between Israel and its God, and finally the setting up of the Law. The books of Psalms, Proverbs, and Kings also have a great importance, because they concern David and Solomon, who are key characters both in the historical lineage (the meeting of King David and the Queen of Sheba being the foundation of the Ethiopian royal dynasty) and in the Bible (for example the displacement of the Ark of the Covenant to Ethiopia). Additionally, a central place is given to all the books that, within the Old Testament, have a pronounced messianic and millenarian content, such as the Books of Daniel, Isaiah, or Jeremiah. The parables contained in the stories of Jonah

---

[4] Although he never refuted them either, and his descendants maintain a close relationship with the Rastafari movement, in particular with the British branches of the Twelve Tribes of Israel.

and the whale, Daniel in the lion's den, or of Nebuchadnezzar's conquest of Jerusalem, which exiled Israel, all make strong sense for the Rastafari movement, and are abundantly cited in reggae music. The second essential text for Rastafari is the Book of Revelation. Of course, this book is not vetero-testamentary; however, by its mystical and imaged writing and its content, it seems closer to the Old Testament (in particular to its messianic parts) than to the New Testament. The Book of Revelation is a singular book within the Bible, and it always takes on a particular importance even for the religious movements that are based on the books of Daniel or Jeremiah, because it is the only book that describes, with so many details, the end of the world, the struggle between Good and Evil and the establishment of the Kingdom of God. The rastas consider the Book of Revelation as the complete and exact description of the future, at a concrete and material as much as metaphorical and spiritual level.

The Rastafari movement therefore uses two essential groups of biblical texts. First, the books that tell the history of Israel, its origins and its past: founding books, historical books (especially Joshua, Judges, and Kings), and poetic books (Psalms and Proverbs).[5] Second, the books that tell the future and the fulfillment of the prophecy: the essential Book of Revelation, accompanied by the prophetic books (Isaiah, Jeremiah, Ezekiel, Jonah) and by certain apocryphal books called "apocalyptic" such as the Ascent of Isaiah, the apocrypha of Ezekiel, and the Ethiopian Book of Enoch. The first group of books tells about the past of Israel, while the second tells about its future; and it is worth noting that the vetero-testamentary parts that are of specific importance for Rastafari are the ones that link this history of origin to the description of the future, whether it concerns justifications of the lineage between the messiah and biblical history, prophetic announcements and oracles concerning Israel, or parables that allow an explanation of the recent past of colonial slavery. Although it sometimes uses the New Testament,

---

[5] The distinction used here is conform to the Catholic habits; another classification goes as following: (1) The Law (Genesis, Exodus, Leviticus, Numbers, Deuteronomy); (2) The Prophets (Joshua, Judges, Samuel, Kings, Isaiah, Jeremiah, Ezekiel, and the Twelve); (3) The Writings (Psalms, Proverbs, Job, Song of Solomon, Ruth, Lamentations, Ecclesiastes, Esther, Daniel, Ezra-Nehemiah, Chronicles).

the Rastafari movement can therefore be considered as a veterotestamentary messianism, with an eschatology essentially based on the Revelation of Saint John.[6]

In *The Sociology of Hope*, Henri Desroche offers a typology of messianic and millenarian movements, which is the combination of three typologies: of persons, of kingdoms, and of computations (Desroche 1979: 87–96). The Rastafari movement can be placed in this typology. The *person* is historically present. Selassie is a claimed messiah, since he has not himself recognized his status of messiah, but has been claimed, by his followers, to be the messiah. Before the coming of the messiah, there has been a vicarious presence in the form of Marcus Garvey, who can be considered as a guide, and is sometimes considered a prophet (through his prophecy concerning the anticipated crowning of a "Black King" in Africa). The *Kingdom* links religious and social factors, with a strong emphasis on socio-economic factors as well as on what Desroche calls a "cosmic" factor. It does so in a very complex way, which links together different times (sacred and profane, religious and historical), as will be observed in details later on in this book. It suffices to say at this point that the millenarianism of the Rastafari movement corresponds to what Desroche points out: "at this stage, the sociology of messianism runs into the sociology of utopia" (Desroche 1979: 91). Finally, the most interesting point is found in the *computation* –that is, in the strategy that unites the person to the kingdom, and especially in the distinction made between pre- and post-millenarianism, "which touch[es] a social process of intervention and a theological conception of grace" (Desroche 1979: 93). Clearly, the Rastafari movement has to be analyzed as a case of post-millenarianism: the coming of the kingdom of God has already started (since the messiah has returned), and is being progressively installed "by an *evolutive* process" (Desroche 1979: 93). There is an historical progression that can be traced until the final advent of the New Jerusalem.

---

[6] The very refusal of apocryphical books by the European Churches (to a different degree: the Orthodox Church accepts more than does the Roman Catholic Church, which itself accepts more than Protestant Churches do), makes them even more susceptible to be true and authentic. Their apocalyptic and mystical content adds to their appeal. However, they are not contained in the King James Version of the Bible and few rastas use them. The only exception is the Ethiopian Book of the Kings, the *Kebra Negast*, which is largely known among the rastas.

Additionally, human collective action contributes to this process, which is a necessary character of post-millenarianism. It is to the question of the coming of the kingdom, and its characteristics and dimensions, that I turn now.

8

Hope and redemption

> When there is no vision, the people they perish
> But whosoever keepeth Jah Jah love, happy is he I say
> Cause he that causeth the poor to go astray
> Shall surely pay this day, shall surely pay this day
> The fire gonna burn and there'll be nowhere to turn.
>
> Dennis Brown, "Oh what a day," 1980
>
> Deliverance will come, come, come, deliverance will come
> For I have seen the land of my father in my visions
> From the hills of captivity's plains.
>
> Dennis Brown, "Deliverance will come," 1978

The major characteristic of millenarian movements is the essential place they give to eschatology—that is, the mythical narrative of the end of the world. Generally, it implies both the destruction of the current world, rendered necessary by its gradual degradation, and the birth of a new, purified and regenerated world. This is the case of the Rastafari movement, whose eschatology is centrally based on the Revelation of Saint John; and interestingly, the eschatological narrative is one of the most central in reggae music.

Degradation of the world and apocalyptic cycle

One essential idea is the progressive degradation of the perfect, original creation of God; as Big Youth sings, "What happened to this sweet sweet world?" ("Jah Jah shall guide," 1985). And, following the millenarian logic, this degradation is unavoidable. In reggae music, the signs of the end of the world are everywhere: natural disasters, wars, famines, misery, and, above all, the presence of the messiah and the cracks in the capitalist system, which had so far been considered indestructible (unemployment, corruption, drugs, violence ...). For Buju Banton,

> Indeed I see pestilence and plague
> but I'm not afraid
> they are looking for what they can take
> come in all size, appear in all shape
> Lord give us the vision to differentiate.
> Buju Banton, "Give I strength," 1997

These signs make it obvious that the world is coming to an end, in a spiral of self-destruction for which men are responsible. For Bob Marley then,

> Way earthly things are going
> anything can happen
> you see men sailing on their ego trip
> blast off on their spaceship
> million miles from reality
> no care for you, no care for me.
> "So much trouble," 1979

Indeed, what reggae music really denounces is not capitalism, industrialization, or progress in themselves, but rather what sustains them: the desire for omnipotence. Because it is contemptuous of the laws of God (who alone possesses the power of life and death, and therefore of creation and destruction) as well as of human beings, progress is unacceptable, and is considered as a crazy race with the destruction of the world (Steel Pulse, "Wild goose chase," 1984). This attempt to be the equal of God signifies the reign of Evil, which brings pollution and confusion, and announces the end of the world, as described in the Book of Revelation: we live in the time of the prophecy, and the Apocalypse announced by the Bible is a near future that has already started. As Morgan Heritage sings,

> I went to the King with that complaint from his children
> which is Zion I Rastafari
> a hard time we suffering down hand the wicked,
> I told him about the way we've been brutalized
> by mental slavery and unjust authority.
> "The King is coming," 1998

Hope and redemption

God knows the pain of his people and the sins of Babylon; but "through a vision" the singer met God and asked him when the suffering will cease; the answer is contained in the title of the song: "The King is coming." It is therefore a song of hope and trust, which comforts the rastas in their beliefs and announces the coming of God on earth and his Judgment:

> The King said here I come, I'm coming for my children
> Here I come, to conquer the dragon
> Here I come, to fire upon the heathen
> ... He said go my son and tell the world
> Tell them to let my people go
> For I'm coming with the judgment to judge the whole entire world
> He said I'm coming to liberate my children
> Who suffer by the hands of the heathen
> Go my son and tell the world, here I come.
> Morgan Heritage, "The King is coming," 1998

With the help of biblical references ("conquer the dragon," "the heathen"), this song describes how God will come down on earth to liberate his people, conquer Evil, and punish the heathen. The present is the beginning of the apocalyptic time, a view that is justified by the presence of earthly signs as well as by a divine sign, through the presence of Haile Selassie. As the early protestants saw in their worldly actions the signs of salvation (Weber 2002), so the rastas see in the earthly world the signs of the apocalypse, which in turn reinforce their beliefs. This apocalyptic cycle is expressed by the increasing reign of Evil on earth (and the consequent suffering of the righteous) and the proximity of the intervention of God. What is going to happen next, according to Rastafari, is described in the Book of Revelation.

The term "apocalypse" comes from the Greek *apokalips* and primarily means "unveiling" or "revelation". Apocalyptic narratives are numerous in the Judeo-Christian tradition. They usually appear during times of crisis, when the prophets unveil the future to reactivate and revitalize the hope and faith of the believers: by telling stories about a painful and troubled present, they emphasize a better future, which will see the advent of the kingdom of God. Central to the apocalyptic eschatology is the Judgment of God, which either rewards or punishes all men. Apocalyptic passages are found in the books of Daniel, Isaiah, Jeremiah, and Ezekiel, as well as in apocryphal books such as the three Books of Enoch, the ascent of Isaiah, and the Books of Ezekiel, Elijah, Baruch, and especially Esdras. Apocalyptic literature has been defined as a specific genre, with its own style that includes vivid imagery and colorful symbolism that call on the imagination; apocalyptic texts are always the narrative of a vision (hence the many "ascents" of the prophets, invited in heaven and then sent back to earth to tell what they have seen). The Book of Revelation, last book of the Bible and therefore of the New Testament, is attributed to Saint John, who would have written it at the end of the first century after Christ: in exile on the island of Patmos, John has a vision of the glorified Christ, who commands him to write a letter to the seven Churches; he is then transported to heaven; the Book of Revelation is the narrative of his vision. However, this book is extremely different from the Gospel of Saint John, and it is probable that it was not written by him, although perhaps under his influence.[1] Indeed, as Hadot points out,[2] the Book of Revelation "appears as an erratic bloc" within the New Testament. The way it treats the theme of the apocalypse as well as its writing style and use of images are very different from those of the New Testament. The writing is indeed full of imagery, and uses dramatic symbolism (such as the evocation of the beast, a terrifying animal with seven heads and ten horns), an omnipresent esoteric discourse (especially a repeated use of the mystical symbolism of numbers), and images that refer to the Old Testament (for instance the twelve plagues of Egypt). The Book of Revelation therefore differs greatly from the rest of the New Testament in that it is "extremely rich in the domains where the Gospels are particularly sober" (Hadot, op. cit.). This concerns, of course, the eschatological theme that occupies a central and essential space in the Book of Revelation, while hardly appearing in the New Testament. In the end, the Book of Revelation is so different from the Gospels that its position after them seems incongruous, and it rather appears "like one of the most ancient forms of the Christian message" (Hadot, op. cit.) ascribed in the long tradition of vetero-testamentary apocalyptic texts.

The Book of Revelation has two parts: the first is an introduction,

---

[1] This is why it is sometimes called "Revelation of Saint John of Patmos."
[2] J. Hadot, article "Apocalypse de Jean" in the *Encyclopedia Universalis*.

and contains the letters written by John to the seven Churches of Asia; the second, which constitutes the essential body of the text, narrates the vision of John and the prophecy it reveals. This prophetic vision is itself divided in four parts, and describes the end of the world in detail: the preliminaries to the great day of God, the punishment of Babylon, the extermination of the pagan nations, and the advent of the New Jerusalem. This text is essential to the Rastafari movement; moreover, it is considered a complete, faithful and exact description of the Apocalypse. Rastas believe that the end of the world is going to happen exactly as described by Saint John: they believe that Haile Selassie is the messiah, the Lamb evoked in the holy text, who has come to announce and execute the Judgment of God. The events described in the Book of Revelation, as well as the symbols it uses, are abundantly cited, and applied to the present times, producing a reading that is both historical (since past or current events are interpreted according to the Book) and symbolic (since the events described in the Book are also interpreted as universal parables). According to the rastas then, the apocalyptic cycle has started with the coming of the messiah, and we now live the last moments of the world "as we know it," which are troubled because the power of Evil is increasing. This theme is prominent in reggae music, as for instance in the following song by Sizzla:

> And now the people shall know that in trusting the Fari they shall no longer suffer
> ... And now the children shall behold the glory and goodness Rastafari has to offer
> ... The whole world shall see the lamb upon his throne come fi conquer di beast
> Then shall the people rejoice in the name of King Selassie and di meek
> The world shall see the lamb upon his throne come fi loose di seven seals
> Then the children rejoice and war haffi cease
> ... Let Rastafari be crowned
> Want to behold King Alpha and Black Queen Omega who a seat upon di throne
> Then I say to myself, let the praises be given and let the trumpets sound.
> Sizzla, "The world," 2000

The trumpets, the beast, the lamb, the seven seals are terms borrowed from the Book of Revelation; Selassie is the Lamb who will break the seven seals and conquer the beast; he must be crowned "unto the ... King Alpha and ... Queen Omega": Alpha and Omega, first and last letters of the Greek alphabet, symbolize the beginning and end of all things, the masculine and feminine associated in fertility, the power of life and the living by excellence, as God said to John at the very beginning and very end of the Book of Revelation: "I am the Alpha and the Omega, says the Lord God, who is and who was and who is to come, the Almighty" (Revelation 1: 8), "It is done! I am the Alpha and the Omega, the beginning and the end. To the thirsty I will give water as a gift from the spring of the water of life" (Revelation 21: 6). For Sizzla, the Apocalypse is a fact, and the text of John is not a mystical writing but the exact revelation of a future that is now close.

As mentioned earlier, the rastas believe they are the descendants of the Twelve Tribes of Israel; this identification also takes on a fundamental messianic meaning within the eschatology, because it is linked to the lost tribes evoked in the Book of Revelation. At the beginning of the apocalyptic cycle, 12,000 members from each of the Twelve Tribes of Israel are marked with a seal on their foreheads (Revelation 7: 3–8). Those who will escape the wrath of God will be a number of twelve times twelve multiplied by 1,000—that is, a total of 144,000 chosen ones.[3] This number has been used by many millenarian movements, which believed they had found the lost tribes: "Some will see in it the optimum number of the millenial reunion" (Desroche 1969: 27).[4] For the rastas, the lineage established with the Twelve Tribes therefore affirms that they are the chosen ones, who will be present during the first resurrection. Gathered in the midst of the countless signs of the end of the world, the 144,000 will reign at the side of Jesus during a thousand years, while the Beast will be imprisoned in the pit (Revelation 19–20, especially 20: 1–3: "Then I saw an angel coming down from heaven,

---

[3] The messianic Jerusalem also has dimensions corresponding to the basic number twelve (Revelation 21): "the city lies foursquare, its length the same as its width," each measuring 12,000 stadiums, with walls of 144 cubits high, twelve foundations for the walls and "twelve gates, and at the gates twelve angels, and on the gates are inscribed the names of the twelve tribes of the Israelites," "And the twelve gates are twelve pearls".

[4] One example among many is found with Jehovah's Witnesses.

holding in his hand the key to the bottomless pit and a great chain. He seized the dragon, that ancient serpent, who is the Devil and Satan, and bound him for a thousand years, and threw him into the pit, and locked and sealed it over him, so that he would deceive the nations no more, until the thousand years were ended"). In the Book of Revelation (7: 5), the list of the Twelve Tribes from which will be counted the 144,000 chosen ones excludes Dan but includes Manasseh. This exclusion of Dan in the Revelation, for which there is no clear explanation in the Bible, remains a mystery that some explain by the links of the tribe of Dan with Satan: Dan is traditionally associated with idolatry and unfaithfulness to God because of his comparison with the serpent in the Book of Genesis ("Dan shall be a snake on the roadside," Genesis 49: 17, a malediction confirmed in the Book of Judges 18: 27, "The Danites ... came to Laish, to a people quiet and unsuspecting, put them down to the sword, and burned down the city"). Primitive Christianity (for instance Irenaeus and Hippolyte of Rome, during the second century after Christ) has retained this Jewish tradition, interpreting that the Antichrist would come from the tribe of Dan, which of course would exclude the Danites from the 144,000 chosen ones and explain that Dan is replaced by Manasseh in the Book of Revelation. Manasseh is usually associated, in the enumerations of the tribes, to the tribe of Ephraim, both being generally included within the tribe of Joseph. The choice of Manasseh over Ephraim in the Book of Revelation is not explained, other than by the fact that Manasseh is Joseph's first-born, and should therefore prevail over Ephraim—and this even though Jacob had given precedence to Ephraim when blessing the sons of Joseph.[5]

Redemption and the articulation justice / injustice

> For the wages of sin is death, but the gift of God is eternal life. (Romans 6: 23)

The end of the world is before anything else synonymous of the Judgment of God, the passage of the Judgment during the second resurrection forming the very key of hope:

---

[5] "Israel stretched out his right hand and laid it on the head of Ephraim, who was the younger, and his left hand on the head of Manasseh, crossing his hands, for Manasseh was the firstborn" Genesis 8: 14.

And I saw the dead, great and small, standing before the throne, and books were opened. Also another book was opened, the book of life. And the dead were judged accordingly to their works, as recorded in the books. And the sea gave up the dead that were in it, Death and Hades gave up the dead that were in them, and all were judged accordingly to what they had done. Then Death and Hades were thrown in the lake of fire. This is the second death, the lake of fire; and anyone whose name was not found written in the book of life was thrown into the lake of fire. (Revelation 20: 12–15)

The promise of the Judgment is essential, because it is the source of all hope against crimes that remain unpunished on earth, such as slavery. For Dennis Brown,

> Oh what a day, oh what a day
> when His Majesty comes again
> to judge everyone
> for all the back-biting
> cheating and lying
> robbing and oppressing the poor
> yes He knows they can't take no more ...
> he that causeth the poor to go astray
> shall surely pay this day, shall surely pay this day
> the fire gonna burn
> and there'll be nowhere to turn
> for wicked ones.
>
> Dennis Brown, "Oh what a day," 1980

God will come down on earth and punish all those who have made his people suffer: he will punish "the back-biting, cheating and lying, robbing and oppressing the poor." There are here both the ideas of justice and punishment: those who have sinned will be judged and none will be able to escape. As Anthony B sings,

> I see you trying to run, but there's no escape
> I see you trying to hide but there's no hiding place
> the works that you have done brings mankind disgrace
> that mean a your time fi get erase ...
> Satan follower
> it seems the righteous are few
> you caught in the middle of the belly of the beast

> and there's no hope for you Babylon ...
> all wicked people shall be burning on the rock my lawd
> me see dem pollution, pure corruption
> exploitation coming from over yonder
> abomination, war and confusion
> hear it ina dem propaganda
> I will be there when the rapture call
> rasta will be there to testify you down fall.
>
> Anthony B, "Wicked people," 1999

All human beings, without exception, will face the judgment of God, whether they live now or long ago, and for the rastas it implies a judgment of all those who sold and enslaved African people:

> Four hundred years of war, Rastafari's been booking for sure
> to save the soul of those who've been believing for so long
> a voice in the wilderness is calling, it's the voice of time up
> step up all my bredren and sistren, it's time to go.
>
> Luciano, "Hold strong," 1999

The expression "four hundred years," when used in reggae music, refers to the four hundred years since the beginning of the slave trade in the sixteenth century. In this song, Luciano recalls that God is omniscient and that he has "been booking," in the Book of Life, which will be used to judge all men during the second resurrection. This is an essential point, because it means that justice will be given by God even when it has not been given by men. The enslavers, not punished on earth, will be punished during the Judgment of God, without possibility of mistake, thanks to the books opened for the second resurrection (Revelation 20: 10–15). Their punishment will be pure and simple destruction, described in reggae music by using all the symbols of the Book of Revelation: reggae songs narrate how the heathen will be burned, chased, thrown in the lake of fire and killed without mercy and without being able to escape (for instance in Sizzla's "Inna dem face," 1997: "The rivers a go stop and all them flesh gonna dry"). The punishment of the heathen will end with the second death, eternal and endless: they will be thrown into the lake of fire, along with the Beast and the false prophet, and will burn for eternity for their earthly works (Revelation 20: 13–15).

In addition to punishment of the oppressors, the Apocalypse is also synonymous with *return*, the return to Zion: "A voice in the desert is calling, time is up / walk my brothers and sisters, it is time to go" (Luciano, "Hold strong," 1999). Among the seven hills of Jerusalem, Zion is the one on which was built the Temple of David and conserved the Ark of the covenant; by extension, within the Judeo-Christian tradition, Jerusalem itself is sometimes called Zion. The term refers to redemption, and the rastas use it in its biblical meaning: Zion is the promised land, the city of God, the messianic Jerusalem (or "New Jerusalem") built after the end of the world and where the righteous will live in peace and harmony, with God among them (Revelation 21–22). For the rastas, Zion symbolizes hope, whether it is religious hope, celestial hope, or a socio-political hope that remains to be built on earth.

Walking to Zion necessarily implies the departure from Babylon, as it is ordered in the Book of Revelation (18: 4–5): "Come out of her, my people."[6] Numerous reggae songs relay this exigency of departure, in relation to the coming of the Apocalypse; for instance, "Run come rally" by Vivian Jackson and the Prophets (1975):

> The sunshine, the dark and the moon shine will turn into
>   blood one of the days
> so run away, come away from the land of Sodom and
>   Gomorrah
> run away, come away from the land of the sinking sand.

The exodus from Babylon is "a necessity and a duty" (Desroche 1969: 30); millenarian movements commonly use this passage, which they variously interpret as a necessary rupture with a Church, with European Gods in colonized countries, or with a social system or a state; or, as is the case with Rastafari, as the rupture with a complex category generically called "Babylon." This passage is considered as an essential call for leaving; but it is not only a question of not being associated with the Evil or of protecting oneself from its possible contamination: it is also a question of departure in order to prepare the coming of the Judgment, during which the wrath of God will destroy Babylon ("Come out of her, my people, so that you do not

---

6 Revelation 18: 4–5: "Then I heard another voice from heaven saying, Come out of her, my people, so that you do not take part in her sins, and so that you do not share in her plagues; for her sins have heaped high as heaven, and God has remembered her inequities."

take part in her sins, and so that you do not share in her plagues," Revelation 18: 4–5).

In the case of Rastafari, the notion of *departure* also implies a *return*: Rastafari is organized around the idea of movement, of walking: from the homeland to the slave plantations, back to the land of origin, and towards Zion, the Jerusalem of redemption. In Hugh Mundell's "Jah say the time has now come" (1978), the way in which the category of "Zion" articulates different simultaneous levels is made explicit:

> Jah say the time has now come
> for all his people to trod Mount Zion
> Jah say the time has now come
> for I and I to live as one
> and yes we are stepping to the land where I and I belong
> sure to escape the destruction of Babylon
> free from the people who have no love in their hearts
> our only violence is their treatment.

First, Zion is the Mount Zion of biblical redemption; second, Zion is the unity and fraternity of mankind, which will follow the times of confusion and division; finally, Zion is the land of origin, Africa. Zion is therefore this "elsewhere," the New Jerusalem but also the lost-and-found homeland. Since the rastas are the chosen people, they have nothing to fear from the Armageddon; on the contrary, the Judgment is now close and they have to get ready:

> Children get ready and trim your lambs
> Israelites get steady, no more time to run
> cause I say
> we moving out of Babylon yeah
> we moving to a higher land deh
> with the power of the higher man
> we moving to Mount Zion.
>   Luciano, "Moving outta Babylon," 1999

This excerpt refers both to a physical elevation (Zion is a hill) and to a spiritual elevation (the elevation of the spirit and soul, which also refers to the Judeo-Christian tradition of the ascent to heaven by prophets and saints). Here is found again the idea that the Armageddon will be terrible for the Babylonians, but inoffensive for the righteous because they are protected by God. The first ones will be thrown in the lake of fire, while the second ones will enter the gates of Zion. In "Seek Jah first" (1997), Anthony B tells what will happen after the victory of the Good over Evil:

> O what a day that will be
> walking down the streets with milk and honey
> hand in hand with the majesty
> Mount Zion were made for you and me
> round the rainbow circle throne
> with the man with the crown I and I sat down.

The righteous will be saved, and they should therefore trust God unconditionally:

> seek Jah first everything will come off time
> Him a di shepherd we a di sheep of his pastures
> know the right and truth fullness higha
> so you pray to the Lord and save ya.

The eschatology developed by the Rastafari movement is therefore characterized by different points. First, *a central position is occupied by the Apocalypse as revealed to Saint John*, which describes the future. It can sometimes be accompanied by other apocalyptic texts but always remains the main text that others only reinforce. Second, there is *an apocalyptic cycle that has already begun*, since the messiah has come in the person of Haile Selassie, which is concretely expressed by the existence of many signs in today's world, signs that conform to the biblical description of the Apocalypse and the fall of Babylon (wars, famines, an increasing Evil, the multiplication of false prophets, etc). Third, this apocalyptic cycle that has already begun is accompanied by *an intense hope for the future*, based on the fact that the Armageddon will save the righteous and punish the heathen, and therefore responds to an earthly suffering of the past and present (slavery, oppression, poverty). The eschatology is therefore centered on the notion of liberation and the abolition of suffering. Fourth, the activation of an intense feeling of future redemption for those who have suffered, associated with the complete (and impossible to avoid) punishment of those who have made others suffer, allows the slave descendants to believe in *a perfect justice to come*, as opposed to a past and present characterized by *injustice*. Fifth, hope and redemption occupy a central and essential place within the eschatology, enabling a response to a painful past through a term-to-term reversal that conforms to the Revelation of Saint John: the world is increasingly dominated by Satan, who increasingly corrupts men and makes them follow him; but after the Armageddon and the final victory of God, the followers of Satan will be punished while those who have resisted him will be rewarded by eternal life and happiness in Zion. Finally, in relation to the specific context of the African diaspora, *the advent of the New Jerusalem, Zion, is tied to Africa* in a very complex way, which does not simply constitute a geographical center but also a multiform identification that simultaneously refers to various times and places—among them the apocalyptic future, and the celestial Jerusalem. Zion is the Promised Land in all its dimensions: lost paradise and land of the ancestors, place of the return in the present and future, religious redemption and eternal life, but also the space of liberation and socio-political redemption in the present and the future, as I will discuss later on in this book.

9
The eschatology as future-present

The messianic character of the Rastafari movement, and especially its apocalyptic representation of the future, deeply influences the daily life as well as worldview of the rastas. What is characterized by a future tense—the end of the world, still to come—is translated into present practices, which are interpreted in its light and bear an apocalyptical meaning. The sacred future typically lies out of time; as Hubert (1905) showed, myth is historicized into linear time, but by being placed at its very beginning (cosmogonies) or at its very end (eschatologies). And yet, in reggae music, the eschatology is everywhere: it defines both practices and representations that belong to the present, contaminating them, as it were, by charging them with meaning. What Hubert shows for festivals and rituals—whose function is, before anything else, to periodically renew the intensity of the myth by repeating it both in time and out of time—applies here beyond the rite. The sacred, in reggae music, erupts everywhere; while the past is called into the present and is thought to define it, as was observed in the second part of this book, the same can be said of the future. But the future provides the present with an intensity that the past lacks: the effervescence of collective redemption, the fulfillment of a long-awaited justice, the final coming of the myth into human time.

The apocalyptic time indeed defines the categories of Good and Evil, which are both earthly and celestial, and are concretely expressed in today's world: the opposition between Good and Evil, rooted in a religious and directly apocalyptic opposition between Babylon and Zion, is also a daily, earthly opposition that implies a necessary return to nature, correlative of the "departure from Babylon." More than any other idea, the concept of Babylon structures the specific way of thinking, living, and behaving adopted by the rastas. They use the term constantly and with passion; for them, Babylon is Evil, the source of all oppression. There is here a strong biblical reference: Babylon, a Sumerian city on the Euphrates river, acquired an increasing importance under the first dynasty (2225–1925 BC), especially during the reign of Hammurabi. Destroyed and then rebuilt by the Chaldeans, it later became the capital of the Neo-Babylonian empire and, under the reign of Nebuchadnezzar, one of the marvels of the world with its suspended gardens. In 587 BC Nebuchadnezzar conquered Jerusalem (confirming the prophecy of Isaiah) and exiled Israel in Babylon for fifty years (2 Kings 24–26), which is when Jeremiah was preaching. After the fall of Babylon, in 539 BC, the Jews returned to their land. In the Bible, Babylon symbolizes the enemies of God, and its King vanity and sacrilege; in the Book of Revelation, it becomes the archetype of Evil. Saint Augustine therefore opposed Babylon the profane to Jerusalem the sacred.

Babylon: a clear-cut definition of the inside and the outside

In reggae music, Babylon is the symbol of decadence, vanity, and enrichment, and of the contempt for God and the order of things, as it is told in the Book of Revelation:

> I saw a woman sitting on a scarlet beast that was full of blasphemous names, and it had seven heads and ten horns. The woman was clothed in purple and scarlet, and adorned with gold and jewels and pearls, holding in her hand a golden cup full of abominations and the impurities of her fornication; and on her forehead was written a name, a mystery: "Babylon the great, mother of whores and of earth's abominations." And I saw that the woman was drunk with the blood of the saints and the blood of the witnesses of Jesus. (Revelation 17: 3–6)

> For all the nations have drunk of the wine of the wrath of her fornication, and the Kings of the earth have committed fornication with her, and the merchants of the earth have grown rich from the power of her luxury. (Revelation 18: 3)

Babylon therefore represents Evil incarnate. A correspondence is established between, on one hand, the prostitute of the Bible, the fornication of "the Kings of the earth," the enrichment of the merchants and the luxury of the prostitute, and on the other hand, what is happening in today's world: Babylon becomes synonymous with Western civilization, capitalism, industrialization, colonialism and neocolonialism, the consumer society, and progress. As summarized by Johnson-Hill (1995: 257), "Babylon is evocative of everything that is wrong with the white western capitalist world ... Babylon symbolizes any system felt to be oppressive." According to Israel Vibration,

> The system is a fraud
> it all started from abroad
> where a bunch of guys get themselves together
> and call themselves world leaders
> some of dem were 'posters
> some of dem were traitors
> and some were human slayers
> while some came as slave buyers.
> "Systematical fraud," 1997

There is a clear reference to colonialism and to the way European nations shared the land and intensified the slave trade. The system is therefore the contemporary world system, rooted in slavery and colonialism, and organized around an opposition between rich and poor, oppressors and oppressed, exploiters and exploited. A clear-cut boundary separates the groups, making a distinction between a dominant Babylon and the ones who suffer. As in "We and them" by Bob Marley, the use of "they," "them," or "dem" is recurrent in the language used in reggae music; there is "them" who have the power and money, and "we" who are exploited and dominated.

This radical differentiation of two worlds foreign to each other is absolutely essential. There are two groups that are not only clearly distinguished, but also fundamentally opposed, since Babylon always tries to dominate, conquer, and kill. Thus, for Bob Marley,

> Babylon system is the vampire
> sucking children day by day
> Babylon system is the vampire
> sucking the blood of the sufferers
> building church and university
> deceiving the people continually
> me say them graduating thieves

and murderers they look out now
sucking the blood of the sufferers.
> Bob Marley & the Wailers, "Babylon system," 1979

Babylon is also a *plan* that corrupts the people and tries to keep them enslaved (physically in the past, mentally in the present) or to destroy them by using religion ("church") and education ("university"). For Anthony B, rastas have to "remember Babylon's wicked plans"[1] and be cautious:

> Rastaman dem waan stop, but Rasta children is on the attack
> well remember the time is so perilous
> rasta children don't leave you tracks in the dust lawd
> cover you tracks no mek babylon see whey yu walk
> watch yu head back cause dem no like when rastaman talk
> nah trust no shadow after dark ...
> from birth dem a fight rastaman
> dem aim fi destroy rasta plan
> pon the river we a go walk go bun Babylon
> no leave no footprint inna the sand rastaman
> remember say dem have we pon file
> dem a program we from we a child.
> Anthony B, "Cover your tracks," 1999

For Anthony B, rastas must fight; the plan of Babylon is also a hidden corruption, a social brainwashing ("dem a program we from we a child"). In "Burn down Sodom" (1996) he adds,

> every day Babylon sit down and plan
> come dem come with wrong invention
> nobody hears dem war
> poison dem a poison the human
> Rasta at the head of iriation
> Rastaman give nobody information
> Rasta longer take no injection.

Babylon is fighting a war that poisons mankind with "wrong inventions"—that is, evil ones. The righteous know that, although

---

[1] "I and I remember / remember Babylon wicked plans." Anthony B, "Jerusalem," 1997.

silent and covered, it is truly a war. This topic is very present within reggae music: there is a conspiracy, a war that does not speak its name, and the evil plans of Babylon are kept hidden by the leaders, who try to make the people believe that they work for their good while in reality they exploit them (hence one of the favorite terms used for "politicians" is "hypocrites"). Rastafari here again acts as a movement of revelation: it denounces the plans of Babylon and the secret war it leads against the righteous, who therefore are like hunted warriors: "rasta children don't leave you tracks in the dust lawd / cover you tracks no mek babylon see whey yu walk / watch yu head back cause dem no like when rastaman talk / nah trust no shadow after dark" (Anthony B, "Cover your tracks," 1999).

Mental slavery and resistance to conspiracy

The "wicked plan" of Babylon is designed to dominate and exploit the poor. For the rastas, history offers a long list of Western wrongdoings, whose apogee was slavery and colonialism. Even if slavery has been abolished, the plans of Babylon have remained the same: they simply use different means. One of the strongest assertions of both Rastafari and reggae is indeed the persistence of slavery. For The Prophets, "No shackles on our feet, no whip on our back / yet I and I must realize we are still being enslaved" ("Warn the nation," early 1970s), and similarly for Bob Marley, "No chains around my feet, but I'm not free / I know I am bond here in captivity" ("Concrete jungle," 1973); and then, more than two decades later, Anthony B reiterates: "Black people don't get weary / dem tek off the shackles an face we / but still we under mental slavery" ("Fire pon Rome," 1996). The simple fact that they are still in exile away from Africa represents a form of slavery and alienation, associated with the economic, political, and cultural domination of Babylon. Exile and oppression produce a mental form of slavery, which differs from actual slavery only in its hypocrisy; it is as much a type of cultural domination that imposes Western culture as it is an economic and political domination exerted by society on individuals, by the Western world on the third world, and by the elite on the people: consumer society, in particular, is viewed as a form of totalitarianism implemented in order to favor the elite, just as the world economy is shaped in such a way that it only increases the riches of the West and the poverty of the

The eschatology as future-present 159

rest. Mental slavery is exerted through the whole social structure, from the education system to religious institutions to the media to the government, which are all viewed as actively participating in a vast enterprise of exploitation; churches, in particular, are seen as conveying false beliefs and a false religion aimed at the mental domination of the oppressed, as is apparent in Sizzla:

> now yuh use dem to stray di minds of di youths
> and as they preach di youths cease from knowing di truth
> but, this is di truth above all circumstances
> I see how yuh constantly building churches.
> Sizzla, "Praise ye Jah," 1997

One of the most essential goals to seek, therefore, is liberation from mental slavery: "Emancipate yourselves from mental slavery / none but ourselves can free our mind" (Bob Marley & the Wailers, "Redemption song," 1980). Liberation is articulated around a necessary departure from Babylon, which produces, in daily life, both a behavior of avoidance (such as the foundation of rural communities or various refusals to participate in the political or social spheres) and engaged struggle (social and sometimes political militancy): indeed, the notion of departure can be variously interpreted as *escape* or as *struggle*. But the notion of avoidance remains present since what matters is to protect oneself from the contamination of Babylon, whether one chooses to passively escape from Babylon or to actively fight it. Through its capacity for corruption and its hypocritical strategies, Babylon is indeed viewed as contaminating. The notion of contamination, associated with the essential notion of pollution, is expressed intensely in the practices of daily life. Rastas must therefore liberate themselves from Babylon:

> Loose out they're running wild through the land
> beware of every step you make or you'll be standing on sinking sands
> the eagle and the dragon symbolize the confusion
> arise o mighty lions, and claim yourselves of this pollution
> set yourself free my brother
> I beg you set yourself free my sister
> emancipate your heart and soul I say
> of the wickedness of this world

> I'm crying freedom
> freedom of heart and soul
> 			Morgan Heritage, "Set yourself free," 1998

The constant correspondence traced between the present and the apocalypse, as well as between the present and the history of Israel, clearly appears in this excerpt. The description of Babylon is made by using images of war and symbols from the Bible, which I now turn to.

Babylon and the symbols used in reggae music

As the archetype of the reign of Evil, Babylon has many synonyms, which are sometimes profane (the system, or the vampire as in Sizzla's "Give them a ride," 1997, Jahmali's "Politics," 1998, or Bob Marley & The Wailers' "Babylon system," 1979) but most of the time rooted in the Old Testament and, especially, in the Book of Revelation. In Morgan Heritage's "Set yourself free" (1998) and in Anthony B's "Conquer all" (1999), the eagle and the dragon are symbols used for Babylon: the eagle, as one of the most-used symbols for empire in history,[2] and the dragon, biblical symbol of Evil, incarnation of Satan: "Then another portent appeared in heaven: a great red dragon, with seven heads and ten horns, and seven diadems on his heads" (Revelation 12: 3), "The great dragon was thrown down, that ancient serpent, who is called the Devil and Satan, the deceiver of the whole world" (Revelation 12: 9). In reggae songs, Satan is often symbolized by the beast (for instance in Sizzla's "The world," 2000), his acolyte, which appears in the Book of Revelation and, in the Judeo-Christian tradition, has long stood for the Roman Empire (as the eagle has).

Indeed, Babylon is often associated with Rome, both in reference to the Roman Empire and to Roman Catholicism. The latter is detested by the rastas because it supported the slave trade, justified slavery, was enriched by colonialism, invaded Ethiopia in the 1930s, whitened the Bible, and so on. It is a song against Rome that made Anthony B famous:

---

[2] The eagle is of course the symbol of the United States of America; but it has a much longer history as the symbol of several empires, from the late Byzantine empire to the Roman empire to the Napoleonic army.

Fire pon Rome
fi Pope Paul an him scissors an comb
Black people waan go home
A Mount Zion a di righteous throne.

"Fire pon Rome," 1996

The Pope symbolizes a religious hierarchy that rastas refuse; they do not recognize his authority, nor his sanctity: "Worship Pope Paul rastaman no" (Anthony B, "Swarm me," 1996). The Pope even becomes evil, a follower of Satan, and therefore has a negative dimension that rastas justify in the Bible itself: in the Book of Revelation, when the angel shows to John the whore in the desert, she is described as "clothed in purple and scarlet, and adorned with gold and jewels and pearls, holding in her hand a golden cup" (Revelation 17: 4). For the rastas, these attributes clearly refer to the Roman Catholic Church, whose hierarchy wears scarlet clothes, holds golden cups, and has amassed gold and jewels. The condemnation of Babylon in the Bible is therefore an explicit condemnation of the Roman Catholic Church, and the whore is Rome, who sold herself to the Devil in order to gain more riches and power (indeed, the participation into slavery and colonization is seen as prostitution).

Babylon is also referred to as Sodom and Gomorrah, as in the song "Burn down Sodom" by Anthony B (1996), because it symbolizes sin and contempt for the law of God, as well as homosexuality, which the Rastafari movement abhors. Another commonly used term is "the West," in opposition to the East, for example in Sizzla's "Black woman and child" or "One away," and in Buju Banton's "Til I'm laid to rest."[3] The West represents the Occidental world, therefore Babylon and Evil, while the East stands for Africa and therefore the Good; additionally, during the trade, the slaves were taken from the East to the West. And, of course, the sun rises in the East, which is traditionally considered as the place of redemption and resurrection. The West, like Rome, must be left, as Jahmali points out in "21st century" (1998): "Nothing for me, here in Rome." Finally, in Jamaican English, "Babylon" also means "policeman," as in "Three

---

[3] "Rastafari from the East" (Sizzla, "Black woman and child," 1997); "Why secret is vain, just make it to the East / for salvation I'm desperate ... the people ina di West di whole a dem gone crazy" (Sizzla, "One away," 1997); "Til I'm laid to rest / I'll always be depressed / there's no life in the West / I know the East is the best" (Buju Banton, "Til I'm laid to rest," 1995).

Babylon" by Aswad (1976). Babylonians are variously called *the wicked* in a strong biblical sense (countless references), *the pagans* or *heathen* (again, countless references), the *pharisee* and *scribes* (Sizzla, "The world," 2000; Buju Banton, "Not an easy road," 1995), *parasites, hypocrites* (Dennis Brown, "Home sweet home," 1980), *scorpions* (Morgan Heritage, "Let them talk," 1998), *vipers* (Paul Elliott, "Save me oh Jah" and "Vipers," 1999), or *rats* (Paul Elliott, "Fat belly rat," 1999).

The notion of pollution is essential: Babylon is synonymous with pollution and the degradation of a world that was once balanced and harmonious. For instance Bob Marley sings,

> That's why we gonna be burnin' and lootin' tonight
> I say we gonna burn and loot
> burnin' and lootin' tonight
> one more saying
> burning all pollution tonight
> burning all illusion tonight.
> "Burnin' and lootin'," 1973

Pollution and confusion characterize Babylon—which again sets up Rastafari as a movement of revelation that makes clarity emerge from confusion, and purity emerge from pollution. For Morgan Heritage, "The eagle and the dragon represent the confusion / arise o might lions, and claim yourselves out of this pollution" ("Set yourself free," 1998). The "mighty lions" are the rastas—that is, those who have *realized* that the world we live in is characterized by confusion, pollution and illusion; they must therefore liberate themselves from Babylon, which can only bring pain and sorrow: "We've got to step away from here / step away, step away from here / sadness and sorrow everywhere / down here in Babylon the youth will only suffer" (Aswad, "Judgment Day," 1979); for Black Uhuru, "Down in Babylon where it's like a battlefield / too much war and gunshot" ("Satan army band," 1978).

The category of Evil, symbolized by Babylon, calls forth a category of the Good, which fundamentally opposes it and is represented by Zion. Originally one of the hills of Jerusalem, Zion quickly came to refer to the city itself, and then to the messianic Jerusalem spoken of in the prophetic and apocalyptic texts. Moreover, the terms of "Zion" and "daughter of Zion" are used in the Bible to speak of the chosen people, for instance in the Book of Isaiah. Logically, the category of the Good, symbolized by Zion, contains the "righteous," those who have chosen God. And it is the concept of Nature that sustains this category: nature as the creation of God, as the natural order of things. To a non-reasonable, vain, and contemptuous evolution, is thus opposed a reasonable, humble, and respectful evolution. For Rastafari, the original creation is how the world should be, the universe in its divine and perfect harmony in which all participate:

> Creation, from the beginning till forever
> we come together to realize the fulness of Creation
> so we grow, from stage one to the other
> and we must move on, like the rivers, like the springs
> we see children come, we see plants, we see animals, we see birds, we see insects
> and everything is reflecting the Almighty Jah
> Jah is the earth and everything that dwells therein
> Jah live, Jah live, can't stop Jah works.
>
> Luciano, "Can't stop Jah works," 1999

This unity of creation, this harmony of each part with the whole, even the smallest, has already been evoked concerning the notion of living God; but now appears the notion of a creation that is in order but also in movement: Evil is precisely the contempt for, and destruction of, this harmonious order.

Two fundamentally opposed categories are therefore elaborated: *Zion / Nature* (category of Good: respect of God, what is good, natural evolution, Rastafari, the pure...) and *Babylon* (category of Evil: contempt for God, what is bad, quest for power, Rome, the West, the impure...). These two categories define the boundaries of the group, since they oppose the righteous (Rastafari) to the heathen (the rest of the world). They also have deep implications for practices and beliefs,[4] and are the foundation of a worldview that opposes truth to lies, revelation to dissimulation, and Good to Evil.

Concluding remarks

The concept of nature is intermingled with religious beliefs and produces the fundamental categories of the pure and impure, Good and Evil; it also influences the conceptions related to the world and

---

[4] In particular those linked to the body: food practices, hygiene, etc.

the individual, the role of the latter, social life, procreation, and death; finally, it has a central role in daily life, especially when it comes to food practices. Additionally, expressed on a continuum that goes from strict to flexible, the presence of the harmony with nature in daily practices and the maintenance of a holistic balance (body/soul, man/nature) also constitutes a social marker, "a means to progressively demarcate the social boundaries of the community," as well as "an ideology of cultural resistance" (Homiak 1995: 174). The adherence to an "Ital" (natural) way of life constitutes an essential social distinction as well as an emblem of resistance to the system.[5] The progressive shift in practices during the process of conversion represents the consequence of a new apprehension of the world, a strong demarcation with non-believers, and an ideological opposition, the refusal to participate in the system. The modification of practices goes hand in hand with a stronger participation in, and adherence to, Rastafari; as the scholarship on religious conversion shows, there is within the process of conversion a simultaneity of the (re)construction of reality, of the modification of practices, and of the collective validation of these changes (Cashmore 1979a; see also Jules-Rosette 1975).

Beyond concrete issues (such as pollution, the destruction of coral reefs, or drugs that invade the islands) that might motivate and legitimate a desire of returning to nature and the foundation of rural communities in the hills, the concept of nature must also be linked to the notion of lost paradise, which has a strong religious dimension. Within a messianist and millenarian problematic, Rastafari indeed

---

[5] The Rastafari way of life obeys two essential exigencies: to live in harmony with nature by maintaining the balance of creation, and to live outside of Babylon. Called *Ital* ("natural") this way of life is based on the essential notions of purity and naturality and on a mystical conception of the body as "holy temple" and inseparable from the soul. Body and soul must be harmoniously balanced and pure. Therefore, the term Ital does not concern alimentation only, but applies to all the practices of daily life and generically means "what is good"; indeed, "Ital conveys a sense of natural, organic purity, as well as cultural authenticity" (Johnson-Hill 1995: 202). Purity, impurity, naturality, and artificiality are of course deeply linked to the notions of Good and Evil. The basic hypothesis is simple: we are what we eat; therefore, alimentation and body practices have to maintain the balance of both the body and soul. The Ital way maintains a physical and spiritual balance and harmony between body and soul, the individual and the group, mankind and God's creation.

promises the advent of a new world that is nothing other than the restoration of an initial world that was slowly degraded by mankind. This new world will be inhabited by the righteous. This lost paradise hence takes the color of natural profusion, which offers abundance and happiness to men, as long as they respect God, their fellow men, and the world around them. This is nothing new (Eliade 1949), but what is interesting in the case of Rastafari is that the notion of lost paradise also refers to a problematic of deracination from and return to Africa, the original land that was lost by the slaves and their descendants. The return to Zion is made both towards *a mythical land* (i.e. nostalgia for a lost paradise, mingled with the idealized image of a mythical Africa) and towards *a real land* (today's Africa, to which one can concretely return). Moreover, the return to Zion symbolizes the struggle for liberation, *now and here on earth*. For the rastas, there is no heaven after death, contrary to what most churches preach, but a heaven on earth, for which each must fight in the present. As the Nigerian artist Majek Fashek sings,

> We are going to the promised land
> I hope you are ready
> promised land is not America
> is not Asia
> promised land is a state of mind
> promised land is not Europe
> is not Africa
> promised land is a state of mind.
>
> "Promised land," 1997

Zion is as much the reward of God after the Armageddon as what can be lived here and now. And therefore the concrete location of Zion does not matter, because its spiritual and symbolic dimension is more important than a place: what matters is to build a better world. To use Taylor's words (1990: 201), "the idea of the millenium, the new Zion, can be reinterpreted as a process of building a new, just and free society. Ethiopia becomes a creative social and political symbol." Because of this dimension, Rastafari must not be analyzed as an escapist movement, but as a movement of resistance that promotes action in order to change the world, while still believing into a celestial Jerusalem to come, which must be prepared and not simply awaited, since the access to the New Jerusalem depends on the actions of each human being during his earthly life.[6] Homiak (1995: 154), referring to his fieldwork, noted that "they were not seeking to withdraw from society or others within the movement. Rather, they were seeking spiritual growth through a mystic alignment with nature and, from this, empowerment with which to confront the dominant system." Indeed, the return to nature is associated with a necessary replenishment in order to fight in the world, not with a strict escape. Moreover, the articulation of the concept of nature with its opposite Babylon, and their association with respectively God and Satan, strongly refer to the eschatology: man's degradation of Creation leads to the end of the world; the quest for a harmony with nature is therefore in itself a proof of faith and a refusal of Evil, both being experienced with Armageddon in mind, for which one has to prepare. Contrary to a common assertion, it is precisely the articulation between a religious narrative of the origin and an apocalyptic representation of the future that, within a particular context that includes the past of slavery, allows the development of an active millenarism that favors socio-political struggle: for the rastas, the point is to await the end of the world (and to survive it), but also to actively participate in its coming.

I will now turn to socio-political engagement and its transmission within reggae music. Examples of the links that exist between music and ideology are numerous, the most famous being, perhaps, revolutionary songs and national anthems, which work as symbols that provide an immediate representation of the ideology to which they are linked: they evoke places, events, emotions, a history, beliefs, and ideals. The case of reggae is interesting because it is a popular musical style that is not, in the beginning, directly linked to political events, parties or movements, although it was born soon after the independence of Jamaica. Nor was it born out of the Rastafari movement, although it was quickly appropriated by the rastas. Additionally, if the tie between reggae and Rastafari is close-knit, it has never been exclusive: from its birth until today, some reggae artists have not been linked to Rastafari. Therefore, one might consider that reggae music is only a tool used by the Rastafari movement. However, it is more than mere use; they are complexly

---

6 Hurbon (1989: 336) emphasizes the same point: "To consider the movement as an escape from social and political struggle, is, in a strict sense, to miss the essential aim of Rastafari." See also Taylor 1990: 200.

tied, mutually influence each other, and are considered as linked in a deep although non-systematic way.

Reggae is a popular music, then, but one which takes an affirmed ideological character, both because its texts echo social or even political engagement, and because it is *considered* as conveying a message and *identified* more or less closely with a religious movement. Moreover, reggae itself claims to be an instrument of knowledge and teaching. Reggae songs often use the terms "to teach" and "to learn," and opposes "reggae schoolroom" and traditional school, the latter being considered a tool of domination that perpetuates slavery and colonization. For instance, Anthony B assimilates reggae music to the "rastaman school":

> Grab a seat and sit down
> rastaman school unno come, student
> time fi gain wisdom
> and kyan yuh ears listen King Selassie I song
> "Rastaman school," 1997

The educative function of reggae music—or at least of "cultural" reggae—is claimed by the artists. This function is also viewed as being inherent to the sounds of music, and not only derived from the content of the texts.

In the case of reggae, the relationship that exists between memory, music, and politics is in fact sustained by the *articulation* made between a construction of the origin and a representation of the future that have essential consequences for daily life. Dynamically associated to the present, this articulation also produces an ensemble of concepts and practices specific to the Rastafari movement. In particular, the dynamic transformation of a traditional eschatology (that is, the Revelation of Saint John) allows its complexification, switching from a passive to an active expectation: redemption is above all the direct result of the actions of each individual on earth, judged by God; it is a distant future as much as a close future blended with the present, transforming into a sort of "double eschatology" that establishes parallels between the Armageddon and earthly struggle, between a judge-like and warrior-like God and each individual, between the messianic New Jerusalem and a symbolic Zion to be built on earth, or between the different levels of an Africa that is simultaneously a paradise both lost and to come, a concrete continent, and a state of mind. This articulation between a rebuilt origin, an expected and awaited future, and a difficult or problematic present (including here the recent past subsequent to the Middle Passage, corresponding in fact to the birth of the diaspora), therefore produces an active millenarism, even though Rastafari has long been described as an escapist movement.

This complexification of the eschatology, and with it the notions of hope and redemption, has coincided with two essential events in the history of Rastafari: the birth of reggae at the very end of the sixties, and the death of Haile Selassie in 1975. It is difficult to determine the exact impact of each of these two events on the eschatological complexification, which brings into the present an eschatology that used to be distant, inaccessible, and ideal. It remains that the death of the messiah has pushed the movement to redefine its beliefs (as seen earlier in chapter 7), while reggae music provided a medium of communication well adapted to a community in diaspora.[7] Reggae also provided a dynamism that Rastafari might have lost with time. Additionally, the relationship that ties reggae and Rastafari has been essential in the active redefinition of the latter: religious-tainted ideological and political engagement finds with reggae music a performing medium of communication and an audience opened to its message. Reggae artists who are linked to the Rastafari movement all consider themselves as having the duty to convey a religious and political message, as being the ambassadors of an identity and a social engagement, and as being messengers with multiple functions. All insist on this role, which they often call "a mission", in the interviews they give.

---

[7] Indeed, music is easy to transport, and it also reaches a large audience, beyond age, class, or gender distinctions as well as beyond the limits of literacy, unlike written media.

10

The construction of a socio-political memory

> Two thousand years of history
> Could not be wiped away so easily
> Two thousand years of history, black history
> Could not be wiped so easily.
> Bob Marley & the Wailers, "Zion train," 1980

> – But wait, nobody no left?
> – It's only we Rasta.
> Steel Pulse, "Tribute to the martyrs," 1979

Reggae music expresses a central will: the recognition of a history of struggle, against slavery, segregation, and colonization. This history starts with the slave trade and is in permanent and continuous construction; while it is logically attached to Jamaica, it also goes beyond its borders. This historical memory has three main goals: first, to reveal a history of resistance considered as having been underestimated as well as hidden by Europeans; second, to restore dignity by showing that resistance started with the first captured slave; and third, to transmit this history of resistance, in particular to generations to come. The notion of revelation is worthy of more lengthy consideration, because it is a founding question for both Rastafari and reggae music. According to them, "half the story has never been told," concerning history in general and more specifically the history of Africa (which, written by Europeans, has been falsified to the point of making people believe that there was no African civilizations until colonial times), the history of the slaves' struggle and resistance, and the history of the African diaspora. Both reggae and Rastafari are organized around the notion of revelation, seeing the world to be woven with lies and believing that the truth still has to be revealed. As Dennis Brown sings,

> We've got to know the truth
> You see, what about the half that's never been told?
> What about the half that's never been told?
> Look how long it's been kept a big secret
> Look how long it's been hidden away
> The half, the half, the half that's never been told.
> U Roy and Dennis Brown, "The half," 1978

This story that has never been told concerns the historical past, but also, and maybe above all, religious truth: if the world does not believe in the status of "righteousness" of the rastas, in the redemption that is promised to them, and in the existence of Jah himself, it is because of the influence of Evil, which turns the people away from the truth and strengthens the domination of Babylon. The Rastafari movement comes as the revelation of this denied, hidden, religious, and historical truth; the notion of revelation is therefore essential to understand it, as was emphasized by Anita Waters (1999: 65). The history of resistance, only "half told," is cherished by the Rastafari movement and transmitted in reggae music, precisely because it has been distorted and mistold. I have distinguished four major themes that build and form this history in reggae music: the Jamaican maroon communities and peasant revolts in Jamaica; Marcus Garvey; the figures of the black struggle in the United States; and finally the independence and anti-apartheid movements in Africa.

Jamaican maroons and peasant revolts, and the figure of the warrior

The Spanish term "cimarrón" (wild, on the loose), which refers to the slaves who escaped the plantations in Spanish colonies, has been borrowed by English ("maroons" in the Caribbean, "runaway slaves" in the United States). Marooning was very frequent in the Caribbean islands, as well as on the South American continent (Price 1979, Mintz 1989), although Europeans often minimized the phenomena to avoid more runaways. Many maroon communities existed, and still do, especially in the forested areas of Venezuela, Suriname, Brazil, and Guyana, and in the hills of the Caribbean islands, especially in

Jamaica. These communities settled in areas that were difficult to access and of little interest for Europeans, such as mountains, forests or jungle, swamps, or rocky areas (Besson 1995a: 302). In Jamaica, since the beginning of the slavery system, runaway slaves found a refuge in the Blue Mountains and the Cockpit Country, which were particularly wild and inaccessible. The first maroons were the slaves abandoned by the Spanish during the English conquest of Jamaica, in 1655. Since this time, independent communities settled in the back-country, far from European plantations. They were based on an economy of survival inspired by traditional African traditions—in particular, the collective sharing of the products of hunting, fishing, and gathering, and subsistence farming.[1] The maroons were not only on the run, they were also at war with the English, fighting for their territory and independence. One of the great chiefs of war was Cudjoe, who coordinated the different communities in their struggle against the English from 1729 to 1739. Cudjoe ended the war by signing a peace treaty that guaranteed the maroon communities' autonomy, hunting and fishing rights, and territorial independence. As occurred elsewhere, the treaty was broken by the colonial forces (Patterson 1979); in 1775 the second maroon war started.

Because they have represented, until today, the archetype of resistance to slavery and a greater cultural and social proximity with the African continent, the maroon communities retain an aura in the eyes of "the others"—that is, the slaves who had not run away.[2] This aura is paradoxical because the maroons are both admired and feared. They are the subject of many stories, and are usually viewed as stronger, more courageous, more heroic, and above all "more African"; they are the warriors who fought the English and remained faithful to their African traditions. But the maroon communities also symbolize an unknown "elsewhere," both appealing and scary. For the Rastafari movement in particular, the maroons represent a powerful referent because they are historical models of resistance, who fought back relentlessly and without compromise, and also because they represent a closeness with the African inheritance. Their way of life—close to nature, autarchic—the survival of many

---

[1] About the history of Jamaican maroon communities, see Kopytoff 1976 and 1977, Price 1979, Campbell 1988.
[2] For a literary point of view, see Banks 1980, and the passage of the escape in Confiant 1988.

African traditions (in particular linguistic), and their pride, make them a model to follow. Moreover, Rastafari considers itself, in a way, as a sort of maroon community of the twentieth century, which resists the oppressor ("Babylon"). This is one identification among several others with which the Rastafari movement defines its place in the contemporary world: the rastaman is the lion in the jungle (Big Youth 1986), a Cudjoe who resists the English (for instance, the French band Nèg' marrons), a Zulu warrrior (for example, Jah Shaka's nickname "the mighty Zulu warrior"), and so forth. Similarly, the traditional Rastafarian matting of the hair called dread locks symbolizes together the mane of the lion, freedom and naturality, and the haircut of the Mau-Mau warriors who resisted the British in Kenya until the 1930s.[3] The symbol of the lion is the most used and probably one of the most powerful; it refers to the King of the animals, symbol of strength, power and nobility, and is also the distinctive symbol of the tribe of Judah as well as one of the honorific titles held by Haile Selassie. The rastas intensely identify with the figure of the warrior, because they consider that they live in a world that is at war, between the forces of Good and Evil. To be a rastaman, therefore, is like being a "mighty warrior" who resists and fights. The notion of war in a situation of adversity remains absolutely essential, although it rarely implies concrete violence, since it is mostly interpreted as a spiritual fight between Good and Evil. The maroon communities, being the heir of a long tradition of resistance and associated to a close relation with both nature and the African roots, therefore constitute an important symbolic referent, which appears in reggae music sporadically.

The maroon inheritance is not the only history to which reggae pays homage. It also narrates the history of the black struggle in Jamaica, which has been particularly important, and of which one hero was Sam Sharpe, a Baptist pastor who had access to the abolitionist movement and devoted his life to teaching the slaves. He organized the rebellion of 1831, which started in Saint James, spread around the island, and lasted eight days. Known as the "Christmas rebellion" because it started on December 28, it followed several others, which took place in Barbados (1816), Trinidad (1819, 1825, and 1829), and Antigua (1831). The rebellion was ferociously repressed; Sam Sharpe was executed in Montego

---

[3] This practice is also found among the *sadhus* in Hinduism.

Bay in May 1832. In 1834, the United Kingdom abolished slavery; according to Campbell (1985: 30), Sharpe significantly contributed to the acceleration of the abolition debate. But the most important symbol of the struggle in reggae music is actually a post-slavery figure: Paul Bogle, a peasant from the parish of St. Thomas. He was a member of one of the free villages that were created in Jamaica after the emancipation of the slaves, in which the inhabitants were struggling for land property rights. In "Tribute to the martyrs" (1979), Steel Pulse sings:

> Is what to Bogle?
> Morant Bay rebellion, standing up feh him rights, dem decide
>   fe hang 'im up
> what?
> truly
> 1865.

Paul Bogle tried to unite the peasants in their struggle against the planters, and asked maroon communities for their help. Using force, the rebellion intensified in 1865, and for a few days the rebels took control of the parish of St. Thomas, around Morant Bay. The government then declared martial law and sent in troops. In October, Bogle was hung, along with others. According to Steel Pulse,

> William Gordon and Paul Bogle led a rebellion cause they
>   used their heads
> but had their necks in a noose
> martyrs of freedom, freedom condemned.
>   Steel Pulse, "Prediction," 1978

The Morant Bay rebellion marked the beginning of the contemporary struggle of the slave descendants in Jamaica, and set the foundation for the development of Ethiopanism, Panafricanism, and Garveyism. As Bob Marley sings,

> I'll never forget no way
> they turned up back on Paul Bogle
> so don't you forget no youth
> who you are and where you stand in this struggle.
>   Bob Marley & the Wailers, "So much things to say," 1977

The Morant Bay rebellion represents, to him, a structural and essential event that determines who and where are good and bad, friends and enemies, oppressed and oppressors. In other words, it functions as an atemporal model of struggle, which provides a template for the present. Therefore, reggae music narrates a history of Jamaica that is made from the side of the oppressed; this history is narrated but also explained and taught, through names, dates, and events. Some characters in this history are honored as models of both struggle and martyrdom. In a way, through reggae music is built a pantheon of martyrs, and their memory is transmitted and honored.

Marcus Garvey

A second theme in reggae lyrics concerns the countless references made to Marcus Garvey; Culture's album *Two Sevens Clash* was actually named after a prophecy attributed to Garvey concerning July 7, 1977. One of the most prolific reggae artists in relation to the evocation of Garvey is Burning Spear, who actually gave his name to one of his first albums (*Marcus Garvey*, 1975).[4] According to Burning Spear, Marcus Garvey has been forgotten, unlike other important characters in Jamaican history:

> No one remember old Marcus Garvey
> no one remember him, no one
> they been talking about Paul Bogle
> they been talking about William Gordon
> they been talking about Norman Washington Manley
> including Bustamante
> no one remember old Marcus Garvey.
> Burning Spear, "Old Marcus Garvey," 1975

But reggae music corrects this mistake: an essential reference for Rastafari, Garvey has a strong presence in reggae lyrics. This presence takes two dimensions: the homage paid to him, and the exposé of his ideology.

The homage to Garvey is found in the references made to him, the

---

[4] Among other songs by Burning Spear, see "Old Marcus Garvey" (1975), "Marcus children suffer," "Marcus say Jah no dead," "Marcus senior," and "Mister Garvey" (1978), "Follow Marcus Garvey" and "Jah see and know" (1980), "Africa," "Every other nation," "Old timer," and "Subject in school" (1995).

multiple citations of his name scattered in reggae lyrics. For instance, in "Hail Selassie" (1997), Sizzla sings

> Hail king Selassie
> Ethiopia son his majesty
> Emmanuel, holy holy
> take us home Marcus Garvey.

He refers to the ultimate goal of Marcus Garvey, the repatriation of the slave descendants back to Africa. In another song he adds, "Marcus Garvey done say it / him seh if the future come, haste" ("Black woman and child," 1997). Sometimes it is a simple reference that introduces the song, which is itself actually not about Garvey, as in "I need a roof" by the Mighty Diamonds (1976) or "Cowboy," once again by Sizzla (1997).

Second, reggae contains references to Garvey's ideology, which form an exposé of his thought, ideas, and actions. For example, Burning Spear sings:

> Marcus Garvey did say
> people, black people
> you can't wait until your back's against the wall
> before you start to inquire, whose fault.
>   Burning Spear, "Marcus children suffer," 1978

In "Mr Garvey" (1978), he describes the importance of Garvey's movement, the UNIA:

> Mister Garvey is so cool
> Mister Garvey is so smooth
> that's why he go to school
> he is the first through black History
> who ever control so much people
> hundreds, thousands, millions
> he cause an eruption.

In "Til I'm laid to rest" (1995), Buju Banton quotes a slogan of the UNIA, "Africa for the Africans, at home and abroad" ("Africa for the Africans / Marcus Mosiah speaks"). Beyond repatriation, the goal of Garvey was the unity of all Africans, from Africa as well as from the diaspora. In "Mama Africa" (1999), not much is said, but much is suggested:

> Who say so?
> Marcus Mosiah
> listen Mr. B
> Marcus tell I
> Black starliner gonna carry us home.
>
> > Anthony B, Buju Banton, and Garnett Silk,
> > "Hello mama Africa," 1999

The first part of this excerpt suggests that what precedes it is not the personal opinion of the artist, but comes from the teachings of Marcus Garvey. The second part suggests a proximity between the words of Garvey and their reading by the artist ("Marcus tell I"). Finally, there is a reference to the Starliner, the sailing line created by Garvey for repatriation, which Culture also mentions in "Black Starliner must come" (1978): "We're waiting / for the black starliner which is to come." At the end of the song "Tribute to the martyrs" (1979) there is a conversation between the members of the band Steel Pulse. It functions on the mode of call and response, and evokes a series of heroes, the martyrs to whom Steel Pulse pays homage. Among them is found a reference to Garvey's Starliner:

> Whah happen to Marcus?
> Marcus say a thing sah
> one God, one aim, one destiny
> Starliner
> Black.

Junior Byles also mentions the slogan "One God, one aim, one destiny" in "Know where you going" (1975). Finally, according to the Mighty Diamonds, "them never loved, them never loved poor Marcus / them never loved him, oh no ... til they betrayed him" ("Them never love poor Marcus," 1976). The use of "them" is typical of the essential distinction made between "us" and "them": Marcus Garvey was not loved because he resisted "them"—that is, the oppressors, the rich, the colonialists—within a problematic of adversity and opposition between the Good and Evil, Zion and Babylon.

Afro-American movements of struggle

Reggae music quickly expanded its interest beyond Jamaica. This expansion is especially visible in the references made to African-American liberation movements, which began to appear in reggae songs as early as the mid-seventies.[5] Dennis Brown for instance, in 1978, dedicated a song to Malcolm X:

> Cause of Malcolm X
> white men got vexed
> they didn't want to see black men progress
> and all along the way
> black men have strength
> searching to find the way
> I wanna know
> how long will it be
> to all my brothers see
> the hidden brutality
> how long will it be
> it's been hidden from our eyes much too long
> we've got to know the truth.
>
> Dennis Brown, "Malcolm X," 1978

Beyond the homage to Malcolm X, the notion of diaspora appears: Dennis Brown links all slave descendants, considered as members of the same group, by using the first person plural ("from our eyes," "we've got to know the truth") and the term "my brothers." In 1979, Steel Pulse wrote a song in honor of George Jackson, a member of the Black Panthers who was jailed in the Soledad prison:

> This one's in memory of Uncle George ...
> George Jackson Soledad brother
> malicious unjust society
> he became revolutionary
> George Jackson Soledad brother.
>
> Steel Pulse, "Uncle George," 1979

---

[5] As well as in Marley's reference to the Buffalo Soldiers, originally the nickname for the "colored" 9th and 10th Cavalry Regiments in the US army, formed in 1866; it later came to refer to all African-American regiments (both cavalry and infantry) that have served since the Civil War.

For Steel Pulse, the Black Panthers are part of a unique and indivisible history, the history of *all* slave descendants. Indeed in "Tribute to the martyrs" (1979), Steel Pulse mentions the Black Panthers, Martin Luther King, and Malcolm X, establishing a continuity between them:

> The Black Panthers
> freedom fighters
> they tried, they died
> Luther King
> he had a dream, Grizzly, he had a dream
> Malcolm X
> lift struggle, lift struggle
> in a pool of blood
> 1965.

This unity of the diverse movements that compose the struggle for liberation is regulalry present in reggae music. According to Burning Spear, all those who have fought against slavery and segregation, independently of the way in which they have, are seen as united, and all provide models that complete each other even though they might seem antagonistic:

> Remember Mister King philosophy
> remember Mister X philosophy
> remember Marcus philosophy.
>
> Burning Spear, "Every other nation," 1995

Here are three philosophies that have to be remembered and conserved; moreover, they should be taught in school, as Burning Spear mentions it in "Subject in school" (1995):

> We want a subject in school on Marcus
> we want a subject
> Malcolm X, Martin Luther King ...
> these three brethren was one brethren
> before your system split them apart.

Not only do the teachings of these three models have to be remembered and transmitted, they have to be in an official way as well. It is therefore a *memory to be transmitted* and a *history to be taught*. This issue is at the heart of the problematic of the falsification of history, which I have already discussed: Burning Spear questions the content of official school programs and makes an important claim; he asks for the history of the slaves' descendants to be taught in school, officially and universally. Additionally, he emphasizes the unity of the struggle, in a very explicit way: "These three brethren was one brethren / before your system split them apart." The conflicts that might have existed between the three men are a consequence of the "system"—that is, of the enemy, which divides in order to reign.

The unity of the struggle, beyond boundaries and differences in their form, also implies a unity of the slaves' descendants, beyond their cultural, national, or geographical differences, and therefore a construction of the notion of diaspora. The appearance of the notion of diaspora within reggae lyrics echoed its elaboration within the Rastafari movement, and took place in the 1970s, although Marcus Garvey had based his ideology on its existence; the increasing interest in the North American struggle and the African movements of independence and against apartheid in reggae songs is an indicator of a progressive construction of a concrete diaspora in reggae music.[6]

African independences and the struggle against apartheid

As Zips (1994: 56) points out, "African identity, pan-African solidarity ... and African redemption was thematized by hundreds, if not thousands, of lyrics, found in the reggae discography." The presence of contemporary Africa in reggae lyrics is expressed through two main themes: the fight for independence, and the struggle against apartheid. The progressive independence of colonized African countries took place between the very beginning of the 1960s and the beginning of the 1980s, and strongly marked both the Rastafari movement and reggae music, for two reasons. First, because they echoed the independence of Jamaica, in 1962, and second, because they symbolized the liberation of the African continent, so important to the rastas, and therefore reinforced their faith in God: Africa, free at last, was the proof that the world was changing, and that God

---

[6] An interesting postscript can be added here: in 2008 and 2009, the candidacy and then election of Barack Obama as the 44th President of the United States was documented in reggae music, among others by Cocoa Tea, Damian Marley, Prince Thompson, and Steel Pulse.

was stronger than Evil. Bob Marley's song "Zimbabwe" is essential in the history of reggae music, not only for its celebration of the independence of Zimbabwe (and of the rest of Africa altogether) but also because it founds a unifying conception of African countries (therefore, a pan-African view) as well as an identification of Africa with the diaspora:

> Every man got the right to decide his own destiny
> And in this judgement there is no partiality
> So arms in arms, with arms, we fight this little struggle
> Cause that's the only way we can overcome our little trouble
> Brother you're right, you're right, you're right, you're so right
> We go fight, we'll have to fight, we gonna fight, fight for our rights
> Natty dread it inna Zimbabwe
> Set it up inna Zimbabwe
> Mash it up inna Zimbabwe
> Africans a liberate Zimbabwe
> No more internal power struggle
> We come together to overcome the little trouble.
> Bob Marley & the Wailers, "Zimbabwe," 1979

In this excerpt, Bob Marley addresses both the people of Zimbabwe ("my brother, you're right"), the united group formed by all Africans ("Africans a liberate Zimbabwe"), and the united group formed by the Africans of the diaspora and those of Africa ("arms in arms we fight," "we come together"). By celebrating the independence of one country, Zimbabwe, Bob Marley also celebrates the liberation—or the duty of struggling for liberation—of the rest of the continent, and finally the construction of a pan-African unity that brings together all the Africans, in and out of Africa. This diasporic and pan-African construction appears explicitly in another song, "Africa unite":

> Africa unite, cause we're moving right out of Babylon
> and we're going to our fathers land
> how good and how pleasant it would be, before God and man
> to see the unification of all Africans ...
> so Africa unite, cause the children wanna go home ...

> unite for the benefit of your people
> unite for the Africans abroad
> unite for the benefit of your children
> unite for the Africans a yard.
> Bob Marley & the Wailers, "Africa unite," 1979

Bob Marley calls forth on the unification of Africa, which also implies the repatriation of the Africans of the diaspora. The diaspora is therefore theorized within the notion of African unity, as a distinct ("abroad") but nevertheless interconnected group ("children wanna go home"). The physical participation of Bob Marley & the Wailers in the ceremony of independence in Zimbabwe marked the concretization of the tie between Africa and the diaspora.

South African apartheid is the second major topic that concerns "concrete" Africa in reggae music. Here again, reggae lyrics express a great closeness between the Jamaicans and black South Africans:

> Ain't gonna sit around and wonder
> what to do
> cause in South Africa here is apartheid
> oh my people ...
> Ain't gonna sit around and wonder
> what to do
> cause in South Africa here is a fire
> on the youth.
> Black Uhuru, "No loafing (sit and wonder)," 1980

Black Uhuru suggests unity ("my people"), the worries about the apartheid regime, and the need for action ("ain't gonna sit around and wonder / what to do"). One of the characters of the anti-apartheid struggle that is the most present in reggae lyrics is Steve Biko:

> Hey what is to Biko?
> Biko detainee in detention
> What?
> 1977
> South Africa.
> Steel Pulse, "Tribute to the martyrs," 1979

Biko was an anti-apartheid militant who was arrested and then killed in prison, the case being closed as suicide.[7] Steel Pulse tells his story in a song written for him:

> Blame South African security
> a no suicide he wasn't insane
> it was not for him to live in Rome
> still they wouldn't leave him alone
> they provoke him, they arrest him
> they took his life away
> but can't take him soul
> then they drug and ill-treat him, and they beat him
> and they claim suicide.
> Steel Pulse, "Biko's kindred lament," 1979

Using the metaphor of Rome, Steel Pulse explains that he was a rebel to the system, here apartheid ("it was not for him to live in Rome"). Steve Biko, young and innocent, became a symbol of the uncompromising struggle against apartheid. The identification with this symbol was marked by a great sense of intimacy, as is apparent in the song, in which his death is described as a personal mourning:

> The night Steve Biko died I cried (and I cried)
> Biko, O Steve Biko died still in chains
> Biko, O Steve Biko died still in chains
> Biko died in chains, moaned for you ...
> I'll never forgive I'll always remember.

Source of pain, his death is also considered as an example that will never be forgotten:

> not, not only I no
> but papa brothers sisters too
> him spirit they can't control
> him spirit they can't control
> cannot be bought nor sold
> freedom increase one-hundred fold.

Steve Biko, who "died in chains," is considered a brother and becomes a martyr; he did not die in vain, but on the contrary will

---

[7] The case was sent back to court by the Commission of Reconciliation in 1999, and amnesty was denied to the individuals implicated in the murder of Steve Biko.

serve as a model, as a symbol that reinforces the struggle. Reggae music documented the South African situation over the course of many years. Almost every important event was mentioned, described, and commented on, in particular, of course, the liberation of Nelson Mandela in 1990 after twenty-seven years of imprisonment.[8] From Steve Biko to Nelson Mandela, South Africa was a central theme in reggae music, and this was due to its strong symbolic character. Indeed, the apartheid regime represented, in a way, the archetype of domination: pushed to the extreme, and based on a colonial and racial construction.

Therefore, there is in reggae music a militant positioning for African unity and freedom, and against colonization and apartheid. This concrete evocation of the African continent is superimposed upon an imaginary evocation of Africa—the land of origin and return, the Jerusalem of redemption. Indeed, Africa had been massively present in reggae lyrics from the beginning, but at the end of the seventies it took on a reality that it did not have before: it became a contemporary continent, where milk and honey do not flow, but that is rather the site of the struggle against colonialism. This new "reality" of the African continent is especially visible in the way artists began to mention specific African countries, instead of a mythical Africa called "Abyssinia" or "Ethiopia": for instance, Buju Banton speaks of Congo, Bostwana, Kenya, and Ghana in "Til I'm laid to rest" (1995), while Anthony B mentions Morocco and Congo in "Conscious entertainer" (1999); Burning Spear evokes Liberia and Sierra Leone in "Subject in school" (1995), and Luciano the Gambia, Nigeria, Senegal, and Tanzania in "When will I be home" (1999). These "two Africas" are neither in contradiction nor in conflict with each other, but complementary. The difficulties faced by many African countries do not discourage the rastas; the reality that is imposed on them does not endanger what Africa represents at a symbolic level. Africa continues to symbolize the origin and to provide hope. Some rastas settled in Shashamane in Ethiopia, and live within the reality of contemporary Africa; others are engaged in social or cultural programs, for instance the artist Jah Shaka in Ghana. It is sometimes difficult, when Africa is evoked in reggae music, to know exactly "which Africa" is spoken of, because the two levels are not completely distinct, but tightly intermingled.

---

[8] For instance in Barrington Levy's hit "Mandela," 1992.

However, this must not be considered as a contradiction: Africa is both a reality and a symbol, a continent in pain and the land of redemption, different countries (which are sometimes at war with each other) and a united "Ethiopia."

Memory of the diaspora, memory of the struggle: Diaspora and universality

This pantheon of martyrs, to which reggae pays homage, illustrates the appearance of a changing and dynamic collective memory in construction, which narrates a history still being made today, and which functions through identifications and symbols—from Cudjoe, who resisted the English in the Cockpit country, to Sam Sharpe, who educated the slaves, to Malcolm X "in a pool of blood," to Steve Biko, who died in detention in a South African jail. This memory of liberation is based on Jamaican history, but not limited to it: it quickly incorporated the struggles against segregation in the USA, for freedom in Africa, and against apartheid in South Africa.[9] Hence, it was, and still is, transformed into a memory of the diaspora, which articulates both a horizontal concept of diaspora in the Caribbean and Americas, and a vertical tie to Africa. As Negus (1996: 106–107) says,

> the *roots* of the contemporary black experience can therefore be traced back to Africa and the sudden brutal disruption introduced by slavery. Yet, the subsequent *routes* that black people have taken and the cultural forms that have been created cannot be understood simply in terms of common origin in Africa ... Gilroy suggests that the cultural and political connections that bind black people together have been continually *created* through identities and practices that have been generated during processes of movement and mediation (Gilroy 1987, 1993).

What Gilroy (1993) calls roots refers to the vertical tie with the land of origin, here Africa; his routes refer to the horizontal ties created

---

[9] Although not part of our corpus, an interesting example is the dub album *International Heroes Dub*, recorded by Overton "Scientist" Brown with the Forces of Music at Channel One studio in 1983–1984, with the following songlist: Marcus Mosiah Garvey, Walter Sisuli, Malcolm X, Mohammed Ali, George Jackson, Desmond Tutu, Nelson Mandela, Martin Luther King, Jomo Kenyatta, Steve Biko, Dedan Kimathi, Kwame Nrumah.

(and still being created) within the diaspora itself. As I mentioned earlier, both the homeland (the roots) and the path shared after exile (the routes) are equally important for the sense of being in diaspora.

The socio-political memory conveyed by reggae music therefore concerns the Africans of the diaspora and the Africans of Africa. Moreover, it is based on a radical distinction between "we" and "them." These two opposed categories fundamentally refer to slavery (slave masters versus slaves) and to race (whites versus blacks), but they have been enlarged to form a memory of resistance that distinguishes Good from Evil. A memory of resistance brings together diverse characters who come from different places and times, from the Jamaican maroons to the Black Panthers, and who are considered as models. In "So much things to say" by Bob Marley, history is presented as being a continuous and timeless model:

> Hey, but I'll never forget no way
> they crucified Jesus Christ
> I'll never forget no way
> they sold Marcus Garvey for rights
> I'll never forget no way
> they turned up back on Paul Bogle
> so don't you forget no youth
> who you are and where you stand in this struggle.
> "So much things to say," 1977

Not only must history be revealed and narrated, it also must serve as a lesson and allow each to know "who you are," and moreover "where you stand in this struggle." The memory conveyed by reggae music is, therefore, a memory that transmits and teaches, within the fundamental perspective of the revelation of truth against a dissimulated or distorted historical reality; it is also a memory that pays homage to all those who have made it, for instance in Steel Pulse's "Tribute to the martyrs" (1979). Reggae can, therefore, convey through its lyrics a socio-political memory, a historical narrative made from the side of the group itself. Not only does reggae recall the days of slavery, it also narrates the tradition of slave resistance and the successive rebellions, and perpetuates the memory of the people who made this history. Moreover, it includes within this tradition the North American and African struggles.[10] This extension of collective memory is both the expression (or consequence) of the construction of a diasporic identity, and one of the elements that build this identity. By evoking (sometimes in an intimate way, for instance in the case of apartheid) the history of Africa, reggae participates in the production of a diasporic unity but also, as it was thought by Marcus Garvey, of a unity between "the Africans of the diaspora" and "the Africans of Africa." By transmitting this memory, reggae assumes both an identitary and educational function, and relays a history that had been transmitted partially, poorly, or not at all. The transmission of the memory of its people also represents an explicit defiance of the dominant history imposed by slave masters and colonialists, and today by the elite. It therefore seems obvious that the sociopolitical memory conveyed by reggae music is also a memory of resistance, within the broader problematic of Western cultural domination, which Rastafari violently opposes. For the rastas, the transmission of history and memory also implies, simultaneously, the transmission of a culture that has been endangered by slavery and colonialism: the narrative of the socio-political history of the diaspora is treated as one essential element within cultural transmission, an element that is both educational and ascribed in protest, since the point is to unveil a history that has been falsified and to transmit a revealed history considered to be true. This revelation then enables consciousness-raising among the people and their political and religious engagement in the struggle for liberation. Returning to the notion of mental slavery, the transmission of a memory of resistance also represents an act of *revelation, liberation and redemption*. In the case of the African diaspora, indeed, the devaluation of African history by the West during several centuries, which served to justify African slavery, alongside religious and pseudo-scientific racial classifications, played an essential role in the domination exercised over the slaves, who were stripped not only of their daily life, culture, kinship, and land, but also of their history. Additionally, the systematic downplay of a part of the history of slavery (i.e. the resistance of the slaves, the existence of countless maroon communities or free villages) constituted a

---

[10] As well as their own local history in the case of non-Jamaican reggae bands—for example in Great Britain, France, Mauritius, Hawaii, etc—although it does not appear in this book.

strong tool of control on the slave populations. The revelation and reappropriation of this dissimulated and travestied history, in other words the transmission of its living memory, therefore constitutes an essential act, which alone can make possible the liberation of its people but also, and foremost, its survival as a people.

Part IV

From revelation to revolution

11

Rhetoric of oppression and social critique

> Can't get no food to eat, can't get no money to spend.
> Burning Spear, "Marcus Garvey," 1975
>
> Open your eyes and look with it
> Are you satisfied with the life you're living?
> Bob Marley & the Wailers, "Exodus," 1977
>
> No need to shift through time and space into reality
> Cause it's right up in your face it is so plain to see.
> Jahmali, "Time and space," 1998

The message contained in reggae music is above all a message of denunciation: the point is to show what is really happening, based on the fundamental distinction made by Rastafari between Good and Evil, between Zion and Babylon. Within a world viewed as a permanent struggle, reggae music *takes a position*: it is essential to know on which side one is ("where you stand in this struggle," Bob Marley & the Wailers, 1977). It also develops a *social critique* and a *denunciation* of oppression, and functions as a social tribune, as a chronicle of resistance. Reggae music works as a trigger, and exhorts its audience to "open your eyes and look with it" (Bob Marley & the Wailers, 1977). As the artists, audience, and scholars are all keen to argue, reggae is therefore a music of resistance, based on a rhetoric of oppression which, although it is influenced by the Rastafari movement, is also shared by artists who are not linked to it, such as Bounty Killer. This rhetoric of oppression defines the terms which govern a worldview and is rooted in the daily reality of the lives of poor people in Jamaica. It also structures the social critique made by reggae music, as well as, more broadly, the way in which reggae is politicized.

The music of the sufferers: Reggae and the rhetoric of oppression

> I started [to sing] ... by crying. Yeah, that's how I started. (Bob Marley, 1973)

Fundamentally, reggae is considered "the music of the poor," and Rastafari their religious movement. Both not only take a stand for the poor, but are also grounded upon, and identify with, the poor. Born in the Jamaican ghettos, reggae echoes their daily life and claims to be the voice of the people, as well as their champion against the oppressors. In "Poor and clean" (1980), Gregory Isaacs affirms that he would "rather be poor and clean / than to live rich in corruption," and adds that "the rich man's heaven, heaven, is the poor man's hell."[1] This sentence might almost be considered the cornerstone of the rhetoric of oppression developed by reggae music since the very beginning of the seventies: the world is made of rich people (the few) and of poor people (the many); Jamaica, still based on a system of a few big land owners for whom many people work ("slave," in the words of Gregory Isaacs), is a deeply unequal society. Reggae music describes the complete control of the rich over economic and political power, and their exploitation of a people for which they have only contempt. It argues that poverty is neither a shameful condition nor in the order of things, but rather is only the consequence of the corruption of an elite that maintains a society based on exploitation, which therefore could be changed. Reggae claims that the rich are able to appear more respectable than the poor, but that in fact they are corrupt and maintain in place a system that has been inherited from slavery and colonization. Finally, reggae is trying to show that power and material wealth do not define a people's worth, and even that they have an immoral effect

---

[1] "So many years I've been slaving in your factory / never had a chance to talk with the boss / and for so long I've been living in this old community / where no one knew my pain yet I've paid the cost / no one knew my pain no, yet I've paid the cost / but I would rather to live poor and clean / than to live rich in corruption (...) a rich man's heaven, heaven, is a poor man's hell." Gregory Isaacs, "Poor and clean," 1980.

on people. In this sense, when linked to the Rastafari movement, reggae music is very close to a "Christianity of the poor" that does not obey religious institutions but only the word of God through the Bible. Furthermore, Rastafari can be considered as a strong critique of consumer society and, more generally, capitalism—Steel Pulse indeed sings, "I and I was not born rich nor poor, I and I was born naked" ("Tribute to the martyrs," 1979). This position strongly resonates for Jamaican people; reggae is their music, it belongs to them, it stands with them against the oppressors, it documents their everyday reality: the rich man's heaven is the poor man's hell.

This narrative is omnipresent within reggae lyrics. For singer Michael Rose, misery is such that there is nowhere to go and no goal to pursue:

> Another day of suffering
> I woke up this morning with the sky as my roof
> I had nowhere to lay my head so the cold ground is my bed ...
> things won't come my way, so it's just another day.
> > Black Uhuru, "Hard ground," 1978

If Bim Sherman describes, in the song "Down in Jamdown," a world filled with pain, misery and shame, for Bob Marley it is a world where the sun never shines:

> They say the sun shines for all
> but in some people world, it never shine at all ...
> so much have been said, so little been done
> they're still killing, killing the people
> and they're having, having, having lots of fun.
> > Bob Marley & the Wailers, "Crisis," 1978

In "Concrete jungle" he adds:

> No sun will shine in my day today
> the high yellow moon won't come up to play
> darkness has covered my life
> where is the love to be found?
> oh someone tell me cause life must be somewhere to be found
> instead of concrete jungle.
> > Bob Marley & the Wailers, "Concrete jungle," 1973

In "Concrete castle king," Dennis Brown addresses the king of the castle, that is, "the rich" who live in the hills above the ghettos:

> Living in your concrete castle on the hill
> you don't know what life is like in the ghetto
> living in a two by four with no place to walk around
> while you're in a castle all alone ...
> cause life isn't easy in the ghetto
> it's hard to keep from getting into troubles ...
> many days we stand in and sun
> waiting for the bus that never come
> you pass by in your fancy car
> wearing a plastic smile and smoking a big cigar.
>
> Dennis Brown, "Concrete Castle King," 1978

Reggae music therefore describes a world based on oppression, or rather the existence of two coexisting worlds that are foreign to each other. Positioning itself on the side of the oppressed—whom Bob Marley calls "the sufferers"—reggae becomes their emblem. The opposition between the oppressors and the oppressed is a continuous leitmotif, the former being fundamentally "against" the latter, as Jahmali makes it explicit:

> They don't wanna see you shine, no
> but I know it's only time
> they have a disease of mind, I know
> the wicked a go see you shine
> they oppress the poor, ain't got much to give
> but the just by faith shall live
> so just have some faith, patiently wait
> for you have Jah Jah on your menu.
>
> Jahmali, "No water," 1998

The rhetoric of oppression developed by reggae music therefore articulates a fundamental opposition between the oppressors and the oppressed (based on the essential distinction of Babylon/Evil and Zion/Good), and the *notion of hope*. Hope is very closely tied to religious redemption, but also takes, at a socio-political level, a strong dimension of struggle and resistance. The rhetoric of oppression therefore offers a report on the current situation, which denounces the domination of the Good (the poor) by Evil (the rich). It also entertains the hope for a better future and the trust in the courage and strength of the poor, who survive and struggle despite oppression. For instance, Anthony B evokes the struggle for satisfying even very basic needs:

> Cloth a fi wear, food a fi eat
> wanna see it, everybody need a place to sleep
> it's a necessity every man a fi seek
> Babylon want stop we
> but we rise and get stronger.
>
> Anthony B, "Universal struggle," 1997

Bushman also mentions the courage of the poor:

> Worries and problems
> but ghetto youth a work hard fi survive
> but then the system keep on giving a fight
> but ghetto youth a holding on.
>
> Bushman, "Worries and problems," 1999

For Buju Banton, one has to survive and not despair:

> Be strong, hold a firm meditation
> one day things must get better
> don't you go down, keep your heads above the water
> say one day things must get better.
>
> Buju Banton, "Close one yesterday," 1997

There is therefore the description of a negative present, but it is always accompanied by hope in the future: "they don't wanna see you shine", but also "the wicked a go see you shine" (Jahmali, "No water," 1998). There is a belief that those who oppress today will pay tomorrow, whether it is on earth or during the Last Judgment: divine redemption, which promises both the punishment of the oppressors and the reward of the righteous, is accompanied by human redemption, in a political form, which is based on the notion of liberation and the promise of the end of oppression and defeat of the oppressors.

Reggae's rhetoric of oppression is therefore revolutionary—although deeply spiritual and religious. Because of its complete rejection of organization, institution, and centralism, and because of its religious attachment, the Rastafari movement cannot easily join revolutionary political movements (although it did so in the case of the Revolution of Grenada). In fact, Rastafari is based on an ensemble of notions that might appear paradoxical. It refuses capitalism (considered as the work of Evil) but has great difficulties in joining any political structures such as unions or parties, and does not trust communism (which is nothing but one more "ism," as Bob Marley or Anthony B state). It supports the struggle against oppression, but is also extremely wary of both politicians and politics. Finally, it is attached to individual freedom but also strongly oriented to collective life (for instance in communities); as Lewis (1986: 5) points out, "although rasta philosophy favors a communal identity, modes of communalism vary among them." However, these apparent paradoxes might rather be considered as a form of consensus, as attempts to find "another way" to live in society. The politicization of reggae music is misleading for traditional politics, because it does not fit into any of the common categories, and harmoniously meshes with religion, sometimes to the point of complete conjunction (for instance, with the correspondence of divine redemption and socio-political liberation). Many young Western "leftists" have been drawn to reggae music, and through it to Rastafari, because of its revolutionary and uncompromised aspect, only to discover that the movement resists any attempt at traditional politicization, is based on a refusal of institutions and dogma, and often supports conservative views, especially concerning relations between men and women.

It seems that the so-called political and/or ideological "paradox" of Rastafari and reggae can be explained in three different ways. First, their undeniable attachment to Jamaican popular culture reinforces positions such as the importance of individual freedom, the mistrust of politics and politicians, and some conservative opinions; the strong refusal of homosexuality (and the violent reaction it provokes), for instance, is also a characteristic of Caribbean popular culture. Second, their "racial" character, based on a clear distinction between whites/oppressors and blacks/oppressed and linked to the colonial context, might explain their lack of an elective affinity with Marxist movements. Indeed, Marxism (for reasons that will not be discussed here) has always had problems in contexts characterized by racial prejudice (for instance the Sandinistas in Nicaragua or the American Communist Party in the USA). The third explanation is the most interesting and the most convincing, and concerns the modernity of Rastafari. For, although it might sometimes be considered conservative or even reactionary, in the end the movement also appears extremely well adapted to the modern world: it is both conservative and revolutionary, "ethnic" and universalist, individualist and communal, deeply attached to the past but resolutely turned towards the future. All these paradoxes might be considered not as such, but rather as efficient adaptations to the contemporary world that are in tune with its requirements for mobility and flexibility. This aspect seems especially obvious in the case of the sense of belonging: Rastafari develops a very powerful sense of belonging, which traces clear-cut boundaries and provides individuals with the intense feeling of forming a community, while keeping individual freedom intact—freedom of movement, of thought, of speech, and of way of life. Similarly, the anchoring in the past is both essential and turned towards liberation, and functions through identification (from the present to the past) rather than inheritance (from the past to the present); moreover, this anchoring in the past does not constitute a refusal of modernity that would be exclusively turned towards the past, but on the contrary allows a projection towards the future. The institutional "disorganization" of Rastafari also probably constitutes its major asset for succeeding in the modern world. The individual's belonging to the movement is not significantly coercive: the way in which men organize is left to the choice of each, and the absence of clergy and dogma leaves significant freedom to individuals, whether it concerns beliefs or practices. This lack of coercion, with a simultaneous intense sense of belonging, is adapted to the modern world, in which "free attachments" allow individuals to belong without their individuality being endangered.

A description of the Jamaican situation

As the music of the poor, reggae echoes daily life in Jamaica. It describes in detail the situation in poor neighborhoods, and has done so since its birth, following the evolution of Jamaican society. More than a description, it is a denunciation of the conditions in which Jamaicans live, and a criticism of the policies implemented by successive governments. From the *shanty towns* of the sixties and seventies, described in the reggae of the time with a strong acuity, until the explosion of violence and poverty in the eighties and nineties, reggae music is a faithful observer of Jamaica's social history, made from the standpoint of the poor:

> The city is congested with robbers and thieves
> and so many homeless youth got nowhere to sleep
> I also see them eating out of rubbishes
> and cocaine smugglers keep on ruling the city.
>   Bushman, "Worries and problems," 1999

Reggae therefore functions as a reality check, which describes increasing poverty:

> When we gonna get some food
> can't even get no water
> all system's gone on red alert, oh Lord.
>   Anthony B, "The mockingbird," 1997

The degradation of life in poor neighborhoods is one central theme in the reggae music of the 1990s (whether it is played by artists close to Rastafari or not), which speaks about hunger, poverty, violence, and above all about the responsibility and culpability of those in power. In "Gangstas think twice" (1997), Anthony B sings

> I call out to the gangstas in the street
> too much people are dying ...
> gangstas think twice
> cause when I look and I see what's going today
> there's no place for the youth to play
> the moral of the society is on the decay
> step by step humanity fail away.

According to Anthony B, the current situation shows how society has become immoral, violent, and is bound to fail—not only in Jamaica, but also for humanity as a whole.

The concrete degradation, which reggae narrates for everyone to see, is considered from the starting point of the apocalyptic degradation of the world, while simultaneously being understood as a confirmation of the eschatologic belief: the current evolution of the world, seen through the lens of decline and depravation, constitutes for the rastas the confirmation that the apocalyptic time has begun, while at the same time, in a double movement, their belief makes them see in the world the signs of the apocalypse. Hence they interpret the world in the light of the eschatology, in a similar way to how, as Weber showed, Calvinists seek signs of their state of grace, and therefore of salvation, in their earthly actions (Weber 2002):

Rhetoric of oppression and social critique

> Totally unsuited though good works are to serve as a means of attaining salvation ... they are indispensable as *signs* of election. ... This means, however, fundamentally, that ... the Calvinist *"creates"* his salvation *himself* ... more correctly: creates the *certainty* of salvation. (2004: 79)

By interpreting current events in the light of the coming end of the world, by reading it in a specific meaningful way, the believer hence creates, or reinforces, his own certainty of the end of time; the world becomes surrounded by *signs*, which are born out of belief and yet indispensable to its existence as well as solidity over time. Wars, famines, poverty, violence, or natural disasters are all considered as indubitable signs of the ineluctable degradation of the world, and the increasing empire of Evil it implies—leading to the climax described in the Book of Revelation. Poverty and violence are also described by Buju Banton in "Untold stories" (1995):

> All I see is people ripping and robbing and grabbing
> no love for the people who are suffering real bad ...
> what is to stop the youths from getting out of control
> filled up with education yet don't own a payroll
> the clothes on my back has countless eye holes ...
> with all the hike in the price
> arm and leg we have to pay
> while our leaders play ...
> I say who can afford to run will run
> but what about those who can't, they will have to stay
> opportunity is scarce commodity in these times I say ...
> it's a competitive world for the low budget people.
>   Buju Banton, "Untold stories," 1995

Buju Banton denounces violence and crime, unemployment, inflation, and above all the responsibility of the government for these conditions. Indeed, with the adherence of Jamaica to the economic development policies of IMF at the end of the 1980s, poverty and inflation increased exponentially. During the 1990s, violence has become an omnipresent component of urban life. In "Fire pon Rome" (1997), Anthony B describes how life has become harder for poor people:

> How much black youth behind iron curtain
> ... Everyday cost a living get harder

> ... Well out of the slum di poor people send mi
> Fi look what a gwaan and don't disagree
> What is the benefit of GCT?
> It benefit you but it never fit me
>
> Anthony B, "Fire pon Rome," 1997

The General Consumption Tax is seen as one more law that affects the poor much more than the wealthy, since it is imposed on everyone regardless of income. Anthony B blames the politicians:

> Mi haffi bun fire fi P.J. Patterson
> him mek certain move and wi nuh too certain ...
> true mi nah go trod inna Babylon order
> haffi bun fire fi di one named Seaga ...
> so many things politicians have stole dem
> still them return with the one Bruce Golding
> saying a brand new party dem forming.
>
> Anthony B, "Fire pon Rome," 1997

P.J. Patterson was the leader of the PNP ("People National Party," center-left) and the Prime Minister since 1992, while Edward Seaga, leader of the JLP ("Jamaican Labour Party," right), had been the Prime Minister between 1980 and 1989—during which time he adopted a pro-American stance, supported the IMF, and sent troops to participate in the American invasion of Grenada in 1983 (in order to counter the Marxist revolution). Bruce Golding left the JLP in 1995 and formed a new party (the National Democratic Movement). According to Anthony B, even Patterson must be "burned," although he belongs to the PNP, a leftist and almost socialist party which claimed to be the party of the "poor" and the "blacks" in the 1970s, in opposition to an elitist JLP. The PNP has also been linked to reggae music and the Rastafari movement, obtaining support from both at the beginning of the 1970s. For instance, for the 1972 election, the PNP hired reggae musicians to tour the island (among them Bob Marley, Peter Tosh, Bunny Wailer, Clancy Eccles, Ken Boothe, Max Romeo, Dennis Alcapone, Delroy Wilson, and Junior Byles); during the 1976 campaign, the PNP employed reggae music and Rastafari in a significant way; Waters (1989: 178–179) shows how it used Rastafari language (calling Seaga "Blind-ga" by using the typical syllable reversal of the dread talk), its referents (Garvey, Selassie, the Back'O'Wall ghetto...) and even its dressing code. For

Anthony B, then, even the PNP must be burned and is just a party like any other, of which the people should be wary: "him mek certain move and wi nuh too certain." Politics, as a whole and without distinction of parties, has therefore lost any credit it might have had before: "so many things politicians have stole dem." According to Anthony B, politicians are less to be trusted than the mockingbird:

> I tell you, I heard more truth than from your politician
> even though the mockingbird is seldom heard ...
> I tell you, I got more views than from your congressman
> even though the mockingbird is seldom heard
> listen to the mockingbird
> for stories unheard ...
> I tell you I got more news than from your television.
> "The mockingbird," 1997

The mistrust of politicians has always been a constant characteristic of reggae music. According to Buju Banton, people in power should not be trusted because the government's economic policies and its positive and optimistic discourse are hypocritical. One fundamental characteristic of politicians, according to reggae music, is that they lie:

> This nine to five is a joke compare to the pressure
> the minister say the economy is getting better
> misleading the people the mass still suffer.
> Buju Banton, "Close one yesterday," 1997

Then again, there is a strong opposition between those in power and the people: if the country is doing better economically, as its leaders proclaim, it remains that the people do not benefit from it and continue to suffer from poverty. This opposition is also a clear-cut distinction: the government is not for the people or of the people, but rather is against the people. And, according to Sizzla, it does not care for police brutality: "Prime Minister no care when police down have up their guns" (Sizzla, "More guidance," 1997). In the ghettos, violence is brutal and permanent: "the youths nah hear dem black brother dem come ya a shot down ... hey, look, black man, mi say stop shot down all you black son" (Sizzla, "More guidance," 1997). There is here both a description of what is going on, and a call for an end of violence, which is addressed to the youth of the ghettos while condemning the government for responding to violence with violence. This song, filled with references to God, also expresses the prominence of the laws of God on the government of men because he never goes against the interest of his people. According to Anthony B, not only does the government remain inactive, but it also produces and maintains the social problems:

> Ghetto youth open you eyes and rise up with the living
> cause the leaders go out in a ism and schism ...
> dem don't like we true we bun counsel and bun M.P.
> dem a bring segregation no unity
> pure promise bout yah and no loyalty.
>
> Anthony B, "Me dem fraid of," 1999

Anthony B points out the opposition that exists between the leaders and the people ("dem don't like we"), the incompetence of the leader, their indifference and even their bad intentions; he also calls for the struggle, in reference to the Rastafari movement: "rise up with the living" ("the living" is an expression used by the rastas to qualify those who know and have seen the truth, in opposition to the "dead" who don't see the world as it is).

Therefore, reggae music describes the current situation in Jamaican and the daily life of the poor; but it also brings forth an explanation of this situation, which is based on a rhetoric of oppression that fundamentally distinguishes between those who have the power and those who do not, a rhetoric that is rooted in eschatological beliefs and in a religious distinction of Good and Evil that uses Babylon as an archetype for corruption and the quest for omnipotency. Indeed, the current situation is compared by the rastas with the biblical text. The founding hypothesis of reggae music, which is also valid for the Rastafari movement, is that the interests of the elite always go against the interests of the people.

Beyond Jamaica

In a 1997 song, Anthony B asserts: "It's a worldwide thing / the whole world cry, the whole world cry" ("Universal struggle," 1997). And indeed reggae does not limit its critique to Jamaica. It also offers a global view of the contemporary world, which is above all marked by a negative finding. According to Buju Banton and Garnett Silk, "I look over yonder, and what do I see? / the whole world is in trouble" ("World is in trouble," 1996). Similarly for Luciano,

> Look at the world and what do we see, hatred and jealousy
> the world has gone crazy for vanity, no love for the
>   Almighty ...
> the world is in agony.
>
> "Punch line," 1999

Thus the world is not only "in trouble," it is also "in agony," "crazy for vanity," and it refuses the law of God—which, of course, refers to the earlier mentioned religious notion of the degradation of the world. With this religious notion in the background, reggae music directly attacks the "new world order," based on the globalization of exchange, the existence of international organizations and private companies, and the increasing power of the West, in particular the United States. According to Jahmali, international organizations are not inherently bad:

> unions are formed for men to speak as one
> NATO to ensure that no one country has autonomy over the
>   other
> United Nations to address issues of war, famine and disasters
> commercially NAFTA and WTO are designed to protect us
>   from ourselves.
>
> "Real issues," 1998

What he criticizes is the fact that these organizations are, ultimately, mechanisms that protect the power of the elite, although they were originally designed to serve the people:

> but still they do not deal with the real issues
> dem nah deal with the real issues
> treating my people like a piece of tissue ...
> dem nah deal with the real issues
> misleading my people down poverty avenue.

The essential opposition between the politicians and the people, the elite and the poor, appears here again, this time at an international level; the "new world order" is considered a large-scale reproduction of the same oppression experienced locally. Jahmali concludes: "the new world order has only created disorder."

Thus, reggae music develops a rhetoric of oppression which is rooted on a binary scheme organized in terms of oppressors and oppressed and rooted in a fundamental opposition between Good and Evil. However, this rhetoric is far from being limited to a simplistic and unreasonable criticism made in Manichean terms. Reggae transmits an argument, a reflection on the contemporary world; it speaks about people's daily life and about what is going on; it shows how people live and experience the decisions taken by governments and international institutions. To use Chude-Sokei's words (1994: 80), reggae describes "micro-realities." And, with this rhetoric of oppression as its basis, reggae also develops notions of struggle and revolution, which are tied to the Rastafari promise of redemption.

12

Only rasta can liberate the people: Resistance and revolution[1]

> Do you know what it means to have a revolution?
> And what it takes to make a solution?
> ... Are you ready to stand up and fight the right revolution?
> Are you ready to stand up and fight just like soldiers?
>
> Dennis Brown, "Revolution," 1985

One of the major consequences of the international commercial success of reggae music is probably the weakening of its revolutionary character in the media. As is the case for most politically engaged musical styles, commercial success threatens the survival of political engagement and, above all, of the authenticity of the style.[2] In the case of reggae music, the enlargement of its audience, in particular within Western markets, has indeed provoked an idealized interpretation of its message: the overriding impression of reggae music today in the popular consciousness is of its pacific tendencies, a sort of "tropical peace and love." However, through its own commitment as well as the way it is seen by its audience, reggae has always been a socially and politically engaged musical style, which conveys a strong and explicit revolutionary message. Indeed, the narrative contained in reggae music is not only a denunciation, as I have shown earlier: it also puts forward a call for political engagement and struggle,

---

[1] Buju Banton, "Hills and valleys," 1997: "Only rasta can liberate the people / Over hills and valleys too / Don't let them fool you / Don't believe for a minute that they are with you."

[2] A great discussion of authenticity is found in Grazian's book on Chicago blues (Grazian 2005).

and even for revolution—a content that is difficult to miss in Bob Marley's "Burnin' and lootin'," for instance. This is also the case for the Rastafari movement. A view that considers it as primarily escapist and insists on interpreting behaviors as a retreat from the world necessarily neglects its deeply revolutionary aspect. For some, the consumption of marijuana seems only an escape from reality, as would the avoidance of "industrial" practices, the refusal to vote, or the founding of rural communities. This view seems to be very far from reality, not only because many rastas live "in the heart of Babylon," but also because practices of removal and avoidance of, or separation from, Babylon do not necessarily imply an escape from this world. Rather, they might represent practices of change, sustained by an acute awareness of poverty and by a rhetoric of oppression that organizes, more than anything else, the Rastafari worldview. The notion of revolution has been present within reggae music since it was born, and has progressively evolved, from a simple notion of the "revolt of poverty" at the very beginning of the seventies to a more complex notion of revolution.

Moreover, the deep attachment to tradition displayed by the Rastafari movement, as mentioned earlier, can wrongly induce an erasure of the notion of revolution in the analysis of Rastafari. It is indeed true that Rastafari strongly refers to a religious tradition, placing itself within a lineage that goes back to the beginning of biblical history. It is also characterized by conservatism in beliefs and practices, by a desire for conformity to a vetero-testamentary morality, and by an opposition to some forms of progress and modernity. However, this traditionalism coexists with a pronounced revolutionary character, concretely expressed by a radical questioning of the order of things. But are tradition and revolution really two opposed notions? The notion of tradition is complex. According to Balandier (1988), tradition is the permanence of an order: "it orders, in all the meanings of the word."[3] Tradition has often been associated with immobility, permanence, and continuity, and opposed to the notion of revolution, which refers to change, movement, and rupture. In an ideal-typical way, the relationship to tradition is therefore expressed in terms of two opposed poles:

---

[3] Balandier, who is writing in French, refers to tradition in all the meanings that the term takes in French: as ordering but also as prescribing, organizing, commanding, and ordaining.

rejection and acceptance. However, the ascription within tradition does not necessarily imply an immutable and fixed repetition of the status quo, but rather a dynamic reference to a lineage. The notion of tradition, therefore, refers once again to a double movement between the past and present: just like memory (and as a matter of fact, the terms tradition and memory have sometimes been used interchangeably), tradition is above all a question of dynamic identification. And dynamic identification invariably implies a symbolic process: tradition is hence what we believe has always been rather than what has always been, and implies an interpretation made by the individual or group. Individuals ascribe themselves to a tradition (from the present to the past) and dynamically identify with it; simultaneously, tradition is also transmitted (from the past to the present), which implies another process of interpretation; indeed, transmission, just like language, presupposes a prior agreement between those who communicate, but also an interpretation and translation by those in communication. Hence, as Hervieu-Léger points out (2000: 145), "any tradition in its relationship to a past, given actuality in the present, always incorporates an imaginative strain." This is particularly obvious concerning the religious movements that claim an essential attachment to tradition while being situated in a revolutionary relationship to the world, such as the Nation of Islam. The tradition to which these religious movements refer is reconstructed, or even reinvented, in light of the interests and requirements linked to their specific history and above all to the present context. Therefore, in many cases there can be a coexistence of a strong reference to tradition and the development of a deeply revolutionary perspective; in such cases, the two notions are not antinomic but rather dynamically articulated.

This dual quality of tradition and revolution characterizes the Rastafari movement. To use Desroche's words, Rastafari invokes the Patriarchs while developing a revolutionary and utopian quest: "It is a well-known fact that apocalypticians refer to the Patriarchs. Always, or almost, imagination asks help from memory" (1974: 199). By referring to Abraham, Jacob, or Noah, Rastafari calls upon an ancient tradition—that of the revelations made to men by God—which, it claims, is continuous and finds its apogee in the Rastafari movement. It even links itself to this tradition in a concrete way, since its members consider themselves to be the descendants of the twelve sons of Jacob. At the same time, this reconstruction of a lineage and adherence to a tradition is first and foremost an identification, which operates above all from the present to the past: it is an act of memory that institutes or restores a continuity between the past and present. The tradition to which Rastafari refers is therefore a reinvented one, which dynamically (re)constructs a continuity and calls upon the past as much as upon imagination— but an imagination that always remains pertinent, is ascribed within historical constraints, and responds to socio-cultural requirements: in the case of Rastafari, the re-reading of the Bible and reinvention of tradition take place within a broad historical problematic marked by slavery and forced exile. Hence, the reinvention of tradition is not a game without rules: it is not made in a historical vacuum or on a fantasist mode, and it is not a simple reactive and desperate attempt to rebuild a continuity damaged by slavery. The issue at stake here is, above all, the ascription within a lineage, which is not made randomly but through logical choices, even if the latter do not always appear logical. As Jenkins points out: "That there are limits to the plasticity of ethnicity, as well as to its fixity and solidity, is the founding premise for the development of an understanding of ethnicity which permits us to appreciate that although it is imagined it is not imaginary" (Jenkins 1997: 169). Thereby, it is essential to understand that it is not tradition in itself that matters, but the ascription within a lineage and the reference to a tradition, which can both be reshaped or even reinvented, and are imagined, not imaginary; in other words, what matters is the process, not the content. According to Hervieu-Léger (2000: 145), utopia "makes of the complete and total break with the old order the condition of access to a new one, which is glimpsed by means of a memory that has been replenished at a source for which greater authenticity is claimed." In the case of Rastafari, the "more authentic" source is constituted by the African roots and by the Biblical text and history, which have to be revealed because they have been modified by history and adapted to the European will to domination and power. Hence, Rastafari is based on a falsified history of which it offers to reveal the hidden truth, and therefore it intensely refers to a tradition that goes back to the Book of Genesis, while modifying it, and therefore using it in a revolutionary mode. This articulation between a profane revolution and the religious revelation brought forth by the Rastafari movement appears very explicitly, and in all its different layers, in reggae music.

The articulation between revelation and revolution

> Revelation reveals the truth, revelation
> Revolution, revolution, revolution
> It takes a revolution to make a solution
> Too much confusion, so much frustration.
>
> Bob Marley & the Wailers, "Revolution," 1974

Rastas do not believe in hell and paradise after death, but, within a very millenarian perspective, they believe in eternal life after Judgment Day for the righteous, while sinners will be punished. However, to them, eternal life (as opposed to the "second death" of the sinners) is not simply a reward one might receive after the Judgment: it must also be obtained here on earth, and man must fight for it—both on an earthly and celestial level. Even within the purely apocalyptic level, man still has to fight in order to help fulfill the prophecy. This religious belief, which refutes the existence of hell and heaven, is also explained by non-religious reasons, linked to the history of Christianity and to the interpretation of power relations. According to the rastas, the belief in hell and heaven after life has been invented and used as a means of domination and oppression; as both Bob Marley and Sizzla sing, two decades apart, Western Churches have entertained the belief in heaven because it leads to the passivity of believers concerning their earthly life conditions.[4] The rejection of paradise and hell, to which the Last Judgment is substituted (eternal life for the righteous, eternal punishment for the sinners, after the return of the messiah and the judgment of God), plays a central role in the constant articulation made, within the Rastafari movement, between eschatology and revolution, because it allows for the coexistence and interdependence of present and

---

[4] "Preacher man no tell me / heaven is under the earth / I know you don't know / what life is really worth ... most people think great God will come from the sky / take away everything and make everybody feel high / but if you know what life is worth / you would look for yours on earth ... we sick and tired of your ism, schism / to die and go to heaven in Jesus name / we know when we understand / Almighty God is a living man / you can fool some people sometimes / but you can't fool all the people all the time" (Bob Marley & the Wailers, "Get up, stand up," 1973); "Now yuh use dem to stray di minds of di youths / and as they preach di youths cease from knowing di truth / but, this is di truth above all circumstances / I see how yuh constantly building churches" (Sizzla, "Praise yeh Jah," 1997).

future, of earth and heaven, of man and God. It is precisely this rejection that allows Rastafari to dynamically and closely articulate social struggle, earthly revolution, and eschatological battle—that is, to articulate religion and politics. In other words, religious utopia, which is placed in a spiritual future and therefore in another time and place (or, as rastas say, "on higher grounds" or "in higher heights," an expression used by Buju Banton as the title of his 1997 album *Inna Heights*), is articulated with an earthly utopia that belongs to a material and human present. Religious utopia and social utopia are even so intermingled within the Rastafari movement that they mutually sustain, feed, and confirm each other: they are superimposed, and rooted in the same struggle between God and Satan, between Good and Evil. Indeed, paradise on earth and New Jerusalem are two concepts that are closely tied together, interdependent, and often intermixed in the words of the rastas as well as in the texts of the reggae artists. The streets "paved of gold" and the earth "where milk and honey flow"[5] contain a strong eschatological meaning, but they also simultaneously work as a parable to refer to a concrete and contemporary "paradise," for which one has to fight. For the rastas, struggle is the affair of everyone, and the notion of resistance is everywhere: resistance to physical slavery in the past, to mental slavery in the present, to Babylon, on the side of God, and for a better life on earth as much as to prepare the Armageddon. This might seem paradoxical; but the underlying notions of Good and Evil are rooted in the opposition between God and Satan and distinguish the people of God from the forces of Satan, and therefore allow the coexistence of revelation and revolution. Associated with the notion of a living God, the notions of Good and Evil articulate the world around the essential notion of struggle: the oppressors struggle to subject and/or kill the righteous, who themselves must struggle for their liberation, whether it is an (almost) immediate earthly liberation, or for a spiritual liberation to come, linked to the Apocalypse.[6]

The notion of revolution is therefore fundamentally articulated around the distinction between Babylon/Evil versus Rastafari/Good.

---

[5] For instance, see Dennis Brown, "Milk and honey," 1978.
[6] This of course is not a characteristic solely of the Rastafari movement; as one example among others, Balandier (1963) emphasizes this "union" between eschatology and revolution in his analysis of Ba-Kongo messianism.

It is ascribed within an essential context of struggle against Evil, expressed at a concrete and earthly level by the fight against the "power" and the institutions, which take a merciless color, due to the radicalness of the distinction between two fundamentally opposed groups (Babylon versus Zion). The rastas are extremely wary of any attempt of organization and centralization, even, or maybe above all, when it concerns their own movement. As Chevannes (1994: 32) says, they "refuse to surrender [their] freedom and autonomy by joining any organization, Rastafari or not. A common explanation is 'wa jain kyan brok' (what is joined can be broken). But in truth it is their ethical value of complete freedom from the force of unnatural rules which informs this resistance." This wariness towards institutions is linked to the fundamental importance of freedom as well as to the fact that any institution is synonymous with the system; it is linked to Babylon, and therefore to Evil. Institutions are archetypically represented by the politicians, the police, and the CIA, extensively used in reggae music, within a direct critique but also with metaphorical goals. For instance, for Jacob Miller,

> the Roman soldiers of Babylon are right behind us
> coming from the North with their pockets full of
>   ammunition
> trying to turn dreadlocks into politician ...
> yes the C, the I, the A.
>   Jacob Miller, "Roman soldiers of Babylon," 1976

1976 was an election year in Jamaica, during which the JLP, then in power, was accused of trying to destabilize the country with the help of the North American CIA, while the PNP was making imperialism the center of its campaign. The JLP was said to receive weapons from the American government. Babylon, Rome, and the CIA are strong symbols, here used to represent Evil, as well as the leadership that oppresses the poor and the politicians who try to use Rastafari in order to win elections. Also in 1976, another example is found in the song "Rat race" by Bob Marley:

> When the cat's away
> the mice will play
> political violence fill the city
> don't involve rasta in your say
> rasta don't work for no CIA.

The point is to show that rastas cannot be associated with a political struggle that they reject, or participate in what Marley calls a "rat race." There is nothing to expect from politicians; and participation in the political system would imply following its rules, which they oppose, and would lead them to be tarnished, in terms of the dialectic pollution/contamination. Jahmali, therefore, attacks politicians:

> Politics, so rotten
> my people have you forgotten
> that it is so bitter
> only the people dem inna di ghetto dem a suffer ...
> politics will never change ...
> we're tired of their manipulation
> while they take advantage, we're caught in the chain reaction
> it's the politics of change abusing the poor man's brain
> so blood thunder, the system is a vampire.
> Jahmali, "Politics," 1998

Jahmali is clear: politicians are corrupt, but politics as a system is corrupt as well, in a structural way; there is therefore nothing to expect from politics as it exists now. This corruption is seen in terms of domination, which refers as much to an ethical principle as to the actual, common understanding of the word corruption: politicians take advantage of the situation; they manipulate and abuse the people. Politics, hence, is seen as a disadvantage for the people; additionally, any attempt at political participation is doomed to fail, because of the structural corruption of the political system.

In "Revolution" (1974), Bob Marley warns the people: "Never make a politician grant you a favor / they will always want to control you forever." This position towards politics implies a withdrawal from political life, but it is not taken in an escapist mode: the opposition to the system is active and not passive. The point is not to cease action, but rather to reject the current system as a whole, to change it without participating in it, to oppose it from the outside, to replace it by another way of functioning. In this sense, the social critique present in reggae music is revolutionary: the point is not to improve the system, but to tear it down in order to replace it with something else. And reggae music, strongly and constantly, becomes the messenger for revolution as much as it is a messenger for revelation: "Jah send I as a messenger," sings Luciano ("Messenger," 1995). Beyond the general opposition to

Babylon, reggae sharply criticizes politicians and the political system, institutions, capitalism, and imperialism.[7] Has the revolutionary character that appears in reggae music, since its emergence, changed? Do young artists refer to the same symbols, do they support the same positions? What about British reggae? The modalities of the notion of revolution and of revolutionary commitment can vary, and I now offer three case studies, which bring forth differences rather than similarities, in a comparative perspective: Bob Marley & the Wailers (a Jamaican reggae band of the 1970s), Steel Pulse (a British reggae band from the 1970s but which still exists today), and Anthony B (a young Jamaican artist who started his career at the beginning of the 1990s).

Resistance and revolution in the 1970s: Bob Marley

> So don't you forget no way
> Who you are and where you stand in this struggle.
> "So much things to say," 1977

Bob Marley, Peter Tosh and Bunny Wailer formed the band The Wailers in 1963. They recorded many singles in between 1963 and 1965 for Coxsone / Studio One; they were then joined by Aston and Carlton Barrett and worked for Lee Perry until 1971. In 1973, the band recorded its first albums, *Catch a Fire* and *Burnin'*, for the Island label; both were commercial successes. Peter Tosh and Bunny Wailer then left the band to start solo careers, while the vocal group *I-Threes* (Rita Marley, Marcia Griffith and Judy Mowatt) joined the remaining members. The band then took the name of Bob Marley and the Wailers, and from this time on had phenomenal success, until the death of Bob Marley in 1981. From the misery of Trenchtown to concert halls around the world, Bob Marley & the Wailers never set aside their socio-political engagement; each album bears the mark of this engagement, even those that have been said to be "light," like *Kaya*. By analyzing their texts, it is possible to build what King and Jensen (1995) have called Marley's rhetoric of redemption. Here, I will only look at the revolutionary aspect of this rhetoric: namely, the call for change and struggle, and its modalities.

---

[7] For example a dub by King Tubby is called "Big Youth fights against capitalism" (Big Youth being the singer of the corresponding vocal version).

In 1973, the Wailers released their two first albums, *Catch a Fire* and *Burnin'*, which reflect the poverty that the members of the band had experienced in the ghettos of Kingston. For many fans, these two albums symbolize raw engagement, and paint a faithful image of the life in Trenchtown; they set the basis for the notion of revolution as it was developed by Bob Marley & the Wailers throughout their musical career. The notion of revolution concerns, first, the evidence of resistance and the necessity of the struggle in the song "Get up, stand up," which has since become legendary:

> Get up, stand up
> stand up for your rights
> get up, stand up
> don't give up the fight.

It is the struggle of "the little ones" against "the big ones":

> If you are the big tree, we are the small axe
> sharpened to cut you down
> ready to cut you down.
> "Small axe," 1973

The oppressed are compared to a small axe, able to cut down a big tree despite its size—that is, the oppressed can defeat the oppressors although the latter appear indestructible. Struggle and resistance are associated with raw rebellion, which is not (yet) theorized nor politicized, as is clearly expressed in "Burnin and lootin'":

> That's why we gonna be burnin' and lootin' tonight
> I say we gonna burn and loot
> burnin' and lootin' tonight
> one more saying
> burning all pollution tonight
> burning all illusion tonight.
> "Burnin and lootin'," 1973

Revolution is not tied to any political movement, nor is it linked to an "after": it is a bursting reaction against oppression, a revolt of poverty rather than a well-defined political or revolutionary project.

Between 1973 and 1976, the notion of revolution, associated with a developing rhetoric of oppression, begins to be more clearly defined and theorized. Several fundamental themes are articulated with each other to form the modalities of the notion of revolution, well expressed in a few lines in "Talkin' blues":

> I've been down on the rock for so long
> I seem to wear a permanent screw
> But I, I'm gonna stare in the sun
> Let the rays shine in my eyes
> I'm a gonna take a just a one step more
> Cause I feel like bombing a church
> Now, now that you know that the preacher is lying
> So who's gonna stay at home
> When, when the freedom fighters are fighting
> "Talking blues," 1974

These themes concern illumination and through it enlightenment ("I'm gonna stare in the sun / let the rays shine in my eyes"), the lies of institutional religion ("the preacher is lying"), struggle ("who's gonna stay at home / when the freedom fighters are fighting") and freedom ("freedom fighters"). Revolution is the direct consequence of poverty and oppression, as it was in *Catch a Fire* and *Burnin'*, and can only happen after a revelation or an illumination that concerns the recognition of oppression, the discovery of the Christian lie, and a truth that, although it finds its source in religion, concerns not only all the levels of human life but also the world as a whole. The Rastafari movement is the trigger of this revelation: it opens the eyes of the people to the full reality of social conditions as well as the religious lie. The notion of revelation was already present in "Burnin and lootin'," which spoke of "burning all illusion": simple revolt or complex revolution, revelation always plays a triggering, essential role, as is strongly expressed when, in the song "Revolution," Bob Marley plays with the phonetic similarity of the two words "revelation" and "revolution": "Revelation reveals the truth, revelation / revolution, revolution, revolution." In the same song, the notion of revolution is developed:

> It takes a revolution to make a solution
> too much confusion, so much frustration ...
> so my friend I wish that you could see
> like a bird in the tree, the prisoner must be free.

The revolt is caused by poverty and oppression, but also by the fact that the system of power is not pure but confused ("too much confusion");[8] as to the goal of the revolt, it is above all liberation. In this song, the notion of revolution is also linked to the Armageddon, and takes a strong religious color:

> so if our fire make it burn
> and if our blood make it run
> rasta deh pon top
> can't you see, so you can predict the flop
> we got the lightning, thunder, brimstone and fire
> kill, cramp and paralyze all weaker conception
> wipe them out of creation.

A correspondence is established between earthly revolution and the struggle of God against Evil, as it is described in the Book of Revelation ("our fire make it burn," "our blood make it run," "lightning, thunder, brimstone and fire"). There is also the certainty that God will be on the side of the revolutionaries, giving them access to his traditional weapons (lightning, thunder, brimstone, fire).

In "So much things to say" (1977), the articulation between the divine struggle and the struggle of men appears again:

> I and I no come to fight flesh and blood
> but spiritual wickedness in high and low places
> so while they fight you down
> stand firm and give Jah thanks and praises
> cause I and I no expect to be justified
> by the laws of men.

Bob Marley refers to the radical distinction that must be made between Good and Evil (later in the song: "who you are and where you stand in this struggle") and to the validation of the righteousness of the revolutionaries, which argues that the only valid justification is the one given by God: "I and I no expect to be justified by the laws of men." This latter point is essential because it implies that the adversity faced on earth has no importance: the word of God alone matters. As long as the people know that they are on the right side of the struggle, they should not worry about what other men say. The struggle of God "in high places" and the struggle of

---

[8] The opposition between purity and impurity, clarity and confusion, appears here as well.

men "in low places" are interwoven; by fighting on earth, men also participate in the victory of God over Evil: "I and I no come to fight flesh and blood / but spiritual wickedness in high and low places." By associating the earthly and divine struggles, Bob Marley develops a notion of active struggle, the necessity of revolution here on earth, which takes the color of war:

> The heathen back deh upon the wall
> rise up fallen fighters
> rise and take your stands again
> cause he who fight and run away
> live to fight another day.
>
> "The heathen," 1977

The very life of the righteous is considered a struggle, a battle fought each and every day, hence the identification of the rastas with warriors or soldiers, although it is not a concrete, armed struggle (in "So much things to say": "I and I no come to fight flesh and blood"). With God at their side, the revolutionary warriors cannot be stopped or defeated:

> No bullet can stop us now
> we neither beg nor we won't bow
> neither can be bought or sold
> we all defend the right
> Jah Jah children must unite
> life is worth much more than gold,
>
> "Jammin," 1977

Here is sketched the necessity of the unity of the "children of Jah"—that is, of the righteous. Marley also emphasizes the goal of the struggle: "life is worth much more than gold"; therefore it is for a better life that the rastas fight, not for material reasons.

This philosophy of struggle, which sustains the thought of Bob Marley, clearly appears in "Zimbabwe" (1979). It is before anything else characterized by its universality: "Every man got the right to decide his own destiny / and in this judgement there is no partiality" (which again refers also to the fact the redemption is gained from the choices of men, not pre-destined). This universality traces clear boundaries between those who choose Good, and those who choose Evil. The former have to unite and fight for their rights:

> so arm in arms with arms we will fight this struggle
> cause that's the only way we can overcome our little trouble
> ...
> we'll have to fight, we gonna fight, we'll have to fight
> fighting for our rights ...
> to divide and rule could only tear us apart.

The revolutionary struggle will therefore be difficult: it will take place in adversity—in link with the rhetoric of oppression evoked earlier: the current world is divided into two groups that have diametrically opposed interests. And, finally, Marley evokes the revelation to come:

> in every man chest there beats a heart
> so soon we'll find out who is the real revolutionaries
> and I don't want my people to be tricked by mercenaries.

The truth will be revealed, the mercenaries uncovered, the righteous recognized, and all will be judged according to their works.

Contestation and resistance in Great Britain: Steel Pulse

> So let's join hands my brethren
> Let's do it for our children and their children
> ... Doesn't justice stand for all,
> Doesn't justice stand for all mankind?
>   "Handsworth revolution," 1978

Steel Pulse is probably the most famous British reggae band. Created in 1975 by David Hinds, Basil Gabbidon, and Ronnie McQueen, all from the neighborhood of Handsworth in Birmingham, the band signed with the record company Island and released their first album, *Handsworth Revolution*, in 1978. It was a phenomenal success; Barrow and Dalton describe it as "devastating," and praise its texts, vocals and music (1997: 333). It is true that Steel Pulse always stood out by their specific sound (especially in the vocals, with numerous call-and-response sections), by their highly politicized texts, and by the strong social commitment of the band's members. In 1979, Steel Pulse recorded *Tribute to the Martyrs*; the band has ever since had a continuous success, in Great Britain and in the rest of the world. The albums *Handsworth Revolution* and *Tribute to the Martyrs* serve as the basis for the analysis I develop in this chapter.

The notion of revolution offered by Steel Pulse in their songs is comparable to the one developed by Bob Marley: a description of the current state of the world, a radical delimitation of two opposed groups through the elaboration of a rhetoric of oppression, the necessity of the struggle, considered both as a consequence of oppression and as a moral duty (which in the case of Steel Pulse also concerns the racism faced by minorities in Great Britain), and its universality, complexly articulated with the liberation of black people. As in the case of Bob Marley, the fight for liberation by the slaves' descendants is transformed into a universal struggle against oppression by the capitalist system. Finally, Steel Pulse's notion of revolution is, like Marley's, rooted in the religious beliefs of Rastafari, in particular its eschatology which, combined with the notion of social liberation, produces a complex notion of revolution, articulated with the notions of Good and Evil, justice and injustice, redemption and hope.

However, the texts of Steel Pulse differ from Marley's because of their politicization, which is highly dependent on the context of the artists: their songs also evoke themes such as racism, the extreme right, and scientific progress. This politicization is Westernized and adapted to the British context, but it remains strongly rooted in Rastafari. In particular, in comparison to Jamaican artists, Steel Pulse give an essential place, in their texts, to the notion of diaspora and the unity between slaves' descendants, African immigrants, and Africans in Africa. The variety of the themes present in British reggae albums indicates that the diaspora is embraced as a whole, as a group that shares the same referents and not only a common origin.[9] This is especially visible with Steel Pulse; their second album (*Tribute to the Martyrs*) contains songs that concern the South African Steve Biko ("Biko's kindred lament"), the North American Black Panther George Jackson ("Uncle George"), the fight against racism in Great Britain and the National Front ("Jah pickney"), and a general homage paid to many heroes of the black struggle in the New World ("Tribute to the martyrs"); their first album (*Handsworth Revolution*) evokes the situation of the Caribbean community in Great Britain ("Handsworth revolution") and the North American Ku Klux Klan ("Ku Klux Klan").

This great variety of themes in British reggae in comparison to

---

[9] See other British artists such as Macka B.

Jamaican reggae is explained by the important contacts that existed between the British left, especially the unions, Rastafari, and reggae music, and by a political engagement or even militancy in reggae and Rastafari not as common elsewhere. Steel Pulse has always stood as a musical band engaged in British social and political life. Additionally, the history of reggae music in Great Britain, since the success of ska and rock steady in the 1960s, has been marked by the crossing of social boundaries, the music being quickly and largely appropriated by white youth while remaining strongly attached to its Jamaican roots. In Great Britain, reggae music is not limited to a Jamaican or Caribbean audience, and many young Britons have identified with it, independently of their origin or colour. This is also the case for the Rastafari movement, although to a lesser extent. The political engagement of Steel Pulse and the variety of themes they evoke is therefore partly the reflection of the context in which they perform, partly the reflection of the "twice diaspora-ization" (Hall 1995) of the Caribbean community. Steel Pulse explicitly expresses the unity of the diaspora beyond geographical boundaries and cultural differences. While this evocation of the diaspora is present in other artists, for instance Bob Marley & the Wailers, as I have mentioned earlier, it remains particularly explicit and probably less "abstract" in the case of Steel Pulse, as well as in British reggae in general, reflecting a different social context.

Revolution, tradition and fin de siècle: Anthony B

The truth inna me song make revolution come.

"Swarm me," 1996

Since 1995, Anthony B has become one of the stars of reggae dancehall. He displays a strong socio-political engagement and adherence to the Rastafari movement; moreover, he is close to the Emanuelites and wears their distinctive turban. As in the case of Steel Pulse, the specific context in which Anthony B has emerged—as other young Jamaican artists such as Buju Banton or Sizzla have—strongly influences the texts of his songs and the modalities of his social and political engagement. While Steel Pulse grounded their ideology on Rastafari religious beliefs and conceptions and, at the same time, were strongly committed to a tradition of struggle that goes largely beyond the boundaries of Rastafari and of the Caribbean community, this is not really the case for Anthony B. The double notion of resistance and revolution is essential in his songs, and is deeply rooted in his religious beliefs, but it is not linked to other, strictly political movements such as Marxism or workers' unions. Anthony B's songs mostly refer to the Jamaican (or Caribbean) situation, and his notion of revolution remains very religious and almost completely foreign to "traditional" modes of political commitment.

Anthony B, like many other current artists, often refers to Bob Marley, which indicates not only an inheritance, but also a historical continuity throughout the forty years of existence of reggae music.[10] Jamaican reggae indeed, as I have mentioned earlier, retraces in its texts its own history and evolution. While Bob Marley & the Wailers were a part of the beginning of both reggae music and the success of Rastafari in the 1960s and 1970s, the young artists of the 1990s and 2000s have a history behind them, which they know and narrate. In particular, they have heard of the attempts at political collaboration by rastamen in the 1970s, and witnessed the evolution of the movement, its expansion within Jamaican society and abroad, and the diverse politics of the successive Jamaican governments as well as their policies towards reggae and Rastafari. For these young artists, the final conclusion of the relationship between Rastafari and reggae on one hand, and politicians on the other, is rather negative:

> Every politician go under rastaman banner
> watch dem a fight over rastaman colour
> one hold pon di green, one pon di red, one pon di yellow
> we a go bruk dem knuckle
> police gi me back di ganja leaf out a you belt buckle
> now dem a bruk like bottle
> over the years rastaman dem a hackle and tackle
> watch out and mi bend dem nozzle
> Anthony B, "Me dem fraid of," 1999

According to Anthony B, the politicians have been, and will always be, hypocritical in their attitude towards Rastafari: on one hand

---

[10] For instance, in "Who shoot first," 1999: "Bob Marley shot the sheriff and mi go shot the deputy / every bad man mi say you life in a jeopardy / gunman no live long look out fi di cemetery / fi di new millennium the twenty first century."

they are trying to use a movement that benefits from an important success as well as from a positive image at the international level ("every politician go under rastaman banner / watch dem a fight over rastaman colour"), but on the other hand they do not adhere to its ideology and beliefs and continue to fight it, especially when it comes to the consumption of marijuana. Additionally, Anthony B recalls the history of the Rastafari movement and the way it has been treated since its emergence in the 1930s: "over the years rastaman dem a hackle and tackle." For him, no trust can be, nor should be, placed in the government, the police, or politicians.

This opposition of Rastafari to politics and politicians forms the very basis of the notions of resistance and revolution developed by the young artists. They adhere to a radical distinction made between Babylonians and the righteous, considered as fundamentally opposed. Resistance must be total, and made on the mode of separation, without any collaboration. Revolution is considered a merciless fight without compromises, of which the outcome can only be the victory of one side on the other, and which refers both to a revolt of the oppressed and, intensely, to religious eschatology. The artist has a radical mission, which makes his songs dangerous:

> I'm in the middle surrounded by media
> Just thru me chant fire bun fi di leader
> Misleadership me say a gwaan all over
> Them waan blow me away like a paper
> Inna me songs when me turn on the fire burning
> Burning hotter than the equator
> That's why dem say me explicit and raw.
> Anthony B, "Swarm me," 1996

If Anthony B is criticized by the media for his violence, it is because he represents a danger for the politicians, who misgovern, with voluntary bad intentions ("misleadership me say a gwaan all over"), and want to keep their power to the detriment of the people, a power that is directly attacked by Anthony B when he criticizes the current order of things. One can see in this excerpt the difference of form between seventies reggae and nineties dancehall; if Anthony B claims to be "explicit and raw," it is to subvert the original meaning taken by the expression in reggae dancehall, which refers to sexual content:[11] he is considered "explicit and raw" because of the truth about social and political realities contained in his lyrics.

The power of words and sound, the power of transmission and politicization of reggae music, is explicitly claimed by the artists, not only Anthony B but also Sizzla ("No other like Jah," 1997) or Buju Banton ("Hills and valleys," 1995), and they claim it both in their songs and in their interviews, as performer and as human being. According to Anthony B, the solution is simple—it is revolution:

> why dem come swarm me, swarm me
> seh we start a revolution army, army
> them no see that them lose, this is the generation them cyaan confused, get the news
> never see me with knife never see me with gun
> the truth inna we songs the revolution come ...
> but we waan a solution
> let's start the revolution.
>
> "Swarm me," 1996

It is a clear and explicit situation: the oppression of the people by the elite must cease, and the only way to change the current system is to make the revolution. The "new generation" to which Anthony B belongs cannot be fooled: it has opened its eyes to the reality of oppression and is therefore ready to fight it (as Bob Marley begged in "Get up, stand up" in 1973). The notion of the revelation of truth is here again absolutely central: it is revelation that enables revolution.

Revolution is therefore grounded in both a past history and a present situation of oppression and suffering, because it is the direct and unavoidable consequence of the slave system but also of ulterior, persisting domination; and this socio-political revolution is inseparable from religious revelation and the apocalypse:

> Stronger stronger than a lion
> Tougher tougher than steel
> Ready now fi di truth it reveal
> ... Now we serve dem dem own poison meal
> Over di years dem a beat we and we never squeal
> Ask dem how di pain and pressure feel

---

[11] For instance, Shabba Ranks' album entitled *As Raw as Ever*.

> Now we a flying fire under dem heel
> Ask dem why dem want all di truth conceal
> Look place fi hide dem a look place fi run.
>
> Anthony B, "Swarm me," 1996

Revolution is seen as a righteous revenge for the suffering inflicted over the years ("now we serve dem dem own poison meal / over di years dem a beat we and we never squeal / ask dem how di pain and pressure feel"). This righteous revenge is religious and, although described in terms of war, it is considered as a spiritual fight: "never see me with knife never see me with gun / the truth inna me song make revolution come / and dem afraid a di fire bun" ("Swarm me," 1996). There is in fact a superimposition of the concrete fight, in the flesh, and of the spiritual struggle, with words, which might seem paradoxical: Anthony B calls forth, simultaneously, on war and peace, on armed struggle and its refusal, all by using a violent and even bloody vocabulary that comes from a biblical, apocalyptic imagery (such as burn, exterminate, break, warriors, fight, battle, etc). This is less a paradox than a reflection of the constant superimposition of the eschatological and earthly levels: earthly struggle is constructed on the model of the Armageddon. Moreover, the war vocabulary used to describe the earthly struggle, beyond being the same vocabulary used to describe the eschatological battle, has an essential metaphorical function: it is used to show the radical, uncompromising, and merciless character that the struggle against Evil must take—and especially the absolute character of the punishment that awaits the oppressors during the Last Judgment. Finally, as for the rastas, words and thoughts are considered as weapons, which are as murderous and dangerous as physical fight. This implies that the latter is not necessary: as Sizzla sings,

> Must put you down
> burning you with words
> power and sound.
>
> "No other like Jah," 1997

It is precisely this assimilation between earthly revolution, spiritual struggle and religious Armageddon that makes possible the sociopolitical engagement of Rastafari, and the construction of a notion of earthly revolution, but also the lack of concrete definition of the latter. Political commitment, including a general opposition to capitalism, or for instance during the revolution in Grenada, does not constitute a dominant position within the Rastafari movement. Of course, the lack of a clear and concrete political project is mostly due to the deep wariness towards institutions and politics, which is characteristic of Rastafari. The rastas tend to form their own communities or to engage in educational or social networks, rather than engaging in politics. References to concrete political projects are therefore largely absent from reggae lyrics, even if Anthony B offers his own vision of what the Jamaican government should be:

> Tell the Government Jamaica house me come for
> Cause we want some truth and rights defender
> Back part a di ghetto give that to Sizzla
> All country mi give to Louie Culture
> Dem a go clean out the heathen wid di Oh Carolina [a famous reggae song]
> To Tivoli we a go move Seaga [Tivoli Gardens is one of the poorest neighborhoods of Kingston]
> In a him seat we a go put in Muta.
> Anthony B, "Me dem fraid of," 1999

This evocation of a government made of reggae artists linked to the Rastafari movement (Sizzla, Louie Culture, Mutabaruka) does not constitute a concrete revolutionary project. The notion of revolution, although clearly defined and precisely defining the enemy and the unacceptable, therefore has great difficulties in being transposed into a concrete and practical political project. And this is true even if the notion of revolution is applied in daily life through social or intellectual engagement, the refusal of certain practices, or the opposition to some social developments. Similarly, the project of repatriation to Africa, constantly evoked with Rastafari and reggae music, only rarely becomes concrete. The lack of a structure within Rastafari as well as its general refusal of any institution or centralization explains the difficulties that rastas have in organizing themselves, although they are very active in local networks and also display an extreme solidarity with each other beyond the local level. The character of utopia itself might also inhibit its concrete realization: the utopian project, whether it concerns repatriation or revolution, seems to have to remain unattainable for its very survival, a point that is also emphasized by Desroche (1969) concerning other millenarian and messianic movements.

Music and ideology: Reggae's function of transmission

The notion of revolution is therefore present in reggae music, throughout its evolution and in Jamaica as much as in Great Britain. While revolution always remains articulated with religious redemption, and this in an essential way, it can be more or less concrete, as well as more or less universal. However, the revolution only very rarely takes a practical dimension, and it does not produce a real political project in the sense acknowledged within contemporary politics, despite a few political attempts in the 1970s, which were quickly abandoned. The notion of revolution—sustained, backed up and considerably influenced by religious eschatology—therefore remains a sort of ideological blank canvas, expressed in a specific worldview (essentially characterized by the notions of structural adversity and necessary struggle), in daily practices (such as the rejection of progress, or the *Ital* way of life), and in usually local social actions (educational networks, forums of discussion, legalization of marijuana), rather than in active, organized, and militant political action. However, even if it does not produce any practical revolutionary project, the blank canvas formed by the rhetoric of oppression, social critique, and notion of revolution—all three being associated with religious redemption and rooted in a tradition of resistance that has been continuous throughout the history of the diaspora—also constitutes a powerful dynamic of politicization that is able to play an important role in the Caribbean area as well as in Western countries. Some Caribbean militants like Walter Rodney or Horace Campbell have emphasized this role of "political dynamic," speaking of the Rastafari movement and reggae music as a "force," as a "conscience" that plays a role of politicization and resistance and functions as a common, transnational, and mobilizing referent across the Caribbean area and the African diaspora scattered in Europe and the Americas. In other words, it is obvious for Rodney or Campbell that Rastafari and reggae hold the capacity of provoking the emergence of political action, even if this emergence has not happened yet, and that they are potential revolutionary forces, not fully expressed but nevertheless present. Campbell (1985) hence argues that Rastafari is a form of "cultural resistance" (through the conservation and transmission of the memory of slavery, of African practices, of a history of resistance...) which has the potential to transform itself into an "organized resistance"—that is, a form of resistance able to express itself through socio-political revolutionary action.[12]

And music plays an important role in the "potential politicization" of the Rastafari movement. First, it assumes a central role in *ideological dissemination*, at the level of social critique as well as of struggle and revolution, this role being associated with the *transmission of a history and a memory* that concerns the Rastafari movement, the diaspora, Africa, and finally the world as a whole, as I have suggested throughout this book. This role is essential, because it compensates for the lack of institutions that characterizes the Rastafari movement—and therefore for its lack of internal institutional transmission, each group or community, and above all each individual, remaining out of the reach of the organizations that exist within the movement. Moreover, the fact that a popular musical style that has been internationally successful since the mid-seventies itself claims to be the medium of transmission for a religious and political message elaborated in a direct link with the Rastafari movement, allows the latter to reach a diversified audience, beyond geographical, ethnic, social, or national boundaries, as well as beyond generational differences, since reggae has existed for over thirty years and constantly renews its audience (which, therefore, comprises diverse generations). Finally, the role of transmission assumed by reggae music allows Rastafari to touch individuals who are already members of the movement, but also those who primarily encountered Rastafari through reggae music, as is often the case with Western listeners. Individuals are able to find, with reggae music, a source of religious information as well as questioning. Reggae music thus has a fast, universal, and international capacity to transmit ideas, in particular through the use of radio, which allows its message to reach isolated places and individuals who cannot afford to buy books or newspapers or cannot read them at all.

Second, reggae music serves to promote cohesion and unification, because it allows individuals to feel a sense of belonging through the confirmation that others "belong" as well. This is an important role, again because of the scattered and non-institutional character of Rastafari, which therefore does not benefit from the more traditional

---

[12] Campbell views Rastafari within a Marxist perspective; he states that his "analysis of the Rastafari is developed to show the identification with Ethiopia as a profound response to the racial repression of capitalism" (1985: 2).

institutional validation of belonging. Through reggae music, even the most isolated individuals can have the sense of belonging to a lively group; they can also validate their beliefs and practices, or compare them with what is said in reggae lyrics.

Reggae music can therefore be considered as the narrative of a history as much as of a memory, as a tool of communication and of transmission of a religious knowledge and socio-political message, as a space of education and politicization, as a discourse of the diaspora and on the diaspora, and as the carrier of a religious revelation and earthly revolution. It is also a musical combination of sounds, which contains, holds, and transmits a sense of home for its audience across the world. This list would not be complete without its first and most essential function: to play music and make people dance, which reggae music itself also considers as a mystical experience that produces and allows spiritual elevation. Through reggae music, hope is entertained and redemption promised. As Buju Banton sings, "There was good and evil. We chose good."

Part V

Conclusion

13

Time and memory

> And now, as I gradually found myself being pulled into the huge, slowly rotating crowd of dancers by the cotton tree, I recalled Mr Mann's story of Columbus and Sir Francis Drake and the two Elizabeths who were actually one, the Africans who were both slave and warrior, and I realized that I had misunderstood him completely: I had thought he was making history up. It hadn't occurred to me that he had been telling the truth. (Banks 1980: 126)

In reggae music, one is able to observe memory at work. The words of the music transmit a memory of the group—a musical memory that traces the boundaries between the inside and the outside, through the use of a specific language and musical techniques, but also and maybe most importantly through covert and overt allusions to previous songs and lyrics or to past or contemporary reggae artists. Reggae music also transmits a multi-leveled memory that relates to historical knowledge—from Jamaican anti-slavery icons to South-African apartheid—but also to religious knowledge—through its close association to the Rastafari movement. Throughout this book, reggae music has been shown to provide a beautiful case study for the analysis of collective memory—a dynamic memory in construction. But it is time now to draw conclusions from this specific case.

In reggae music, memory now appears as complex process. Indeed, the construction of a "time-memory" mobilizes an articulation of both historical and mythical times: a continuity is built between the mythical origin and the present, between the mythical origin and the apocalyptic future, and ultimately between religious utopia and profane utopia (Figure 13.1).

My study started in the present: this is the referent for sociological analysis, the point taken as the source for data. In the second part

Figure 13.1: Memory in reggae music

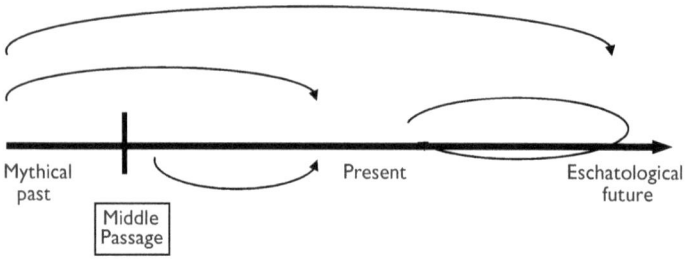

of this book ("Remembering the past"), I showed that reggae music conveys a narrative of the past, which gives the latter a fundamental function in shaping the present. But in my analysis this "past" quickly took on a both sacred and profane dimension. Indeed, on the one hand, the Middle Passage is constructed as a founding event, which works as a rupture in the representation of time: it defines a before, and an after. Both this event and the subsequent history of slavery in the New World are considered as weighing heavily on the definition of the group in the present. This interpretation of the past constitutes the defining moment in the history of the group and therefore its boundaries: it is around it that the identity of the group is defined *in the present*. Hence, a linear influence, from what I have called the "close past" (intercalated between the Middle Passage and the present) upon the present, is *constructed* as defining the group. But, on the other hand, there is also a leap into a mythical past, which I have called "far past," and which is also considered as defining the present. Hence the Bible works not only as a parable, but literally as a history repeated in the present: the strength of the identification allows an irruption of the mythical past in the present, both at the symbolic level (for instance by establishing constant parallels between events in the bible and events in the present) and at what could be called a concrete level: here again, a linear influence is traced from the far past to the present, in particular through the recognition of continuous lineages.

In the third part of this book ("Revealing the future"), I turned to representations of the future in reggae music, and more specifically to the issue of the mythical future—that is, eschatology. I showed that the memory conveyed by reggae music is *also* about this leap into the future, which Nancy Huston has elegantly called a vertiginous projection.[1] And here the way in which it works is a little more complicated: I distinguished again between a far and a close future, which have to do with the sacred and profane spheres. The far future is mythical; it is the eschatology *stricto sensu*. The close future is in some respect a part of the present: it is a profane, soon-to-come future—in a few months, in a few years, but here on earth and somewhat on the same plane as the present (Figure 13.2).

Figure 13.2: Close past and close future

I showed, in the third part, that the eschatological future stands as the end of time—that is, the end of profane, or historical, time. And here one of the characteristics of the eschatology is that it is nourished by the far past, in a fashion typical of myths of the end of the world. Indeed, the cosmogony and the eschatology are one and the same myth, relegated to the far past and future; they are equivalent, in the sense that they both and together constitute the sacred, only repeated and reenacted in rituals in historical time (Hubert 1999 [1905]; see also Desroche 1969 and Eliade 1954, 1957). But there is more to it. The eschatology is not, in the case of reggae music, something that is far away and separate from the present: to a certain extent, it overflows the sacred plane and spills into the profane, historical plane. This irruption takes place in two ways: first, through the preparation necessitated by the coming of the end of the world, hence the present and close future are somewhat contaminated by the sacred by becoming preparatory phases; second, through the appearance of signs that indicate that the end of the world is near, and that the eschatology is already taking place, hence the present and close future become the first stage of the eschatology—thereby becoming a time of transition.

---

[1] "L'humanité n'est même rien d'autre que cela—cette capacité d'aller en avant et en arrière, de noter les récurrences, de faire des rapprochements, d'apprécier des motifs. Nous savons être présents dans le passé et passés dans le présent. Et même, vertigineusement, nous projeter dans l'avenir." (Huston 1993:84).

But there is more—and it relates to the conception of the present and near-future as encapsulated in a phase of transition towards the mythical future. Indeed, the eschatology, instead of producing passive expectation in the present, produces active behavior: it becomes superimposed on a very profane revolution: this is what I showed in the fourth part of this book ("From revelation to revolution"). Whether this revolution has to do *exclusively* with the preparation for eschatological times, or whether it overflows the sacred to become a profane revolution in its own right, the relationship between historical and eschatological times produces action *in the profane world*.

This is where we left our enquiry, at the end of the fourth part of this book. But I would like to return to three issues which are crucial to clarify the construction of memory and the overarching representation of time found in reggae music: I will start with a discussion of the ways in which memory works; I will continue with a discussion of the difficult relationship between sacred and profane time; and finally I will return to memory, attempting to articulate it with time.

A point of departure can be found in Maurice Halbwachs' theoretical account of collective memory. The growth of "memory studies," both in and out of academic scholarship, has spurred a renewed interest in Halbwachs, as has also his recognition as an authoritative figure in the conceptualization of memory. And, indeed, this authority is well deserved: he was the first sociologist to work specifically on the question of memory. But in order to reflect more deeply on the concept of collective memory, I want to explore the theoretical tradition of which he was a part. It seems strange that only rare references, within memory scholarship, are made to prior conceptualizations of time found in the essays written by Hubert and Mauss, as well as to the reflections scattered in Durkheim. This seems strange for two reasons: first, because it might prove fruitful to reflect upon memory and time together, or at least in relationship to each other; second, because an understanding of Halbwachs would surely gain from an inquiry into earlier Durkheimian thought. His work, indeed, can be considered as one part of a multi-faceted collective project on time, which therefore justifies reading the totality of the project as opposed to solely a part of it. The *general project* is focused on the study of time as the rhythm of social life, through the setting of a regular (although non-measurable) succession of "high" and "low" peaks in the intensity of social life. *One dimension* of this project is found in Durkheim and Hubert, and concerns the analysis of the "high" peaks; *another dimension* of this project is found in Halbwachs, who took up the question of time where earlier Durkheimians had broken off their inquiries—that is, at the precise level of the routine, the profane, the low-key moments of social life.

My argument, though, is not only a theoretical one. My analysis of reggae music has shown the ways in which social memory is constructed and transmitted within a process of interpretation; Halbwachs' postulate of a dynamic memory that is alive and in permanent redefinition, in relationship with what matters in the present, has been confirmed. However, throughout the analysis, how often have we drifted away from memory and into the representation of time? Does it matter that the memory conveyed by reggae music also leads the scholar into an analysis of articulated, specific, collective representations of the past, the present, and the future? Indeed, through the analysis of collective memory, or perhaps around it or alongside it, a second set of conceptual issues has been raised: the articulation not only of profane tenses but of sacred tenses, and further the articulation between profane and sacred time. The collective memory at work in reggae music is also about a particular representation of time; a time that succeeds in articulating past and present but also profane and sacred. And it is at this point that the need for reflecting upon time arises; in particular, Hubert's discussion of sacred time will prove enlightening.

I

In terms of temporality, there is one tension within my analysis throughout this book; it lies between revolution and tradition. The strength of tradition lies at the heart of reggae music, and in particular of the Rastafari movement as it appears within reggae music; but tradition is dynamically appropriated and, moreover, reinterpreted. This brings us to a double paradox, or rather to two seemingly paradoxical dimensions.

A first dimension of this paradox lies between (re)invention and tradition: it is expressed through the cohabitation of religious *bricolage* with the identification with a traditional historical lineage. Indeed, Rastafari intensely and essentially refers to a religious tradition;

however, there is also a dimension of non-conformity to this same tradition, through the addition of new or not always consensually accepted elements (for instance the apocryphal books or the traditions that come from Ethiopian Christianity), and above all through a novel interpretation of an already existing lineage and history (through a rereading of the Bible, as well as a rereading of profane history that completes and confirms religious history). This original, new, and non-conformist ascription into a religious lineage that already exists is made within an essential perspective of revelation: Rastafari reveals the truth, which had been dissimulated, of an established tradition. Hence the ascription within tradition—seen as a desire to conserve what in the past is considered as authentic—nonetheless coexists with a dynamic process of interpretation and selection: clearly, this tension is not exactly paradoxical; tradition is invented as much as it is handed down, as Hobsbawm and Ranger (1992) have shown.

A second dimension of this paradox is found between revelation and revolution as opposed to tradition, and this tension is decisive in the emergence and evolution of the Rastafari movement. Since its birth, Rastafari has positioned itself both as a movement of revelation and revolution and as a strongly traditional movement. The point is, in fact, to undermine an established "false tradition" by revealing the "true tradition." Revelation and revolution are expressed on interwoven religious and socio-political levels. Hence the term revelation is used on two semantic levels: first in its profane dimension, as the uncovering of the truth; and second in its religious dimension—that is, a specifically sacred uncovering of true beliefs and practices.[2] Indeed, revelation is religious and belongs to the sphere of the sacred: it concerns the revelation of the true content of the Bible, which includes the Ethiopian Kebra Negast, as well of its correct reading; it also concerns the revelation of the evil character of European Churches. But revelation is also profane: it concerns the revelation of a falsified history, of the wrongdoings of European countries, and so on. And here it is not simply a case of "reading" the profane world as bearing the signs of the sacred: there exists, in reggae music, a critique on both the profane and sacred levels.

---

[2] *To reveal* indeed takes two meanings, one profane and the other theological: (1) to disclose something hidden or kept secret, and (2) to make known by sacred means. The term comes from the Latin *revelare*, to draw back the veil.

This double revelation allows and induces revolution—that is, action *in this world*—and here action is once again both sacred, since it questions the false interpretation and wrong use of the religious tradition, and profane, since it concerns a religious redemption that implies the destruction of the world "as we know it" and its replacement by a new, purified, and replenished world, but also a socio-political redemption expressed by an earthly revolution in the present (Figure 13.3).

Figure 13.3: Continuity and discontinuity in the representation of time

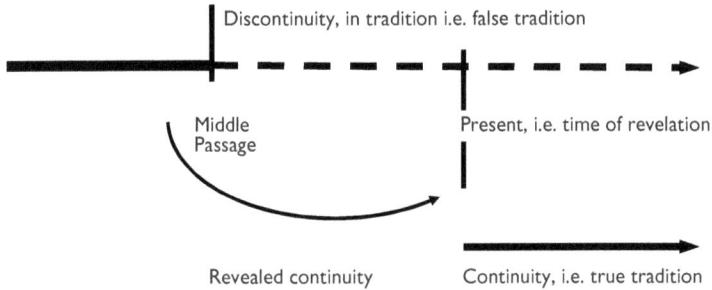

Therefore, three terms are articulated: tradition, revolution, and revelation. All three are related to a fundamental dimension: "drawing back the veil," uncovering the truth that has been kept hidden or secret—that is, all three are related to the profane sense of the term "revelation." What appears to be a static reference to the past—the uncovering, recovering, and transmission of a tradition—in fact has to be considered as a dynamic ascription; it is mobilized in the present through a charismatic process of rupture rather than a traditional process of continuation. Indeed, Weber's characterization of the charismatic type of authority as being fundamentally organized around discontinuity works well here: as I showed in the third and fourth parts of this book, reggae music denounces the false truth of an established tradition, on both the profane and the sacred levels; it is as much about the falsification of history, colonial lies, and capitalist false promises, as it is about the false beliefs and practices of Western Christianity. I have seen, throughout this book, that the denunciation conveyed by reggae music could very well be expressed in the words Weber uses to make the charismatic leader speak: "It is written... but I say unto you..." (Weber 1978: 243). Both Rastafari and reggae music are fundamentally situated within this radical rupture with traditional authority; and, as Weber states, it is precisely because of the rupture it entails that charismatic authority constitutes a revolutionary force: it is organized around rupture (i.e. around revolution), while traditional and legal authorities are organized around continuity (Weber 1978: 244).

And yet, reggae and Rastafari call on both rupture and continuity; the rupture, here, is thought through the *reestablishment of lost continuity*. The notions of revolution and tradition are usually considered antinomic, but here they coexist in a non-paradoxical mode: it is about the revelation of a tradition that has been falsified and its replacement; hence, tradition is interpreted in a strong revolutionary mode: revolution concerns the restoration of an ancient tradition (or one considered to be ancient). Desroche (1979) has pointed out this mechanism in his work on millenarian movements, asserting that the revelation they bring forth, although characterized by rupture, also often calls on figures of the past to legitimate the break in the present. This is also something that Hervieu-Léger (2000) has emphasized in her consideration of religion in modernity: according to her, what characterizes "believing" is the dynamic identification to what she calls a "chain of memory"—that is, the invocation of the authority of a tradition in support of the act of believing (2000: 76). And yet this ascription, she asserts, does not necessarily imply continuity: "It is not the continuity in itself that matters but the fact of its being the visible expression of a lineage which the believer expressly lays claim to and which confers membership of a spiritual community that gathers past, present, and future believers. In certain cases, breaking continuity may even be a way of saving the essential link with the line of belief" (2000: 81). In the case of reggae music, this is indeed what is happening: the very rupture provoked by the revelation in the present is also, ultimately, an act of continuity: it breaks historical time, irremediably, into a before and an after; and yet this very break implies the reestablishment of a continuity thought to be lost. In other words, it is by invoking tradition that a revolutionary change occurs.

At this point, switching back to Halbwachs is helpful. It is not, indeed, simply about handing down an intact tradition in a linear way; it is about interpreting, revealing, and enlightening this tradition. As Gadamer (2003) argued, tradition is always being renewed through interpretation; hence it is "handed down" through interpretation. Memory, precisely, is characterized by this active process of interpretation: Halbwachs argues not only for selection, but also for reconstruction in the light of the present morphology of the group. In the case of reggae music, an active process of interpretation is associated with the fundamental importance of a rupture with the established traditions, but also with the transmission of a lost tradition. And in turn this leads us to Weber: the ability to speak anew is precisely the strength of charismatic authority; but here to speak anew also means to speak anew within the past. Hence a radical rupture—which refers to false beliefs, texts, interpretations, and practices—takes place simultaneously with a claim of returning to the real tradition. Thus in reggae revolution takes place within tradition.

II

We are here, therefore, within the memory conceptualized by Halbwachs; a memory that functions between the present and the past, a memory claimed as fundamental by the group in order to exist in the present; finally, a memory that is about the dynamic interpretation of the past. But there is more. Reggae music constructs memory by articulating a *reappropriation of the past* (which can be made on a mode of reinvention) with a *representation of the future*. Indeed, it is precisely the transmission of memory that allows the construction of a representation of the future, perhaps simply because memory establishes a continuity in time that is necessary to envision a future. Hence memory is about three movements: from the past to the present, from the present to the past, and both past and present projected into (and thereby enabling) the future. The shift in my argument from representations of the past onto representations of the future, in the second and third parts of this book, has shown this continuity; although memory is a narrative of the past, its most important function might be, indeed, that this narrative actually refers to the present and thereby enables a representation of the future to arise. After all, talking about the exigencies of the group in the present also implies that these exigencies are part of its projection in the future. Thus memory is not only a process that takes place between the past and the present, in a circular movement; it also leaps into the future, as shown in the solid arrows in Figure 13.4.

Figure 13.4: The temporal process of memory

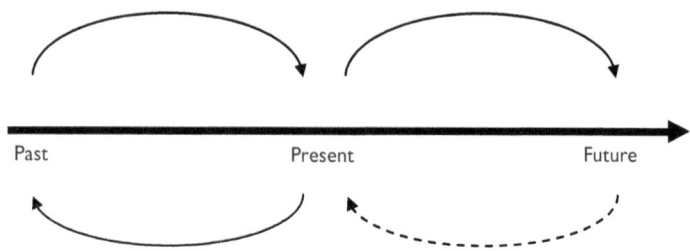

In the case of reggae music, however, the future is not a straightforward category; it is both multi-leveled (close and far, historical, and mythical) and multi-textured (profane and sacred); it is both religious, in a pronounced messianic and millenarian mode, and socio-political (i.e. earthly and profane). In fact, the eschatological representation of the future itself provokes the emergence of socio-political commitment, which possesses strong revolutionary tendencies: the two dimensions, religious and political, of the representation of the future are dynamically imbricated, and this imbrication rebounds back onto the present time, onto the present of the earthly near future, onto the present of daily life. Hence to the three solid arrows in Figure 13.4, has to be added a fourth arrow that shoots back from the future into the present. In other words, in Weberian terms, there is an inner-worldly orientation, since the eschatology produces action in the historical present: social action is oriented towards this world.

It is indeed the link built between the past, present, and future that conditions the essential distinction made between Good and Evil, a distinction that forms the foundation of Rastafari's relationship to the world and the way in which it contemplates the different times and levels as being simultaneous and interdependent. Indeed, these two categories are defined by the mythical past (the Bible), by the profane past (slavery and colonization), by the profane present (the political and economic situation), and finally by the eschatology. In a way, the representation of time conveyed in reggae music allows for a merging not only of the past, present, and future, but also of the profane and the sacred; the interplay found between the different levels allows for their simultaneous coexistence. Again, a diagram might be helpful (Figure 13.5).

First, there is an interdependence of times through the influence of the different times on those which are ulterior, thereby building a

Figure 13.5: Sacred and profane articulations in the representations of time

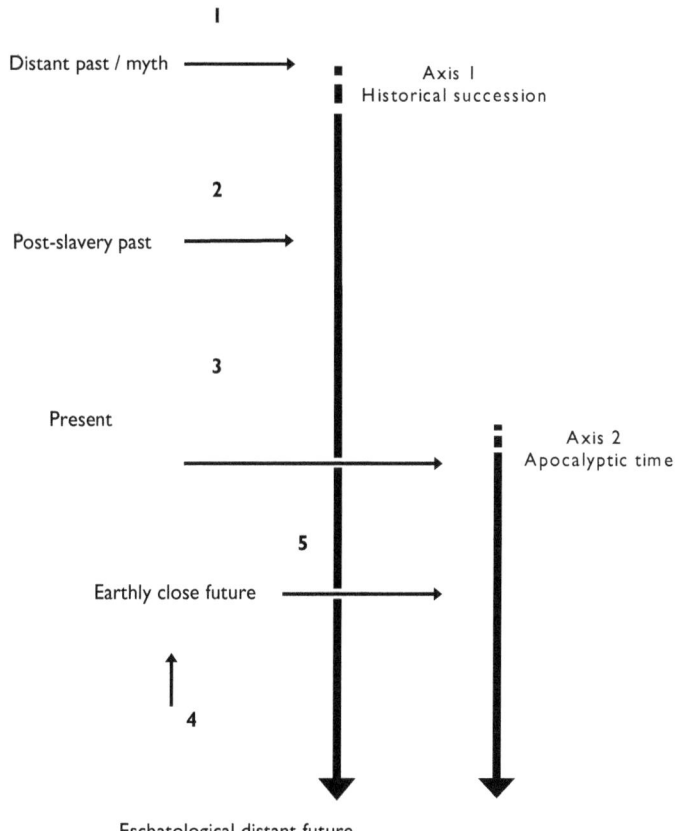

temporal succession made in continuity (axis 1: from the distant past to the distant future). For instance, the biblical lineage is considered as continuous, from the creation of the world to the establishment of the New Jerusalem (arrow 1). What has happened in a close past (the slave trade, slavery, and the history of the diaspora as such, starting with its founding event—that is, the forced exile provoked by enslavement) is considered as having an essential influence on the present (arrow 2), but also on the future since this past conditions both the modalities of resistance and revolution (earthly future) and the modalities of the Last Judgment (eschatological future). Finally, the present influences the future, since Rastafari claims to be a trigger, and since its actions participate in an earthly liberation as well as in a religious redemption that must be prepared (arrow 3).

Second, apocalyptic time (axis 2) is of paramount importance. While it is a distant, religious future, it is also, and perhaps above all, a present, since the messiah has returned, an event which announces the beginning of the apocalypse. Apocalyptical time has therefore already begun. Some rastas link and interpret each current event in relation to passages in the Book of Revelation, and most share a broad understanding of the wars, famines, or natural disasters that mark the present world as being clear signs of the increasing empire of Evil as described at the beginning of the Book of Revelation. If the world we live in has not yet reached the time of the millennium, which will be followed by the Last Judgment and the establishment of the New Jerusalem, the present remains the time of the pre-millennium apocalypse. Finally, this same apocalyptic time strongly influences the present and near future (arrow 4), because the religious categories that are essential in the development of the apocalypse (e.g. Good and Evil in struggle against each other) also define the categories that are essential in the development of human intervention and in the modalities of the distinction made between the oppressors and the oppressed. In a way, the earthly world is traced over religious distinctions and conceptions—which explains the permanent irruption of the sacred, for instance in the description of the current world that is made by reggae music. Additionally, the earthly struggle is considered to influence the divine struggle (arrow 5). The imbrication of earthly and divine actions, visible as much in their mutual influence as in their definition on the basis of the same categories and as in the partial superimposition of the different times, gives to Rastafari its dynamic and active character, which contradicts the common view that considers it as a form of passive escapism.

Therefore, Rastafari considers the succession of three complementary and sometimes simultaneous tenses (past, present, future), which are not viewed as independent but as interdependent and mutually influential. As a matter of fact, these times are not even considered as succeeding each other in a linear way. Not only does the past weigh on the present, through an interplay of influence and shaping, but the present also has to take the past into account, to use it and transmit it, in order to allow the very existence of individuals as a people. This taking into account of the past by the present implies the influence of the present on the past that is being transmitted, on a past that the present *narrates* and therefore interprets, modifies, and orients. Moreover, the articulation made between the construction of the origin, historical continuity, and the representation of an eschatological future, is the very *nodal point* that organizes the existence of the Rastafari movement in the present, in particular by motivating its active relationship to the world.

The constant association made between the time of origin and eschatological time would almost allow one to speak of a circular time which, as Eliade (1954) analyzed at length, reproduces a lost past in the future, and is organized by the fundamental notion of a cycle, from birth to death, from beginning to end, which allows regeneration and a new beginning. In the case of Rastafari, though, this circular time remains marked by a fundamentally historical conception of the temporal flow: a historical time (past, present, future) characterized by change, and by the deep rupture provoked by slavery, is situated within the (circular) return to an original time. How can we understand this? How can a circular time and a linear time coexist with the same intensity? This is where Hubert's analysis proves most helpful. In his *Essay on Time*, Hubert is interested in "religious time"; he starts with a paradox slightly different from ours: while the sacred, through rites, is necessarily situated in time, there seems to be a discrepancy, and even an antinomy, between sacred time and profane time.

> Given, it was said, that rites and mythical events take place in space and time, it is necessary to ask how the theoretical separation of time and space can be reconciled with the infinitude and immutability of the sacred, in which rites and mythical events take place too. (Hubert 1999 [1905]: 43).

The sacred indeed implies infinity, absoluteness, and immutability; it transcends the spatial-temporal dimension of the profane world, and thus time itself. Hubert notes that mythical events "seem to take place outside of time or—what comes to the same thing—within the total extent of time" (Hubert 1999 [1905]: 46). However, these "timeless" or "out of time" events are articulated with or reintegrated into chronological time: rites have a beginning and an end, they are repeated; cosmogonies and eschatologies can be seen as an attempt to integrate eternity within a chronology (Hubert 1999 [1905]: 46). It is precisely this attempt at rearticulating sacred time with chronological time that Hubert questions in this essay: how can the eternity of the sacred be represented in time? There is no doubt that the formulation of this paradox, which of course is part of the Durkheimian crucial distinction between the sacred and the profane as being two radically different and separate spheres, suits our case study well. Instead of speaking of a coexistence of circular and linear time in reggae music, we could indeed reformulate this phenomenon as the coexistence of sacred time and profane, or rather as the presence of sacred time within profane time.

In Hubert's analysis, the presence of sacred time within profane time is discussed through what he calls the rejuvenation of myths. Myths are "imagined within time" (Hubert 1999 [1905]: 46); for this reason, rites function as a commemoration of myth (placed far in the past), as a repetition of a past event. Rites become temporal but also eternal repetitions of the original myth. However, myths are also rejuvenated: "Instead of commemorating a mythical fact, going back to the beginning of time, they commemorate a historical fact. Moreover, the rejuvenated myth always becomes the point of departure for the periodic celebration of the rite, since either the memory of previous periods is obliterated, or else a new and more efficacious consecration of the chosen date is imagined" (Hubert 1999 [1905]: 47). Hubert gives several examples of a myth being replaced by a historical or semi-historical figure or of a "time-worn" saint being replaced by a "younger" one (Hubert 1999 [1905]: 47). There is here, therefore, an irruption of *history* into *eternity* (as well as an irruption of the sacred into the profane): "Myths are rejuvenated in history, drawing on elements of reality which consolidate the belief of which they are the object as myths. But this is not because mythical truth is poorly distinguished for believers from the historical truth that the myths embody; it is because they need to be situated in time with a precision that must increase with the growing precision of the representation of things in time" (Hubert 1999 [1905]: 48). This leads the reader directly into Halbwachs on the issue of memory; indeed, Hubert argues that rituals are adjusted to the expectations of the present; if saints become "worn out," it is not simply that they have been here too long: it is also, and above all, that they no longer make sense intensely enough to the group. Hence, they are replaced by a newer figure—that is, by a figure more adapted to the group in the present. Myth is imagined in time, as examples of the rejuvenation of myths show. So the sacred, indeed, is articulated within time: that is the function of religious calendars, which are not intended to measure time, but to provide rhythm, a rhythm that is necessary for the repetition of rites and the reproduction and reenactment of myths: "In sum, mythic eternities are periodic" (Hubert 1999 [1905]: 49). In a long chapter, Hubert offers a complex analysis of this periodicity, of this rhythmic organization of time:[3] sacred time is divided into parts that, although not equivalent in terms of duration, are still considered equivalent—because what matters is the periodicity, the rhythm, rather than a measurable chronological segmentation:

> Time ends by being represented as a sequence of points which are equivalent to each other and to the intervals which separate them, these intervals themselves being equivalent; and as a sequence of parts of unequal length, nested within one another and equivalent in the same way, each point and each period standing respectively for the whole. In this way, religious and magical actions can cease without being completed, be repeated without changing and be multiplied in time while remaining unique and above time, which is really nothing more than a sequence of eternities. (Hubert 1999 [1905]: 60)

The peculiar representation of time brought forth in reggae music does allow for an irruption of the sacred into the profane; as a matter of fact, the eschatology is here in the present, in everyday life; and it is here *wholly*. Indeed, the sacred does not come partially; when it appears, it appears entirely; eternity bursts within linear, historical time. Here there is something really crucial for an understanding of the representation of time in reggae music, and the articulation of eternity within the chronology that characterizes it. It is not, indeed, that little particles of the sacred are powdered onto historical time, as it were; it is not simply that history allows a little bit of sacred here and there: in the past with the identification to the Book of Exodus, or in the far future with the Book of Revelation; in the present during prayer or rituals, or with the earthly coming of the messiah. *The eschatology comes in entirely.* It is imagined within history, and yet it is irremediably foreign to history. The articulation of the sacred and the profane produces the

---

[3] He discusses five characteristics of sacred time; see 1999 [1905]: 51–61.

possibility for simultaneous sameness and difference, continuity and change, eternity and chronology: "magic and religion ... have put the sacred into time and in this way have established the uninterrupted chain of eternities along which their rites can be dispersed and reproduced while remaining unalterably identical" (Hubert 1999 [1905]: 78). As William Styron's character Nat Turner or Russell Banks' character John Brown read their own life in the Bible, so does reggae music: the sacred comes in, wholly, entirely.[4] When the Psalms are chanted in reggae music, they are not just a piece of the sacred; they are the whole of it; when Israel Vibration sings about the Red Sea, the bloody ocean, Pharaoh and the certitude of "walking the streets of glory" in the future, the biblical story and apocalyptical redemption are not just parables or references that simply enlighten the present: the sacred comes into the present, it imposes itself, it submerges the profane.[5] Indeed, the sacred "is theoretically indivisible, and ... as soon as it manifests itself, it does so entirely" (Hubert 1999 [1905]: 43).

Here we need to come back to the distinction between the sacred and the profane, set up as central to the Durkheimian analysis of religion. By definition, this distinction is so radical that each element excludes the other; hence, they cannot coexist in the same place, and neither can they coexist in the same time (Durkheim 2001 [1912]: 38, 312–313). It is precisely this impossible coexistence that leads to the necessity not only for the spatial-temporal specificity in rituals (which cannot be conducted anywhere nor at anytime) but also for rites of entry and exit, which allow for the passage between the two spheres. And yet, the sacred appears within profane time: in rituals, in festivals, and in cosmogonies and eschatologies. The latter is what is of importance to us here; and our analysis is complicated by the fact that, unlike rituals, the eschatology is not bound by rites of entry and exit in a straightforward way. When a ritual is undertaken, preparations are made: the ceremonial officer might fast, shave, wear special garments, and so forth; by doing so, he ensures a safe passage from the profane to the sacred sphere (Mauss and Hubert 1981 [1899]: 19–28; see also Mauss and Hubert 1905, Durkheim 1912). Conversely, because the ritual—whether sacrificial or magical—consecrates the participants and ties them

---

[4] Styron 1992 [1967]; Banks 1998.
[5] Israel Vibration, "Walk the streets of glory," 1978.

Time and memory

to each other, equivalent rites of exit are needed for the passage back to the profane sphere to occur, and to occur safely (Mauss and Hubert 1981 [1899]: 45–48; Durkheim 1912). Religious rituals can be considered as openings within linear time;[6] what have to be negotiated, hence, are both the conditions of this opening (through prescriptions concerning space, time, tools, etc) and the passage into the opening and back. But in the case of cosmogonies and eschatologies, we are facing something slightly different. First, we are in the presence of the myth itself, not in its reenactment. Second, we are in the presence of a boundless time. There is no prescribed opening, taking place in specific time and place, with a beginning and an end, and a passage into the sacred followed by a passage back to the profane. Indeed, cosmogonies and eschatologies are placed far away, in historical time and yet slightly aside from it. To some extent, cosmogonies and eschatologies enclose historical time, which becomes *a profane opening* within the eternity of sacred time. Hence it could be said that the cosmogony is a rite of exit—from the sacred to the profane; and the eschatology is a rite of entry—from the profane back into the sacred (Figure 13.6).

Figure 13.6: Myths, rites, and historical time

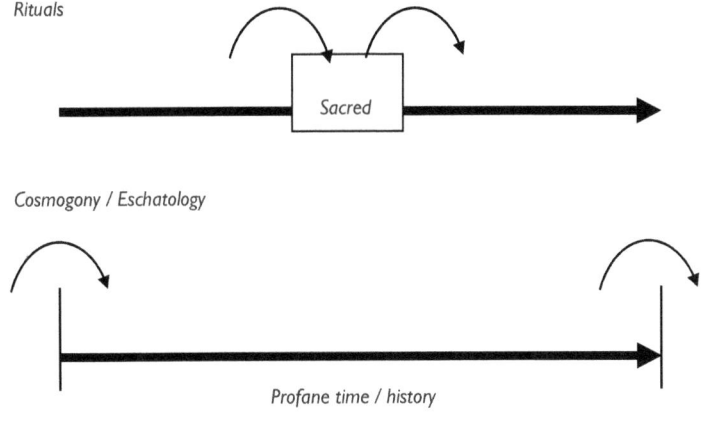

---

[6] See also Eliade, for whom liturgical time (e.g. rituals) is the periodical recovery of the *illud tempus* of the creation, of the beginning (1963a: 208). For him, rituals allow man to live in the sacred, in the "other time" of the myth.

And yet the irruption of eschatological time into the profane, present time does not happen without active preparation either; indeed, the passage has to be negotiated: one has to be aware of the coming of the sacred, and to undertake specific preparations in order to successfully manage this passage; hence reggae singer Luciano enjoins his listeners to get ready and trim their lambs ("Moving outta Babylon," 1999). Leaving Babylon, this injunction so often found within reggae lyrics, is not a metaphor; it is the preparation that one has to undertake with care when (or rather because) one knows that the eschatological time is here, or near. Here, or near: there lies a fundamental nuance. The end of the world is often pushed back, to a liminal time that lies somewhat between the profane future and the sacred; hence it is thought of as being both in historical time—a condition of successful belief, since it *has to be coming*—and out of reach. It is almost here, but not yet, to use Ernst Bloch's expression (1995); it is both here and not. But in other cases, the end of the world is here and now. And of course, this is what is happening in reggae music. The present tense is used—"we're moving to Mount Zion" (Luciano, "Moving outta Babylon," 1999)—present events are interpreted as signs of the gradual end of the world, and the presence of evil is felt.

The eschatology, hence, invades profane time. And that seems to be an insoluble problem, which often leads to the dismissal of millenarian religious movements and their reduction to pathology, or to escapism. In his discussion of the sacred at the beginning of the *Elementary Forms*, Durkheim opens up an unexplored path into the other-worldly dimensions of the religious phenomenon: "The two worlds [i.e. sacred and profane] are conceived of not only as separate but also as hostile and jealous rivals. Since the condition of belonging fully to one is fully to have left the other, man is exhorted to retire completely from the profane in order to live an exclusively religious life" (Durkheim 2001 [1912]: 37). According to him, this is the source of monasticism, or religious suicide. Is it here a question of impossible reconciliation? Is it only that the two spheres are so radically different, and yet so intimately linked in the sense that they cannot exist without the other, that a choice has to be made between the two? This would leave us with only one possible answer: in reggae music, the sacred overcomes the profane, and the eschatology comes to replace the present. Yet this is not satisfactory, for, as this study has shown, the Rastafari movement cannot be characterized as a strictly speaking other-worldly inclination, nor as an escapist religious movement. The "bursting sacred" provokes activity; indeed, it allows the coexistence of millenarian awaiting and earthly action, as shown in the fourth part of this book. Rastafari sets up a representation of origins as well as of the future, by transmitting a memory that has been truncated by slavery but is nonetheless necessary to the survival of the people, and which is, therefore, to be found, to be conserved, and to be transmitted. It is precisely the belief in the eschatology that allows for profane, this-worldy activity, perhaps simply because the end of the world requires preparation.

So if the irruption of the sacred can be reconciled with the profane, as seems to be the case in reggae music, how can we explain it? An excursus into Mauss and Hubert's study of sacrifice can be helpful here. They argue that sacrifice is a system in which *everything comes together*: through slaughter, the victim, which, it was ensured, was both consecrated and in contact with the profane world (Mauss and Hubert 2001 [1905]: 31), realizes the fusion of the profane and the sacred: "Thus this process of drawing together the sacred and the profane, which we have seen come about progressively through the various elements of the sacrifice, is completed in the victim" (Mauss and Hubert 2001 [1905]: 32). Rituals are not *simply* a leap into a radically different time and space: they are a leap *contextualized in the profane*. Weber is helpful here once again, with his central assertion that religion is, ultimately, about the profane world: "The most elementary forms of behavior motivated by religious or magical factors are oriented to this world ... Thus, religious or magical behavior or thinking must not be set apart from the range of everyday purposive conduct" (Weber 1978: 399). This worldly orientation of religion is found even in the case of the virtuoso:

> Only the religious virtuoso ... strove for sacred values, which were 'other-worldly' as compared with such solid goods of this world, as health, wealth, and long life. And these other-worldly sacred values were by no means only values of the *beyond*. This was not the case even when it was understood to be so by the participants. Psychologically considered, man in quest of salvation has been primarily preoccupied by attitudes of the here and now. (Weber 1958: 345–346)

So I would argue that the problem has to be seen in a new light: it is not that the sacred and the profane can, or cannot, coexist; it is not that men have to choose between one or the other, or remain limited to accessing the sacred through rituals; it is that sacred time can indeed irrupt into profane time, including into the present. But this irruption requires very specific conditions. Within the (out of) time and space of the ceremony, a link to the profane world has to be maintained. This has to do with the social function of religion; indeed, we can pause on Durkheim and attempt to look at what he is saying from a different angle. If religion is an ensemble of beliefs and practices that have to do with the sacred, it also has to do with a binary classification of the world into *both* the profane and the sacred. Hence, it could be argued that the primary function of religion is precisely to link the profane and the sacred—even though this link might be one of opposition. This point is made in the introduction to the *Elementary Forms*; it is also contained in the demonstration that religious phenomena are fundamentally social, whether we speak of sacrifice, magic, prayer or totemism (Mauss and Hubert 1981 [1899], Mauss and Hubert 2001 [1905], Mauss 2003 [1909], Durkheim 2001 [1912]). Religious practices and representations concern and address the sacred (Durkheim 2001 [1912]: 38; see also Mauss 2003 [1909]: 53–54); but they are also fundamentally oriented towards the profane or, to use Weber's vocabulary, towards this world. The necessity—or command—of maintaining a *link* to the profane world, in sacrifice, is a witness to this orientation; and as a matter of fact sacrifice is indeed defined as a "means of communication between the sacred and the profane worlds through the mediation of a victim" (Mauss and Hubert 1981 [1899]: 97). Hence while the nature of the sacred and the profane implies that they exclude each other, the function of the distinction lies within profane time, interests, and preoccupations, or at least it is attached to them: indeed, the distinction is fundamentally social; it is a social category of thought. Further, the analysis of totemic rites provided by Durkheim (2001 [1912]: 303–417) also throws light on the issue: the three categories he describes—negative, positive, and piacular—all have a double function: one that concerns the passage into or out of the sacred sphere, or the sacred itself, and one that concerns social life. Needless to say, Durkheim's argument that the totem really represents society, and thereby that the sacred really is the social, points to the importance of the articulation of the profane and sacred spheres, as opposed to the sole importance of the sacred. Ultimately, religious beliefs and practices concern the sacred; but the category disappears if the articulation with the profane is broken. As a matter of fact, it is precisely *the radical distinction*, and the care taken by men in maintaining it through negative cults, that validates the very importance of *the articulation itself*. Indeed, as Durkheim has shown, to keep the sacred and the profane separated through elaborate prohibition practices also implies to enable a *passage* between the two spheres—that is the double function of the negative cult. And if these two spheres have to be distinguished with such care, it is also because they are irremediably linked and do not have any sort of existence without one another.[7]

Weber provides a second pathway to look at the articulation of the sacred and the profane, which allows an understanding of the way in which the sacred provides a basis for (and illuminates) profane action. He does not use these eminently Durkheimian terms, of course, but he nonetheless constructs a relation between values and action, which in certain respects parallels the distinction made by Durkheim between representations and practices. Ultimate values (related to the sacred, whether it be the eschatology, religious beliefs, etc) orient action in this world—that is, the sphere of the profane. Hence in Weber it is no longer a question of exclusion: the sacred, through the meaning it infuses into social action, participates in the profane by orienting it. The development of charismatic authority (in our case, Haile Selassie, for instance), the *bricolage* of tradition, a revolutionary orientation of the political and social struggle, all are particularly enlightening illustrations of Weber's theory of social action as being *meaningfully oriented* by values that can, nevertheless, have their origin in what Durkheim would call the radically different sphere of the sacred.

Profane and sacred times, therefore, need each other; the case of eschatology, although it possesses specificities that distinguish it from periodic rituals, festivities and ceremonies, is still part of this

---

[7] There is more. Arguably, the *raison d'être* of the distinction lies in its enabling the human species to be a little more than an animal. The sacred allows man to reach beyond profane life; the alternation of profane and sacred moments is needed for the revitalization of social life; but it also allows individuals to share in something higher, which reaches before and after, above, within and without individual consciousness. In reggae music, the irruption of the sacred into the present sustains hope; it also revitalizes social life by providing exaltation before the difficulties of the past of slavery, and of the present.

dialectic. Its irruption within historical time is more radical than the temporary gap of rituals; indeed, it is not a reenactment of the myth, but the myth itself; and the irruption of the myth implies much more intense—or irremediable—a rupture. But, ultimately, it allows man to get out of himself; it allows the group to share in togetherness. The communion, though, is not experienced as temporary. As in periods of persecution, the irruption of the eschatology in the present allows an articulation of two parallel spheres: the profane and the sacred, suffering and healing, sorrow and happiness, defeat and victory, slavery and redemption. As many reggae songs assert, the promise is one of *reversal*—the current world, upside-down, will be re-ordered by the sacred.[8] Hence the world, for the group, becomes simultaneously false and true, empty and full, linear and circular. The profane sphere is illuminated by the sacred, as a result of being not exactly the eschatology, but its preparatory phase. The imminence of the end of the profane world provokes tremendous intensity, not only in individual consciousnesses but also in the collective consciousness.[9] Sacred enlightenment solidifies the group. Any drawback, attack, or failure that touches it reinforces the intensity, and is used—following Hubert's rejuvenation of saints—as a renewed sign of its unity. Memory, perhaps, is found here in its most salient form: both the old and the new are incorporated within a sacred continuity based on both tradition and its radical rupture; any event, any person, any moment is susceptible to become represented as a part of collective consciousness, and to be used as an emblem of the irreducibility of the group.

And yet intensity cannot last. The exhaustion it brings calls on more quiet times, on a return to the reparative calmness of the profane. It remains to be seen how this transition will be negotiated in the case of reggae music and more specifically in the case of the Rastafari movement—and for this analysis, incidentally, Weber is more useful than Durkheim, precisely because of his focus on social

---

[8] As in Bob Marley's "Ride natty ride" (1979). The biblical promise is that those who were last will become first (Mathew 19: 30; 20: 16).

[9] The intensity is further heightened, in our case study, by the fact that the eschatology is considered unique: it will happen only once, unlike eschatological beliefs found in various other cases. According to Eliade, this is the "capital innovation" of the Judeo-Christian tradition: both the cosmogony and the eschatology are unique events; hence, they are historicized (Eliade 1963a: 86).

action. Edmonds (2003) has provided an argument for the cultural routinization of Rastafari; on the religious level, one step has been taken, following the disappearance of Haile Selassie; and yet, it has not decreased the intensity of the eschatological beliefs: on the contrary, it has been interpreted, once again, as another confirming sign. The profane remains illuminated by the sacred; and a study in routinization (beyond its cultural dimension) remains to be done, which is not the object of this book. What is of interest to us here, rather, is the Durkheimian hypothesis of the fundamentally social quality of time, and of its rhythmic function, to which I now turn.

III

After this necessary excursus on the relationship between sacred and profane times, it is now time to shift to what has become, finally, of crucial interest: the question of time in relationship to memory. It is important to note, before going further, that this preoccupation arose from the specific object of this book—that is, from the data used as a basis for analysis. Indeed, it is sacred time, in particular the eschatology, that has pushed the analysis of memory beyond its usually accepted boundaries: on the empirical level, there has been an overflow that forced sociological enquiry into the issue of time. But what is time? It is understood that time is a representation; moreover, it is what Durkheim calls a collective concept (Durkheim 2001 [1912]). In other words, it is an overarching category of thought, which frames the group's ideal imagination. Collective representation is a crucial concept in Durkheimian sociology; in the preface to the second edition of *The Rules*, Durkheim refers to the criticisms made to the first edition and asserts, indeed, that social life in its entirety is made of representations (Durkheim 2004 [1895]: xi).[10] The notion becomes, after 1895, central to Durkheim's reflection on the social quality of thought (Durkheim 1974 [1898, 1911], Durkheim and Mauss 1967 [1902]) and on religion (Durkheim 2001 [1912]). Fundamental to his analysis is the articulation between the internal and the external: collective representations are social facts; they are situated precisely in the tension between the collective and the

---

10 "Alors que nous avions dit expressément et répété de toutes les manières que la vie sociale était tout entière faite de représentations, on nous accusa d'éliminer l'élément mental de la sociologie" (Durkheim 2004 [1895]: xi).

individual; they are both constructed and given, in the sense that they do not belong to the individual and yet do not exist without him; they belong to the social sphere, related and yet not reducible to the individual sphere. Collective representations are ideas, and are articulated with practices; together, they form social life. Religion, hence, is formed out of religious beliefs and rites, and the interaction between them; this is a recurrent theme in Durkheimian analyses of religious phenomena.[11] In the introduction to *The Elementary Forms* Durkheim reflects on the notion of category of understanding, which forms the point of departure for his elaboration of collective representation:

> At the root of our judgments, there are certain fundamental notions that dominate our entire intellectual life. It is these ideas that philosophers, beginning with Aristotle, have called the categories of understanding: notions of time, space, number, cause, substance, personality, etc. They correspond to the most universal properties of things. They are like solid frames that confine thought. Thought does not seem to be able to break out of them without destroying itself, since it seems we cannot think of objects that are not in time or space, that cannot be counted, and so forth. The other ideas are contingent and changing, and we can conceive of a man, a society, or an epoch that lacks them; but these fundamental notions seem to us as almost inseparable from the normal functioning of the intellect. They are, as it were, the skeleton of thought. (Durkheim 2001 [1912]: 8–9)

Durkheim's elaboration of the notion of collective representation answers the Kantian problem of categories of understanding; he leaves Kant, though, insofar as he argues that collective representations, although they organize human thought, are variable and changing. *The Elementary Forms* present a complex, and sometimes ambiguous, argument. Durkheim rejects apriorism, and therefore the Kantian assumption that there exist universal, static, unchanging categories of understanding; yet collective representations, or at least some of them, remain necessary to the very existence of mankind as such (Durkheim 2001 [1912]: 16–17). Temporal, spatial, or classificatory representations are the product of society: they arise,

---

[11] Hence the analytical structure of the studies on sacrifice, magic, and totemism (Mauss and Hubert 1981 [1899], 2001 [1905]; Durkheim 2001 [1912]).

as it were, traced over social organization; in return, they express the social as well (Durkheim 2001 [1912]: 441). Hence the spatial organization of the Bororo village has something to say about that people's social organization, as well as about their general representation of space (Lévi-Strauss 1992 [1955]: 215–246); the religious beliefs of the Arunta have something to say about the group: they express society as well as being its product (Durkheim 2001 [1912]). What remains as a constant is the need for a category of time or space: no matter what form it takes, it necessarily exists (Durkheim 2001 [1912]: 440). And here Durkheim takes an interesting step: society is "a specific reality" but it is not "an empire within an empire"; it is part of nature as well as nature's "highest expression" (Durkheim 2001 [1912]: 17). And he furthers his argument in a footnote on the same page:

> Hence the rationalism that is immanent in a sociological theory of knowledge stands between empiricism and classical apriorism. For the first, the categories are purely artificial constructs; for the second, on the other hand, they are naturally given; for us, they are works of art, in a sense, but an art that imitates nature even more perfectly. (Durkheim 2001 [1912]: 17, footnote 22)

Hence categories are fundamental to thought itself; but they are not static: they are "works of art" that arise within the social sphere, not entirely constructed and yet not entirely given. Durkheim is able to reconcile their conditioning role in thought with their variation and fundamentally social origin, and in doing so he maintains the reference to "the nature of things." He concludes indeed that "the fact that the ideas of time, space, genus, cause, and personality are constructed from social elements should not lead us to conclude that they are stripped of all objective value. Quite the contrary, their social origin leads one indeed to suppose that they are not without foundation in the nature of things" (Durkheim 2001 [1912]: 18). And at this point he comes back to the issue of time. Time, he says, is a representation; hence it is socially constructed, on the basis of the rhythm of social life; but "if there is a rhythm of collective life, one can be certain that there is another in the life of the individual and, more generally, that of the universe" (Durkheim 2001 [1912]: 18, note 23). For him therefore, and once again, social time is a work of art, an imitation of something that exists in nature as well, but an imitation that works with a surplus; this surplus, of course, has to do with the social, with the life of the mind, with meaning and the ability of men to think beyond themselves. Time is a necessary category; but the form in which this category functions depends on the work of representation and differentiation, which are both causally rooted in social life. Hence, time imitates nature, but it is grounded in society; and it is also one of those "crucial" representations that Durkheim calls "categories" or "concepts" in *The Elementary Forms*. It organizes thought by providing men with a mental frame.

It is necessary, at this point, to pause for a moment to examine two crucial points in Durkheim's argument: the equation of time with rhythm, and the universality of this rhythm. Here Durkheim is building upon Hubert's essay on sacred time, which postulates periodicity as the function of religious time (Hubert 1999 [1905]), but also on Mauss' essay on the morphology of Eskimo society,[12] which analyzes a case of double social structure that revolves in time (Mauss 2004 [1906]). First, there is *a double social morphology*, which can be summarized as an opposition between winter and summer, based on a general distinction between concentration and dispersion; the distinction is as much geographical and demographic as it is symbolic and social (Mauss 2004 [1906]: 76). A period of dispersion of single family units throughout the land is distinguished from a period of gathering which "dissolves" the individual and the familial into larger units; a period of emotional deprivation, with an absence of religious activity, is distinguished from a period of extreme emotions and thoughts, with intense religious, social and sexual activity, which Mauss qualifies as "continuous exaltation"; finally, a period of limited sociability is distinguished from a period of intense sociability. Second, this *double social morphology is rhythmic*: there is a continuous succession of apogees and perigees, which therefore creates a rhythm between successive high and low levels of intensity.

The final layer of analysis concerns *the existence of this social rhythm in all societies*. Mauss starts by comparing cases where, although the distinction is not as marked as it is in Eskimo societies, seasonal variation in social structure nonetheless exists:

---

[12] The term "Eskimo" is now considered derogative, as opposed to "Inuit." However, for the sake of remaining close to the text, I will use it when referring to Mauss' essay and hypotheses.

in particular, Native American societies of the west coast, but also the transhumance in European mountains, where each year men leave the village with the cattle for higher pastures in the spring and come back at the end of summer. He also mentions the general hypoactivity of the summer and hyperactivity of the winter found in urban areas, while in rural areas it is the opposite: the isolation of the winter, spent inside, is followed by a concentration of social and religious activities in the summer. Mauss, therefore, suspects that seasonal change, and the rhythm it endows to social life, is a general characteristic found in most, if not all, societies:

> All this suggests that we have come upon a law that is probably of considerable generality. Social life does not continue at the same level throughout the year; it goes through regular, successive phases of increased and decreased intensity, of activity and repose, of exertion and recuperation. We might almost say that social life does violence to the minds and bodies of individuals which they can sustain only for a time; and there comes a point when they must slow down and partially withdraw from it. (Mauss 2004 [1906]: 78–79)

Note that the terms used by Mauss, "exertion and recuperation," lead straight to Durkheim's notions of exhaustion and effervescence, explored in *The Elementary Forms*:

> Society cannot revitalize the awareness it has of itself unless it assembles, but it cannot remain continuously in session ... The form of this cycle is apt to vary from one society to another. Where the period of dispersion is long or the dispersion is very great, the period of congregation is prolonged in turn, and there are veritable orgies of collective and religious life ... This is true of the Australian tribes and of several societies in the American North and Northwest. Elsewhere, by contrast, these two phases of social life follow one another more closely, and the contrast between them is less marked. The more societies develop, the less is their tolerance for interruptions that are too pronounced. (Durkheim 2001 [1912]: 353–354)

In other words, both Mauss and Durkheim argue that the intensity of collective life is too exhausting and *must* lead to a sort of "individual rest," just as the profusion of the sacred cannot sustain itself indefinitely and has to lead to a profane routine, as it were, intercalated between moments of religious intensity.[13] The rhythmic

---

13 Interestingly, Durkheim sees profane routine as being intercalated between

succession of "high key" and "low key" moments in social life would therefore be *necessary* to the very existence of social life. The case of the Eskimo society thereby becomes not an exception but a case that, because of its physical environment, is simply more marked than elsewhere (Mauss 2004 [1906]: 79): because seasonal change is so great, and so limiting to the activities of men, it also appears more clearly to the observer. The findings of the Durkheimians are therefore crucial: time is a *social system of representation* whose primary function revolves around the notion of *rhythm* rather than *measurement*. The function of the representation of time is to set up a succession of high and low peaks within social life, which allow for an irruption of the sacred within the profane—or for a profane rest after a moment of sacred ebullition. And time functions as an overarching category that organizes thought and, in Durkheim's words, "governs and contains":

> The rhythm of collective life governs and contains the various rhythms of all the elementary lives of which it is the result; consequently, the time that expresses it governs and contains all the individual times. It is time as a whole. (Durkheim 2001 [1912]: 443)

Hence time is equated with rhythm; in fact, the possibility of measuring the passing of time in a linear way can be understood as a consequence of installing a rhythm. Let's now examine the second important point made by Durkheim, which concerns the fact that social time is a "work of art" that imitates a rhythm found universally, in nature and in individuals. At the end of his essay, Mauss comes back to one central point made by Hubert: indeed, this rhythm of social life coincides with natural changes, often linked to seasons; however, Mauss, like Hubert, argues that this coincidence is only a secondary confirmation, not the primary basis or origin of social rhythm: "Instead of being the necessary and determining cause of an entire system, truly seasonal factors may merely mark the most opportune occasions in the year for these two phases to

---

sacred times, and not the latter as "breaking up" profane time. This movement in his thought, starting from the sacred, reveals his focus on intensity and the impossibility of it being sustained over a long time rather than on the need for profane routine to be revitalized by moments of intensity. This idea seems fundamental: time is thought not as a dull routine that makes intense moments necessary, but rather as a sacred intensity that has to "rest from itself" on a regular basis.

occur" (Mauss 2004: 79).[14] This point is of crucial importance: it opens the door not only to the primacy of the social, an explicit claim made by the Durkheimian school, but also to this primacy *even when natural phenomena are used*. Mauss is not denying the importance of the latter's role in the representation of time, the establishment of calendars, and the rhythm born therewith; however, this role is one of *convenience*, which comes simply as a confirmation—almost as a felicitous coincidence. This is a central point: the establishment of a balance between "natural facts" and their simple role of coincidence with "representations"; in other words, natural phenomena are neither the cause nor the origin of social representations; they are only used in conjunction with them. The function of the coincidence between social representations and natural phenomena has to be found in efficiency rather than in imitation or causality.

I want to come back, at this point, to the simultaneity of circular and linear time in my case study, mentioned earlier. Circularity is a characteristic of sacred time, in the sense that sacred time is, in any of its parts, similar to the whole; and further examination of cosmologies and eschatologies, for instance in the work of Mircea Eliade (1954), also leads to a cyclical process insofar as, even when there is no repetition and when the eschatology brings the end of historical time, the eschatology is either an end that brings a new beginning, or a return to the original cosmogony. Linearity, on the other hand, is characteristic both of historical time and of what Jean-Pierre Vernant, in his work on Ancient Greece, calls memory—that is, individual time (Vernant 1996 [1965]). Mnemosyne, the deity of memory, is associated with poetry; indeed, in a beautiful demonstration, Vernant shows the affinity between the poet and memory: remembering is equated both with knowing and seeing,[15] and the poet is the one who is able to be present to the past, of which he has an immediate experience (Vernant 1996 [1965]: 112). And yet memory does not allow one to live in the past; Vernant uses the image of the bridge to explain further the way memory works. According to him, and echoing Halbwachs, it is not from the present that memory takes one away, but from the visible world: "we get out of our human universe, in order to discover behind it other regions

---

14 See the original in Mauss 1973 [1906]: 473.
15 There is a striking etymological closeness in French between the terms to know (*savoir*) and to see (*voir*). See Vernant 1996 [1965]: 112.

of being, other cosmic levels, usually inaccessible ... To explore the past is to discover what is hidden in the depths of being" (Vernant 1996 [1965]: 116).

For Vernant, both memory and history have to be seen as human acquisitions that parallel the rise of individuality. Both have to do with finitude and irreversibility, with the linearity found from birth to death. Time, on the other hand, is characterized by circularity, by the idea of an infinite cycle. Vernant shows that the appearance of an exaltation of Chronos, understood as "the radical negation of human time" (Vernant 1996 [1965]: 128) is linked to a crisis in the representation of time that arises along with a new image of man around the seventh century BC. He provides a striking hypothesis:

> The time that is sacralized is time that does not age, time immortal and imperishable, as it is celebrated in the Orphic poems under the name Chronos Ageraos. Like another mythical figure, the river Okeanos, which encircles the entire universe in its untiring course, Chronos is a snake whose body forms a circle, a cycle that, by enfolding the world and binding it together, makes the cosmos a single eternal sphere, despite the appearances of multiplicity and change ... The development of a mythology of Chronos alongside that of Mnemosyne [*the deity of memory*] seems to correspond with a period of difficulty and anxiety regarding the representation of time. Time becomes the subject of doctrinal preoccupations and assumes the form of a problem when a domain of experience of time is found to be incompatible with the ancient conception of a cyclical becoming, which applied to the whole of reality, regulating at once seasonal activity, the timing of festivals, and the sequence of generations (in other words: cosmic time, religious time, and human time). (Vernant 2006 [1965]: 130–131)

The rise of a focus on individual being, on the emotional life of individuals, also destabilizes a representation of time until then characterized by an integration of human time within the cyclical organization of cosmic time. Man becomes dominated by death. According to Vernant, memory then becomes a way of escaping the irreversibility of human life: remembering, he asserts, is not motivated by an interest in the past; the function of memory is to transform individual time, to reinsert human time into cosmic periodicity and divine eternity (Vernant 1996 [1965]: 130, 134).

Memory as knowledge, memory as a bridge that links man to the deeper regions of his being, or memory as a struggle against the finitude of human time: these transformations of the idea of memory in Ancient Greece all point to an interesting hypothesis—namely, that memory has to do with human agency. I do not pretend, in this book, to solve a question that Blaise Pascal deemed impossible to answer,[16] but only to open up possible paths towards a reflection on time, memory, and the pertinence of the use of the latter term in social theory. Vernant takes us back to Durkheim in a very interesting, double way. He establishes two fundamental distinctions between time on one hand, and history and memory on the other. (Figure 13.7)

Figure 13.7: Vernant's distinctions between time, and memory and history

Time	Memory and history
Cyclical and eternal	Linear and finite
Coercive (outside of human agency)	Manipulated (within human agency)

Vernant's first distinction is reminiscent of the distinction made by Durkheim, Mauss, and Hubert between sacred time and profane time, which I discussed at length earlier. His second distinction is of even more interest, because it brings us back to Durkheim's apparent distinction between some collective representations and others. Indeed, in *The Elementary Forms* Durkheim repeatedly singles out some representations, such as time or space, which he asserts are categories that form "the skeleton of thought" (Durkheim 2001 [1912]: 8–9). The distinction between time and memory also leads to this paradox: both are representations (i.e. they belong to the sphere of ideas, of thought; they are shared; they are not given, but constructed) and yet the difference between these two sets of representations might have to do with practice and/or agency. Let me push this idea further.

---

[16] "Time is of this sort. Who can define it? And why undertake it, since all men conceive what is meant in speaking of a time, without any further definition?" (Pascal 2004: 432–433).

Can we consider memory as a practical idea? Could we argue that, in a way, we inhabit time but construct memory? Or that time structures thought in a coercive way while memory possesses more flexibility? The emergence of the use of the term "memory" in the social sciences, as well as its political and social uses in the contemporary world, would point indeed to agency as a fundamental component of the concept. Memory is not only what groups *think* of the past, it is most importantly what groups *do* with it, and how they use it in the present, as well as in order to build a future. The link between the uses of memory and the emergence of individuality in Ancient Greece is not fortuitous: memory can be seen, in many ways, as the expression of human agency, as the practice arising from the human desire to control time, or at least to act upon it. The contemporary preoccupation with the individual, indeed, can be seen as providing the environment for what could be called an obsession with memory observed in the past couple of decades, whether in scholarship, politics, or social movements. Both individuals and groups claim their right to the expression and recognition of their own memory, a claim that may be primarily understood as a claim for agency. Memory is claimed by the "I"— whether individual or collective—in opposition to others or, more importantly, in opposition to what lies beyond individual agency; it implies a claim for uniqueness and subjectivity, for particularity in opposition to a larger universal. And claims for the expression and, more importantly, for the *recognition* of one's memory, always imply the fight for individual agency, for the recognition of the particular and the unique. This is articulated with coercion by time, a cyclical and eternal time which does not allow the recognition of individuality and eludes particular experiences. In a way, memory can be understood as the attempt to gain recognition within and against this "negation of human time" represented by Chronos; it comes to symbolize the acknowledgment that individuals and groups matter, despite their finitude, despite their particularity. Claiming memory, for the group as for the individual, is an act of agency—and whether this act is illusory or not is of little importance, because what matters is the fact that it allows for *experiencing agency.*

Parallels can be drawn here. Memory against time, agency against coercion, individuals against groups, and groups against society. Memory is precisely about the recognition of the group, and beyond, of unique experiences. By claiming its memory, the group claims its own point of view, its own vision, its own experience. It is not a coincidence that the rise of claims of particularity (among them, memory) has accompanied a rise in individualistic theories in the social sciences (including an increasing focus on individual and collective experience) and disaffection with those currents of thought seen as "coercive" and "universalistic," such as Durkheimian sociology or Lévi-Straussian structuralism. And neither is it a coincidence if scholarship on memory participates in the elaboration and reproduction of an eminently normative concept: the equation of memory with agency, in the contemporary context, makes it highly seductive. I would argue, then, for the following distinction between time and memory. Both are constructed—in the sense that both are representations that depend on meaning and their link with practices, and are not given nor inherent but changing and dynamic; in Durkheim's words, both are works of art. But memory points towards agency while time points towards coercion, in the sense that memory lies on the side of practical action, while time can be seen as a structuring representation. Time, to use Durkheim's felicitous expression, forms the "skeleton of thought" (Durkheim 2001 [1912]: 9), onto which memory grafts itself. The seeming distinction that Durkheim makes, indeed, between some representations and others has to do with the structuring function that some have over thought. It could be argued that this book's case study provides an enlightening illustration of how memory is structured by time, if we use as a point of departure the fact that sacred time—in our case study both the cosmogony and, above all, the eschatology—illuminates profane time. Similarly, time can be said to illuminate memory: the intersection between the profane and the sacred can be found precisely here; the sacred gives the profane a new texture. Everyday life, once the light (and shadows) of an "out-of-time" is shed upon it, becomes something else; the memory of things past, the experience of the present, and the expectation of the future, are guided, organized, and perhaps structured, by the representation of time specific to reggae music and the Rastafari movement. We find here another way to resolve the seeming paradox raised by the radical dichotomy between the profane and the sacred: indeed the sacred is not "really" here, and yet it wholly organizes the here. Temporal, spatial, and classificatory representations provide a structural frame outside of which no thought can exist. Memory, on the other hand, can be analyzed as a claim to resist the frame of time, as an attempt by the particular to claim its importance within (or without) the universal. In the past few decades, memory has become increasingly associated with political struggles and social recognition; mirroring Vernant's analysis of Ancient Greece, memory has once again become a shelter from both time and death.

Annex 1: List of songs mentioned, by artist

The Abyssinians
1976: Satta amassa gana; African race; Declaration of rights; Abendigo.

Alcapone, Dennis
1973: DJ's choice.

Andy, Horace
1972: Skylarking.

Anthony B
1996: Raid di barn; Repentance time; Burn down sodom; Rumour; Hurt di heart; Fire pon Rome; Swarm me.
1997: Universal struggle; Waan back; Jerusalem; Seek Jah first; Rastaman school; The mockingbird; Gangstas think twice.
1999: Cover your tracks; Cut out that; Who shoot first; Our father; Dem a question; Wicked people; Conquer all; Conscious entertainer; Me dem afraid of.

Aswad
1976: Concrete slaveship; Three Babylon.
1979: Not guilty; Judgment day.

Baby Cham
1999: Desperate measures.

Bailey, Admiral
1987: Punany.

Banton, Buju
1993: Murderer.

1994: God of my salvation.
1995: Untold stories; Not an easy road; Til I'm laid to rest.
1997: Hills and valleys; Love sponge; Destiny; Give I strength; Close one yesterday.
1999: 23rd Psalm; Di women dem phat.
... with Garnett Silk.
1995: Complaint.
1996: World is in trouble.
... with Morgan Heritage.
2000: 23rd Psalm.
... with Luciano.
2000: We'll be alright.

Beenie Man
1999: Better learn.

Bennett, Ike, & the Crystalites
1969: Stop that man.

Big Youth
1973: Cool breeze.
1985: Jah Jah shall guide.

Black Uhuru
1978: Time to unite; Satan army band; Hard ground.
1980: No loafing (sit and wonder).
1985: Solidarity.

Blender, Everton
1996: Lift up your head.

Bounty Killer
1998: Caan believe me eyes.
1999: Anytime.

Brown, Barry
1979: Enter the kingdom of Zion.

Brown, Dennis
1973: Westbound train.
1977: Children of Israel.
1978: Jah can do it; Milk and honey; Deliverance will come; Malcolm X; Concrete castle king; How could I leave.
1979: Ain't that loving you.
1980: Home sweet home; Oh what a day.
1983: Your love got a hold on me.
1985: Revolution.

Burning Spear
1975: Slavery days; Marcus Garvey.
1978: Marcus say Jah no dead; Marcus children suffer; Mr Garvey.
1980: Jah see and know.
1995: This man; Old timer; Every other nation; Subject in school.

Bushman
1999: Live your life right; Worries and problems.

Byles, Junior
1975: Know where you going.

Capleton
1994: Tour.
1998: Pure sodom.

Clarke, Johnny
1976: Be holy my brothers and sisters.

Culture
1978: Zion gate; Black Starliner must come.
1979: Too long in slavery.

Culture, Stevie
1998: No more.

Eastwood, Clint, and General Saint
1983: Stop that train.

Elliott, Paul
1999: Save me oh Jah; Vipers; Fat belly rat.

Fashek, Malek
1997: Promised land.

The Gladiators
1976: Look is deceiving.

Isaacs, Gregory
1979: Slave market.
1980: Poor and clean.
1983: Night nurse.

Israel Vibration
1978: Walk the streets of glory.
1997: Systematical fraud.
1998: So much youths.

Jackson, Vivian, and the Defenders
1972: Love thy neighbour.
... and the Prophets.
1975: Run come rally; Covetous men.

Jahmali
1998: Politics; 21st century; Time and space; No water; Real issues.

Keith and Tex
1967: Stop that train.

Knooks, George
1978: Tribal war.

Levy, Barrington
1992: Mandela.

Luciano
1994: One way ticket.
1995: It's me against Jah.
1997: Messenger.
1998: Sweep over my soul; Jonah.
1999: Jah blessing; Hold strong; When will I be home; Moving outta Babylon; Can't stop Jah works; Punch line.

Marley, Bob, & the Wailers
1961: Judge not.
1964–65: Wings of a dove.
1973: Pass it on; Rastaman chant; Small axe; Slave driver; Get up stand up; Concrete jungle; Burnin' and lootin'.
1974: So Jah seh; Revolution; Talking blues.
1976: Night shift; Want more; Who the cap fit; I shot the sheriff; Rat race; One love; Crazy baldheads; Jah live.
1977: The heathen; Slave driver; Jammin'; So much things to say; Exodus.
1978: Crisis.
1979: Ride natty ride; Survival; So much trouble; Africa unite; Zimbabwe; Babylon system.
1980: Forever loving Jah; Zion train; Redemption song.
1981: Rastaman live up.
1983: Buffalo soldier.

The Mighty Diamonds
1976: I need a roof; Them never love poor Marcus; Why me black brother why.
1982: Pretty woman.

Appendices

Morgan Heritage
1998: Liberation; What man can cry; Exalt Jah; Let them talk; The King is coming; Set yourself free.
1999: Buss up barriers.
... with Tony Rebel.
1998: People are fighting.

Mundell, Hugh
1978: Jah say the time has now come.

The Prophets
Early seventies: Warn the nation.

Ranglin, Ernest
1998: Stop that train.

Rebel, Tony
1991: Fresh vegetable.
1994: Teach the children.
1997: Jah by my side.

Reid, Junior
1989: One blood.

Romeo, Max
1976: War inna Babylon.

Sanchez
1994: Brown eye girl.

Scotty
1971: Draw your brakes.

Shabba Ranks
1991: Trailer load of girls.

Sherman, Bim
1979: Down in Jamdown.

Silk, Garnett
1994: Lion heart.
1995: Lord watch over our shoulder.
1994: A man is just a man.
... with Anthony B and Buju Banton.
    1999: Hello mama Africa.

Sizzla
1997: Hail Selassie; Praise yeh Jah; Black woman and child; One away; Cowboy; Give them a ride; More guidance; No other like Jah.
1998: Ancient memories.
2000: Strength and hope; The world.

The Slickers
1972: Johnny too bad.

The Spanishtonians
1965: Stop that train.

Steel Pulse
1978: Handsworth revolution; Prediction; Ku Klux Klan.
1979: Tribute to the martyrs; Biko's kindred lament; Uncle George; Jah pickney.
1984: Wild goose chase.

Stephens, Tanya
1997: Yuh nuh ready fi this.

Taylor, Rod
1978: Ethiopian kings.
1979: Look before you leap.

Tiger
1992: Yu dead now.

Toots & the Maytals
1968: Do the reggay.

U-Roy
1991: True born African.
… with Dennis Brown.
  1978: The half.

Wailing Souls
1977: They don't know Jah.
1978: Jah Jah give us life.

Washington, Glen
1998: Jah glory.

Yellowman
1984: Belly move.

Zebra
1998: Selassie warning.

Annex 2: Albums in the corpus

The following list includes compact-disc availability in the United States as of January 2009. The reader will note that some of these albums are not available any more, while some are available only as imports (interestingly, from Japan or the UK). Additionally, many available albums are actually remastered issues—and some have been criticized for the remastering's poor quality, for instance Dennis Brown's *Visions*.

1973
Bob Marley & the Wailers, *Burnin'*. Island B00005KB9R.
Bob Marley & the Wailers, *Catch a Fire*. Island B00005KB9T.

1974
Bob Marley & the Wailers, *Natty Dread*. Island B00005KB9X.

1975
Burning Spear, *Marcus Garvey / Garvey's Ghost*. Available as import, Universal Japan B000O78XWG.

1976
The Abyssinians, *Forward on to Zion*. Reissued under the title *Satta Massagana*, Heartbeat B00000042Q. Both original and reissue unavailable.
Aswad, *Showcase*. Available as import, Universal Japan B000FDF20K.
Bob Marley & the Wailers, *Rastaman Vibration*. Island B00005KBA0.
The Gladiators, *Trench Town Mix Up*. Frontline B00004W1DW.
Johnny Clarke, *Rockers Time Now*. Unavailable.
The Mighty Diamonds, *The Right Time*. Remastered, Frontline B00005BHY8.

1977
Bob Marley & the Wailers, *Exodus*. Island B00005LANG.

Burning Spear, *Dry and Heavy*. Available as import, *Dry and Heavy / Man in the Hills*, Universal B00024Z9PK.
Dennis Brown, *Wolves and Leopards*. Reissued, Blue Moon B000007MQI. Both original and reissue unavailable.
U Roy, *Rasta Ambassador*. Frontline B000000I0X, also available as remastered, Frontline B00005BHY5.

1978
Black Uhuru, *Black Sounds of Freedom*. Shanachie B000000DZD, also available as remastered, Greensleeves B000FVQWU6.
Bob Marley & the Wailers, *Kaya*. Island B00005MKA1.
Burning Spear, *Social Living*. Remastered, Island B00009KTWC.
Culture, *Two Sevens Clash*. Shanachie B000000DXK; also a remastered issue, Shanachie B000QTD0AC.
Dennis Brown, *Visions*. Remastered, VP Records B000VQQYEY.
Hugh Mundell, *Africa Must be Free by 1983*. Sanctuary Records B000000Q7W.
Israel Vibration, *Same Song*. Sanctuary Records B000000Q96.
Steel Pulse, *Handsworth Revolution*. Available as import, Island UK B000025NI2.

1979
Barry Brown, *Superstar*. Unavailable.
Bob Marley & the Wailers, *Survival*. Island B00005MKA3.
Culture, *International Herb*. Remastered, Frontline B00005BJC6.
Gregory Isaacs, *Soon Forward*. Frontline B00005KB4N.
Steel Pulse, *Tribute to the Martyrs*. Available as import, Island UK B000026AOE.

1980
Bob Marley & the Wailers, *Uprising*. Island B00005A7X0.
Burning Spear, *Hail Him*. Remastered, Frontline B000062URD.
Dennis Brown, *Joseph's Coat of Many Colours*. Unavailable.
Gregory Isaacs, *Lovers Rock*. Unavailable.
Israel Vibration, *Survive*. Unavailable.

1995
Buju Banton, *Til Shiloh*. Remastered, Island B000068FTE.
Burning Spear, *Rasta Business*. Remastered, Burning Music B00020HBXM.

1996
Anthony B, *Real Revolutionary*. Unavailable.

1997
Anthony B, *Universal Struggle*. VP Records B000001TO7.
Buju Banton, *Inna Heights*. Penthouse Records B000001TQC.
Luciano, *Messenger*. Unavailable.
Sizzla, *Black Woman and Child*. Greensleeves B0000086JR.
Sizzla, *Praise Ye Jah*. Exterminator Records B00000582A.
Tony Rebel, *If Jah*. VP Records B000001TNY.

1998
Garnett Silk, *Collectors*. Unavailable. Can be replaced by another compilation, *Reggae Anthology: Music is the Rod*, VP Records B00066VTUI.
Jahmali, *El Shaddai*. Unavailable.
Morgan Heritage, *Protect us Jah*. VP Records B000001TM7.
Sizzla, *Freedom Cry*. VP Records B00000DMYQ.

1999
Anthony B, *Seven Seals*. VP Records B00000K04X.
Bushman, *Total Commitment*. Greensleeves B00000IMRS.
Luciano, *Sweep Over my Soul*. VP Records B00000I183.
Paul Elliott, *Save Me Oh Jah*. Available as import, Redbridge Records B0000256RF.

Compilations
Junior Byles & Friends, *129 Beat Street* (1975–78). Blood & Fire Records B00000BII2.
Rod Taylor, *Ethiopian Kings* (1975–80). Unavailable.
Yabby You & Friends, *Jesus Dread* (1972–77). Blood & Fire Records, unavailable.

Bibliography

Adam, Barbara. 2004. *Time*. Cambridge: Polity.
Alleyne, Mervyn C. 1988. *Roots of Jamaican Culture*. London: Pluto Press.
Anglès, Eric. 1994. *Les tambours de Jah et les sirènes de Babylone: Rastafarisme et Reggae dans la société jamaïcaine*. France: Fondation Nationale des Sciences Politiques.
Anthias, Floya. 1998. "Evaluating `diaspora': Beyond ethnicity?" *Sociology*: 32 (3), pp. 557–580.
Arendt, Hannah. 1993 [1954]. *Between Past and Future: Eight Exercises in Political Thought*. New York: Penguin.
Austin-Broos, Diane. 1987. "Pentecostals and Rastafarians." *Social and Economic Studies*: 36 (4), pp. 1–39.
Back, Les. 1987. "Coughing up fire: Soundsystems, music and cultural politics in S.E. London." *Journal of Caribbean Studies*: 6 (2), pp. 203–218.
—— 1996. *New Ethnicities and Urban Culture*. London: UCL Press.
Back, Les, et al. 1998. *Lions, Black Skins and Reggae Gyals*. Goldsmith University of London: Critical Urban Studies Occasional Papers.
Balandier, George. 1963. *Sociologie actuelle de l'Afrique Noire*. Paris: Presses Universitaires de France.
—— 1988. *Le désordre. Eloge du mouvement*. Paris: Fayard.
Banks, Russell. 1980. *The Book of Jamaica*. New York: Houghton Mifflin.
—— 1998. *Cloudsplitter*. New York: Harper Collins.
Banton, Michael. 1987. "Are the Rastafarians an ethnic group?" *New Community*: 16 (1), pp. 153–157.
Barrett, Leonard E. 1988 [1976]. *The Rastafarians*. Boston: Beacon.

Bibliography

Barrow, Steve, and Peter Dalton. 1997. *Reggae: The Rough Guide*. London: Rough Guides.
Barth, Frederick. 1969. (ed.) *Ethnic Groups and Boundaries: The Social Organization of Culture Difference*. Boston: Little, Brown and Company.
Bastide, Roger. 1958. "Le messianisme raté." *Archives de Sociologie des Religions*: 5, pp. 31–37.
—— 1970. "Mémoire collective et sociologie du bricolage." *L'Année Sociologique*: 3ème série, 21, pp. 65–108.
Behague, Gérard H. 1994. (ed.) *Music and Black Ethnicity: The Caribbean and South America*. Miami: North South Center Press/ University of Miami.
Bergmann, Werner. 1992. "The problem of time in sociology: An overview of the state of theory and research on the sociology of time, 1900–82." *Time and Society*: 1(1), pp. 81–134.
Besson, Jean. 1995a. "Religion as resistance in Jamaican peasant life: The Baptist Church, Revival world-view, and Rastafari movement." In Chevannes (ed.), *Rastafari and Other African-Caribbean Worldviews*, The Hague: ISS, pp. 43–75.
—— 1995b. "Free villagers, Rastafarians and modern Maroons: From resistance to identity." In Hoggbergen (ed.), *Born out of Resistance: On Caribbean Cultural Creativity*, Utrecht: Isor Publications, pp. 301–313.
Bloch, Ernst. 1995. *The Principle of Hope*. Cambridge: The MIT Press. Three volumes.
Borges, Jorge Luis. 1998. "The garden of the forking paths," in *Collected Fictions*, New York: Penguin, pp. 119–128.
Bourdieu, Pierre. 1986 [1979]. *Distinction*. New York: Taylor and Francis.
Brah, Avtar. 1996. *Cartographies of Diasporas: Contesting Identities*. London: Routledge.
Breiner, Lawrence A. 1986. "The English bible in Jamaican Rastafarianism." *The Journal of Religious Thought*: 42 (2), pp. 30–55.
Brown, Samuel E. 1966. "Treatise on the Rastafarian movement." *Caribbean Studies*: 6 (1), pp. 39–40.
Brynda, Bianca. 1994. "Roots daughters. Rastawomen and their experiences in the movement." In Kremser (ed.), *Ay Bobo. African-Caribbean Religions*, Vienna: 2nd International Conference of the Society for Caribbean Research, pp. 77–100.
Butler, Kim. 2001. "Defining diaspora, refining a discourse." *Diaspora*: 10 (2), pp. 189–219.

Caillois, Roger. 1950 [1939]. *L'homme et le sacré*. Paris: Gallimard.
—— 2001. *Man and the Sacred*. Champaign: University of Illinois Press.
Campbell, Horace. 1980a. "The Rastafarians in the Eastern Caribbean." *Caribbean Quarterly*: 26 (4), pp. 42–61.
—— 1980b. "Rastafari: Culture of resistance." *Race & Class*: 22 (1), pp. 1–22.
—— 1985. *Rasta and Resistance: From Marcus Garvey to Walter Rodney*. London: Hansib.
Capone, Stefania. 1999. "L'Afrique réinventée ou la construction de la tradition dans les cultes Afro-Brésiliens." *Archives Européennes de Sociologie*: 40 (1), pp. 3–27.
Cashmore, Ernest. 1977. "The rastaman cometh." *New Society*: August 25, pp. 382–384.
—— 1979a. "More than a version: A study of reality creation." *British Journal of Sociology*: 30 (3), pp. 307–321.
—— 1979b. *Rastaman: The Rastafarian Movement in England*. London: Allen and Unwin.
—— 1981. "After the rastas." *New Community*: 9 (2), pp. 173–181.
—— 1994. "The de-labelling process: From lost tribe to ethnic group." In Chevannes (ed.), *Rastafari and Other African-Caribbean World-views*, The Hague: ISS, pp. 182–195.
Cassidy, Frederic. 1968. *Jamaica Talk*. London: Macmillan.
Chevannes, Barry. 1976. "The repearer of the breach: Reverend Claudius Henry." In Henry (ed.), *Ethnicity in the Americas*, The Hague: Mouton, pp. 263–290.
—— 1977. "Review article: The literature of Rastafari." *Social and Economic Studies*: 26 (2), pp. 239–262.
—— 1989. "Rastafari: Toward a new approach." *New West Indian Guide*: 64 (3/4), pp. 127–148.
—— 1990. "Toward an Afro-Caribbean theology: Principles for the indigeneisation of Christianity in the Caribbean." *Caribbean Quarterly*: 37 (1), pp. 45–54.
—— 1994. *Rastafari: Roots and Ideology*. Syracuse: Syracuse University Press.
—— 1995. (ed.) *Rastafari and Other African-Caribbean World-views*. The Hague: ISS.
—— 1999. "Between the living and the dead: The apostheosis of Rastafari heroes." In Pulis (ed.), *Religion, Diaspora and Cultural Identity: A Reader in the Anglophone Caribbean*, London: Routledge, pp. 337–356.

Chude-Sokei, Louis. 1994. "Post-nationalist geographies: Rasta, ragga, and reinventing Africa." *African Arts*: 27 (4), pp. 80–84.

Clarke, Steven. 1980. *Jah Music: The Evolution of Jamaican Popular Music*. London: Heinemann.

Clifford, James. 1994. "Diasporas." *Cultural Anthropology*: 9 (3), pp. 302–338.

—— 1997. *Routes: Travel and Translation in the Late Twentieth Century*. Cambridge, MA: Harvard University Press.

Cody, Cheryll Ann. 1982. "Naming, kinship, and estate dispersal: Notes on slave family life on a South Carolina plantation, 1786 to 1833." *The William and Mary Quarterly*: 39 (1), 192–211.

Cohen, Robin. 1994. *Global Diasporas: An Introduction*. London: UCL Press.

Confiant, Raphaël. 1988. *Le nègre et l'amiral*. Paris; Grasset.

Connerton, Paul. 1987. *How Societies Remember*. Cambridge: Cambridge University Press.

—— 2000. "Lieux de mémoire, lieux d'oubli." In Huglo *et al*., *Passions du passé: recyclages de la mémoire et usages de l'oubli*, Montreal: L'Harmattan, pp. 51–92.

Constant, Denis. 1982. *Aux sources du reggae: musique, société et politique en Jamaïque*. Paris: Editions Parenthèses.

Cooper, Carolyn. 1994. "Lyrical gun metaphor and role play in Jamaican dancehall culture." *The Massachusetts Review*: 35, pp. 429–447.

—— 1995. *Noises in the Blood*. Durham, NC: Duke University Press.

—— 2004. *Sound Clash: Jamaican Dancehall Culture at Large*. New York: Palgrave Macmillan.

Davie, Grace. 1997. "Believing without belonging: A framework for religious transmission." *Recherches Sociologiques*: 28 (3), pp. 17–38.

Davis, Stephen. 1992 [1977]. *Reggae Bloodlines*. New York: Da Capo Press.

Daynes, Sarah. 2001. *Le mouvement Rastafari: mémoire, musique et religion*. Thèse de Doctorat en Sociologie, Paris: Ecole des Hautes Etudes en Sciences Sociales.

—— 2003. "The musical construction of the African diaspora: The case of reggae and Rastafari." In Bennett, Hawkins, and Whiteley (eds), *Music, Space and Place: Popular Music and Cultural Identity*, Aldershot: Ashgate, pp. 25–41.

de Albuquerque, Klaus. 1977. *Millenarian Movements and the Politics of Liberation: The Rastafarians of Jamaica*. Ph.D. thesis, Virginia Polytechnic Institute and State University.

Déchaux, Jean. 1997. *Le souvenir des morts. Essai sur le lien de filiation*. Paris: Presses Universitaires de France.
Desroche, Henri. 1960. "Les messianismes et la catégorie de l'échec." *Cahiers Internationaux de Sociologie*: 35 (1), pp. 61–84.
—— 1969. *Dieux d'hommes*. Paris/La Haye: Mouton.
—— 1973. *Sociologie de l'espérance*. Paris: Calmann-Lévy.
—— 1974. *Les religions de contrebande*. Paris: Mame.
—— 1979 [1973]. *The Sociology of Hope*. London: Routledge & Kegan Paul.
Durkheim, Emile. 1893. *De la division du travail social. Etude sur l'organisation des sociétés supérieures*. Paris: Alcan.
—— 1898a. "De la définition des phénomènes religieux," *L'Année sociologique*: II, pp. 1–28. [Translated as "Concerning the definition of religious phenomena" in *Durkheim on Religion*, Oxford: Oxford University Press, 2006, pp. 74–99.]
—— 1898b. "Représentations individuelles et représentations collectives," *Revue de Métaphysique et de Morale*, vol. VI. [Translated as "Individual and collective representations," in *Sociology and Philosophy*, New York: The Free Press, 1974, pp. 1–34.]
—— 1911. "Jugements de valeur et jugements de réalité," *Revue de Métaphysique et de Morale*, vol. XIX. [Translated as "Value judgments and judgments of reality," in *Sociology and Philosophy*, New York: The Free Press, 1974, pp. 80–97.]
—— 1912. *Les formes élémentaires de la vie religieuse: Le système totémique en Australie*. Paris: Alcan.
—— 1974. *Sociology and Philosophy*. New York: The Free Press.
—— 1982. *The Rules of Sociological Method*, New York: Free Press.
—— 1997. *The Division of Labor in Society*. New York: Free Press.
—— 1998. *Lettres à Marcel Mauss*. Presented by P. Besnard and M. Fournier. Paris: Presses Universitaires de France.
—— 2001. *The Elementary Forms of Religious Life*, New York: Free Press.
—— 2004 [1895]. *Les règles de la méthode sociologique*. Paris: Presses Universitaires de France.
—— 2006. *Durkheim on Religion*, ed. W.S.F. Pickering. Oxford: Oxford University Press.
Durkheim, Emile, and Marcel Mauss. 1902. "De quelques formes de classification: Contribution à l'étude des représentations collectives." *L'Année Sociologique*: VI, pp. 1–72.
—— 1967. *Primitive Classification*, Chicago: University of Chicago Press, 1967.

Edmonds, Ennis Barrington. 2003. *Rastafari: From Religious Outcasts to Culture Bearers*. Oxford: Oxford University Press.
Eliade, Mircea. 1949. *Le mythe de l'éternel retour*. Paris: Gallimard.
—— 1954. *The Myth of the Eternal Return*. Princeton, NJ: Princeton University Press.
—— 1957. *The Sacred and the Profane*. New York: Harcourt.
—— 1963a. *Aspects du mythe*. Paris: Gallimard.
—— 1963b. "Mythologies of memory and forgetting." *History of Religion*: 2 (2), pp. 329–344.
Evans-Pritchard, Edwards E. 1937. *Witchcraft, Oracles and Magic among the Azande*. Oxford: The Clarendon Press.
—— 1939. "Nuer time-reckoning." *Africa*: 12 (2), pp. 189–216.
—— 1969. *The Nuer: A Description of the Modes of Livelihood and Political Institutions of a Nilotic People*. Oxford: Oxford University Press.
Forsythe, Dennis. 1999 (1983). *Rastafari. For the Healing of the Nations*. New York: One Drop Books.
Frazier, Franklin. 1997 [1955]. *Black Bourgeoisie*. New York: Free Press.
Frith, Simon. 1987. "Why do songs have words?" In White (ed.), *Lost in Music: Culture, Style and the Musical Event*, London: Routledge, pp. 77–106.
Gadamer, Hans-Georg. 2003 [1960]. *Theory and Method*. New York: Continuum.
Garrison, Len. 1979. *Black Youth, Rastafarianism and the Identity Crisis in Britain*. London: Acert Project Publication.
Gilroy, Paul. 1986. *There Ain't No Black in the Union Jack: The Cultural Politics of Race and Nation*. London: Hutchinson.
—— 1990/91. "It ain't where you're from, it's where you're at: The dialectics of diasporic identification." *Third Text*: 13, pp. 3–16.
—— 1991. "Sounds authentic: Black music, ethnicity, and the challenge of the changing same." *Black Music Research Journal*: 11 (2), pp. 111–136.
—— 1993. *The Black Atlantic: Modernity and Double Consciousness*. Cambridge, MA: Harvard University Press.
—— 2000. *Against Race: Imagining Political Culture Beyond the Color Line*. Cambridge, MA: Harvard University Press.
Gjerset, Heidi. 1994. "First generation Rastafari in St. Eustatius: A case study in the Netherlands Antilles." *Caribbean Quarterly*: 40 (1), pp. 64–77.
Glazier, Stephen D. 1994. "New religious movements in the Caribbean: Identity and resistance." In Hoggbergen (ed.), *Born

out of Resistance: On Caribbean Cultural Creativity, Utrecht: Isor Publications, pp. 253–262.
Goethe, J.W. von. 1963. *Elective Affinities*. Chicago: Henry Regnery.
Gordon, Edmund T. 1998. *Disparate Diasporas. Identity and Politics in an African-Nicaraguan Community*. Austin: University of Texas Press.
Grazian, David. 2005. *Blue Chicago: The Search for Authenticity in Urban Blues Clubs*. Chicago: University of Chicago Press.
Griffiths, Dai. "From lyrics to anti-lyrics: Analyzing the words in pop song." In Moore (ed.), *Analyzing Popular Music*, Cambridge: Cambridge University Press, pp. 39–59.
Habekost, Christian. 1986. *Dub Poetry*. Germany: Michael Schwinn Publishers.
—— 1994. "Rasta 'pon top but raggamuffin rule. The change of a style." In Kremser (ed.), *Ay Bobo. African-Caribbean Religions*, Vienna: 2nd International Conference of the Society for Caribbean Research, pp. 101–118.
Halbwachs, Maurice. 1925. *Les origines du sentiment religieux d'après Durkheim*. Paris: Stock.
—— 1939. "Individual consciousness and collective mind." *American Journal of Sociology*: 44 (6), pp. 812–822.
—— 1941. *La topographie légendaire des Evangiles en Terre Sainte: Etude de mémoire collective*. Paris: Presses Universitaires de France. [Translated in *On Collective Memory*, Chicago: University of Chicago Press, 1992.]
—— 1962. *Sources of Religious Sentiment*. New York: Free Press.
—— 1980. *The Collective Memory*. New York: Harper & Row.
—— 1992. *On Collective Memory*. Chicago: University of Chicago Press.
—— 1994 [1925]. *Les cadres sociaux de la mémoire*. Paris: Albin Michel. [Translated in *On Collective Memory*, Chicago: University of Chicago Press, 1992.]
—— 1997 [1950]. *La mémoire collective*. Paris: Albin Michel.
Hall, Stuart. 1995. "Negotiating Caribbean identities." *New Left Review*: 209, pp. 3–14.
—— 1996. "The West and the rest: Discourse and power," in Hall *et al.* (eds), *Modernity: An Introduction to Modern Societies*, Oxford, Blackwell.
—— 1999. "Thinking the diaspora: Home-thoughts from abroad." *Small Axe*: 6, pp. 1–18.
Hannerz, Ulf. 1987. "The world in creolisation." *Africa*: 57, pp. 546–558.

Bibliography

Hansing, Katrin. 2001. "Rasta, race and revolution: Transnational connections in socialist Cuba." *Journal of Ethnic and Migration Studies*: 27 (4), pp. 733–747.
Hausman, Gerald. 1997. *The Kebra Negast: The Lost Bible of Rastafarian Wisdom and Faith from Ethiopia and Jamaica*. New York: St. Martin's Press.
Hebdige, Dick. 1974. *Reggae, Rastas and Rudies: Style and the Subversion of Form*. University of Birmingham: Centre of Contemporary Cultural Studies.
—— 1979. *Subculture. The Meaning of Style*. London: Methuen.
—— 1987. *Cut'n'mix. Culture, Identity and Caribbean Music*. London: Routledge.
Hepner, Randal L. 1998. *Movement of Jah people: Race, Class, and Religion among the Rastafari of Jamaica and New York City*. Ph.D. dissertation, New York: New School for Social Research.
Herskovits, Melville. 1941. *The Myth of the Negro Past*. New York: Harper & Row.
Hervieu-Léger, Danièle. 1999. *La religion en mouvement. Le pèlerin et le converti*. Paris: Flammarion.
—— 2000 [1993]. *Religion as a Chain of Memory*. New Brunswick, NJ: Rutgers University Press.
Homiak, John P. 1985. *The Ancient of Days Seated Black: Eldership, Oral Tradition and Ritual in Rastafari Culture*. Ph.D. dissertation, Waltham: Brandeis University.
—— 1994a. "From yard to nation: Rastafari and the politics of eldership at home and abroad." In Kremser (ed.), *Ay Bobo. African-Caribbean Religions*, Vienna: 2nd International Conference of the Society for Caribbean Research.
—— 1994b. "Rastafari voices reach Ethiopia." *American Anthropologise* 96 (4): 958–963.
—— 1995. "Dub history: Soundings on Rastafari livity and language." In Chevannes (ed.), *Rastafari and Other African-Caribbean World-views*, The Hague: ISS, pp. 127–181.
—— 1999. "Movements of Jah people: From soundscapes to mediascapes." In Pulis (ed.), *Religion, Diaspora and Cultural Identity: A Reader in the Anglophone Caribbean*, London: Routledge, pp. 87–124.
Hobsbawm, Eric. 1972. "The social function of the past: Some questions." *Past & Present*: 55, pp. 3–17.
Hobsbawm, Eric, and Terence Ranger. 1992. *The Invention of Tradition*. Cambridge: Cambridge University Press.

Hope, Donna P. 2006. *Inna Di Dancehall: Popular Culture and the Politics of Identity in Jamaica*. Kingston: University of West Indies Press.

Hubert, Henri. 1905. "Etude sommaire de la représentation du temps dans la religion et la magie". *Annuaire de l'Ecole Pratique des Hautes Etudes, Section des Sciences Religieuses*, pp. 1–39. [Translated in *Essay on Time*, London: Berghahn Books, 1999.]

—— 1999. *Essay on Time*. London: Berghahn Books.

Huglo, Marie-Pascale, Eric Mechoulan and Walter Moser (eds). 2000. *Passions du passé: recyclages de la mémoire et usages de l'oubli*. Montreal: L'Harmattan.

Hurbon, Laënnec. 1986. "New religious movements in the Caribbean." In Beckford (ed.), *New Religious Movements and Rapid Social Change*, London: Sage, pp. 146–176.

—— 1989. *Le phénomène religieux dans la Caraibe*. Montreal: Editions du Cidhica.

Huston, Nancy. 1993. *Cantique des plaines*. Paris: Actes Sud.

Jedlowski, Paolo. 2001. "Memory and sociology: Themes and issues." *Time and Society*: 10 (1), 29–44.

Jenkins, David. 1997. *Black Zion: The Return of Afro-Americans and West-Indians to Africa*. London: Wilwood House.

Johnson-Hill, Jack A. 1995. *I-sight, the World of Rastafari: An Interpretative Sociological Account of Rastafarian Ethics*. London: ATLA/The Scarecrow Press.

Jones, Simon. 1988. *Black Culture, White Youths. The Reggae Tradition from JA to UK*. London: Macmillan.

Jones, Steve. 2000. "Music and the internet." *Popular Music*: 19 (2), 217–230.

Jules-Rosette, Benetta. 1975. *African Apostles: Ritual and Conversion in the Church of John Maranke*. Ithaca, NY: Cornell University Press.

Kandinsky, Wassily. 1989 [1954]. *Du spirituel dans l'art, et dans la peinture en particulier*. Paris: Denoël.

—— 2008. *Concerning the Spiritual in Art*. Teddington: Echo Library.

Katz, David. 2003. *Solid Foundation: An Oral History of Reggae*. New York: Bloomsbury.

Kebede, Alemseghed, *et al*. 2000. "Social movement endurance: Collective identity and the Rastafari." *Sociological Inquiry*: 70 (3), pp. 313–337.

—— 2001. "Decentered movements: The case of the structural and perceptual versatility of the Rastafari." *Sociological Spectrum*: 21, pp. 175–205.

King, Stephen. 1997. *Redemption Song in Babylon: The Evolution of Reggae and the Rastafarian Movement*. Ph.D. dissertation, Bloomington: Indiana University.
—— 2002. *Reggae, Rastafari, and the Rhetoric of Social Control*. Jackson: University Press of Mississippi.
King, Stephen, and Richard Jensen. 1995. "Bob Marley's redemption song: The rhetoric of reggae and Rastafari." *Journal of Popular Culture*: 29 (3), pp. 17–36.
Kitzinger, Sheila. 1966. "The Rastafarian brethren of Jamaica." *Comparative Studies in Society and History*: 9, pp. 33–39.
—— 1969. "Protest and mysticism: The Rastafari cult in Jamaica." *Journal for the Scientific Study of Religion*: 8 (2), pp. 241–262.
Kopytoff, Barbara. 1976. "The early political development of Jamaican Maroons societies." *The William and Mary Quarterly*: 35 (2), pp. 287–307.
—— 1977. "Colonial treaty as sacred charter of the Jamaican Maroons." *Ethnohistory*: 26 (1), pp. 45–64.
Lafaye, Jacques. 1987. *Quetzalcoatl and Guadalupe: The Formation of Mexican National Consciousness, 1531–1813*. Chicago: University of Chicago Press.
Lake, Obiagele. 1994. "The many voices of Rastafarian women: Sexual subordination in the midst of liberation." *New West Indian Guide*: 68 (3/4), pp. 235–257.
—— 1998. "Religion, patriarchy, and the status of Rastafarian women." In Clarke (ed.), *New Trends and Developments in African Religions*, London: Greenwood Press, pp. 141–158.
Lalla, Barbara and Jean D'Costa. 1990. *Language in Exile: Three Hundred Years of Jamaican Creole*. Tuscaloosa: The University of Alabama Press.
Lanternari, Vittorio. 1960. *The Religions of the Oppressed*. New York: Mentor Books.
Lavabre, Marie-Claire. 1994. "Usages du passé, usages de la mémoire." *Revue Française de Science Politique*: 44 (3), pp. 480–493.
Leach, Edmund. 2001 [1953]. "Cronus and Chronos." In Hugh-Jones and Laidlow (eds), *The Essential Edmund Leach. Vol. 1: Anthropology and Society*, New Haven, CT: Yale University Press, pp. 174–181.
Lemaitre de Sacy, Louis-Isaac. 1998. *La Genèse*. Paris: Mille-et-Une-Nuits.
Lévi-Strauss, Claude. 1950. "Introduction à l'oeuvre de Marcel Mauss." In Mauss, *Sociologie et Anthropologie*, Paris: Presses Universitaires de France, 1973.

—— 1955. *Tristes Tropiques*. Paris: Plon.
—— 1962. *La pensée sauvage*. Paris: Plon.
—— 1966. *The Savage Mind*. Chicago: University of Chicago Press.
—— 1992. *Tristes Tropiques*. New York: Penguin.
—— 2001. *Introduction to the Work of Marcel Mauss*. London: Routledge.
Lewis, Linden. 1989. "Living in the heart of Babylon: Rastafari in the USA." *Bulletin of Eastern Caribbean Affairs*: 15 (1), pp. 20–30.
Lewis, William F. 1986. "The Rastafari: Millenial cultists or unregenerate peasants?" *Peasant Studies*: 4 (1), pp. 5–26.
—— 1993. *Soul Rebels. The Rastafari*. Prospect Heights, IL: Waveland Press.
—— 1994. "The social drama of Rastafari." *Dialectical Anthropology*: 19, pp. 283–294.
Littlewood, Roland. 1993. *Pathology and Identity: The Work of Mother Earth in Trinidad*. Cambridge: Cambridge University Press.
Llewelyn-Watson, G. 1973. "Social structure and social movements: The Black Muslims in the USA and the Ras-Tafarians in Jamaica." *British Journal of Sociology*: 24 (2), pp. 188–204.
—— 1974. "Patterns of Black protest in Jamaica: The case of the Rastafarians." *Journal of Black Studies*: 4 (3), pp. 329–343.
Lloyd, A.L. 1975. *Folk Song in England*. London: Paladin.
Malinowski, Bronislaw. 1926–27. "Lunar and seasonal calendar in the Trobriands." *Journal of the Anthropological Institute of Great-Britain and Ireland*: 56–57, pp. 203–215.
Mannheim, Karl. 1978 [1928]. "The Problem of Generations," in *Essays on the Sociology of Knowledge*, New York: Oxford University Press, pp. 276–322.
Manuel, Peter, and Kenneth Bilby. 1995. *Caribbean Currents: Caribbean Music from Rumba to Reggae*. Phildadelphia, PA: Temple University Press.
Manuel, Peter, and Wayne Marshall. 2006. "The riddim method: Aesthetics, practice, and ownership in Jamaican dancehall." *Popular Music*: 25 (3), 447–470.
Martin, Peter. 1995. *Sounds and Society: Themes in the Sociology of Music*. Manchester: Manchester University Press.
—— 2007. *Music and the Sociological Gaze: Art Worlds and Cultural Production*. Manchester: Manchester University Press.
Mauss, Marcel. 1973 [1906]. With Henri Beuchat. "Essai sur les variations saisonnières des sociétés Eskimos. Etude de morphologie sociale." In Mauss, *Sociologie et Anthropologie*, Paris: Presses Universitaires de France.

—— 1968 [1909]. "La Prière." In Mauss, *Oeuvres*, vol. I, "Les fonctions sociales du sacré," Paris: Editions de Minuit.
—— 2003. *On Prayer*. Oxford: Berghahn Books.
—— 2004. *Seasonal Variations of the Eskimo: A Study in Social Morphology*. London: Routledge.
Mauss, Marcel, and Henri Hubert. 1968 [1899]. "Essai sur la nature et la fonction du sacrifice." In Mauss, *Oeuvres*, vol. I, "Les fonctions sociales du sacré," Paris: Editions de Minuit. [Translated in *Sacrifice: Its Nature and Functions*, Chicago: University of Chicago Press, 1981.]
—— 1909 [1905]. "Esquisse d'une théorie générale de la magie." In Hubert and Mauss, *Mélanges d'histoire des religions*, Paris: Alcan.
—— 1981. *Sacrifice: Its Nature and Functions*. Chicago: University of Chicago Press.
—— 2001. *A General Theory of Magic*. London: Routledge.
Meillassoux, Claude. 1992 [1986]. *The Anthropology of Slavery. The Womb of Iron and Gold*. Chicago: University of Chicago Press.
Merriam, Alan P. 1964. *The Anthropology of Music*. Evanston, IL: Northwestern University Press.
Metraux, Alfred. 1989. *Voodoo in Haiti*. New York: Pantheon.
Miller, William Watts. 2000. "Durkheimian time." *Time and Society*: 9 (1), pp. 5–20.
Mintz, Sidney. 1989. *Caribbean Transformations*. New York: Columbia University Press.
Misztal, Barbara. 2003a. *Theories of Social Remembering*. Maidenhead: Open University Press.
—— 2003b. "Durkheim on collective memory." *Journal of Classical Sociology*: 3 (2), pp. 123–143.
—— 2004. "The sacralization of memory." *European Journal of Social Theory*: 7 (1), pp. 67–84.
Mooney, H.F. 1954. "Song, singers and society, 1890–1954." *American Quarterly*: 6, pp. 221–232.
Mthembu-Salter, Gregory, and Simon Dalton. 2000. "Jamaica: The loudest island in the world," in *Rough Guide to World Music Vol. 2*, London: Rough Guides, pp. 430–456.
Mülhmann, Wilhelm. 1968. *Messianismes révolutionnaires du tiers-monde*. Paris: Gallimard.
Mulvaney, Rebekah Michele. 1987. *Rastafari and Reggae: A Dictionary and Sourcebook*. Westport, CT / London: Greenwood Press.
Murell, Nathaniel Samuel, *et al*. 1998. *Chanting Down Babylon: The Rastafari Reader*. Philadelphia, PA: Temple University Press.

Negus, Keith. 1996. *Popular Music in Theory. An Introduction*. Cambridge: Polity.
Nettleford, Rex. 1972. *Identity, Race and Protest in Jamaica*. New York: William Morrow.
Nowotny, Helga. 1992. "Time and social theory: Towards a social theory of time." *Time and Society*: 1 (3), pp. 421–454.
O'Brien Chang, K. and W. Chen. 1998. *Reggae Routes. The Story of Jamaican Music*. Philadelphia, PA: Temple University Press.
Owens, Joseph. 1976. *Dread, the Rastafarians of Jamaica*. London: Heinemann.
—— 1978. "Literature on Rastafari: 1955–1974." *New Community*: 6 (1/2), pp. 150–164.
Pascal, Blaise. 2004. "On the geometrical Spirit," in *Thoughts, Letters and Minor Works (Harvard Classics Part 48)*. Whitefish, MT: Kessinger Publishing, pp. 427–443.
Patterson, Orlando. 1967. *The Sociology of Slavery: An Analysis of the Origins, Development and Structure of Negro Slave Society in Jamaica*. New York: McGibbon and Kee.
—— 1979. "Slavery and slave revolts: A socio-historical analysis of the first Maroon war, Jamaica 1655–1740." *Social and Economic Studies*: 19 (3), pp. 289–325.
—— 1982. *Slavery and Social Death: A Comparative Study*. Cambridge, MA: Harvard University Press.
Pollard, Velma. 1982. "The social history of dread talk." *Caribbean Quarterly*: 28 (4), pp. 17–40.
—— 1990. "The speech of the Rastafarians of Jamaica in the Eastern Caribbean." *International Journal of the Sociology of Language*: 85, pp. 81–90.
—— 2000. *Dread Talk: The Language of Rastafari*. Montreal: McGill-Queen's University Press.
Potash, Chris. 1997. (ed.) *Reggae, Rasta, Revolution: Jamaican Music from Ska to Dub*. New York: Schirmer / Macmillan.
Poulter, Sebastian. 1998. *Ethnicity, Law and Human Rights. The English Experience*. Chapter 9: "Rastafarians." Oxford: Clarendon Press.
Prahlad, Sw. Anand. 2001. *Reggae Wisdom. Proverbs in Jamaican Music*. Jackson: University Press of Mississippi.
Pratt, Ray. 1990. *Rhythm and Resistance: Explorations in the Political Uses of Popular Music*. New York: Prager.
Price, Charles Reavis. 2003. "Social change and the development and co-optation of a Black antisystemic identity: The case of Rastafarians in Jamaica." *Identity*: 3 (1), pp. 9–27.

Price, Richard. 1979. (ed.) *Maroon Societies: Rebel Slave Communities in the Americas*. New York: Anchor Press / Doubleday.

Pulis, John W. 1993. "Up-full sounds: Language, identity, and the world-view of Rastafari." *Ethnic Groups*: 10, pp. 285–300.

Raboteau, Albert. 1980. *Slave Religion*. New York/Oxford: Oxford University Press.

Reckord, Verena. 1977. "Rastafarian music: An introductory story." *Jamaica Journal*: 11 (1/2), pp. 3–18.

—— 1982. "Reggae, Rastafarianism and cultural identity." *Jamaica Journal*: 46, pp. 70–79.

Ricoeur, Paul. 1988. *Lectures on Ideology and Utopia*. New York: Columbia University Press.

—— 1991. *From Text to Action: Essays in Hermeneutics, II*. Evanston, IL: Northwestern University Press.

—— 2006 [2000]. *Memory, History, Forgetting*. Chicago: University of Chicago Press.

Rousso, Henri, and Eric Conan. 1994. *Vichy, un passé qui ne passe pas*. Paris: Seuil.

Rowe, Maureen. 1976. "The woman in Rastafari." *Caribbean Quarterly*: 26 (4), pp. 13–21.

Ryle, John. 1976. "Rastaman in the Promised Land." *New Society*: December 24/31, pp. 535–538.

Safran, William. 1991. "Diasporas in modern societies: Myths of homeland and return." *Diaspora*: 1(1), pp. 83–99.

Savishinsky, Neil. 1994a. "The Baye Faal of Senegambia: Muslim rastas in the promised land?" *Africa*: 64 (2), pp. 211–219.

—— 1994b. "Transnational popular culture and the global spread of the Jamaican Rastafarian movement." *New West Indian Guide*: 68 (3–4), pp. 259–281.

Sebba, Mark. 1993. *London Jamaican: language systems in interaction*. London: Longman.

—— 1996. "How do you spell patwa?" *Critical Quarterly*: 38, pp. 50–63.

Seeger, Anthony. 1994. "Whoever we are today, we can sing you a song about it." In G. Behague (ed.), *Music and Black Ethnicity: The Caribbean and South America*, Miami: North South Center Press/ University of Miami, pp. 1–16.

Segre, Sandro. 2000. "A Weberian theory of time." *Time and Society*: 9 (2/3), pp. 147–170.

Semaj, Leahcim T. 1980. "Rastafari: From religion to social theory." *Caribbean Quarterly*: 26 (4), pp. 22–31.

Shepherd, John *et al*. 1977. *Whose Music? A Sociology of Musical Language*. London: Latimer.

Simpson, George Eaton. 1955a. "The Ras Tafari movement in Jamaica: A study of race and class conflict." *Social Forces*: 34, pp. 167–171.
—— 1955b. "Political cultism in Western Kingston, Jamaica." *Social and Economic Studies*: 4, pp. 133–149.
—— 1962. "The Ras Tafari movement in Jamaica in its millenial aspect." *Comparative Studies in Society and History*: supplement II, pp. 160–165.
—— 1984. "Religion and justice: Some reflections on the Rastafari movement." *Phylon*: 46 (4), pp. 286–291.
Smith, M.G., Roy Augier and Rex Nettleford. 1960. *Report on the Rastafari Movement in Kingston, Jamaica*. Kingston: Institute of Social and Economic Research.
Sorokin, Pitrim A., and Robert K. Merton. 1937. "Social time: A methodological and functional analysis." *American Journal of Sociology*: 42 (5), pp. 615–629.
Stokes, Martin. 1994. (ed.) *Ethnicity, Identity and Music: The Musical Construction of Place*. Oxford: Berg.
Stolzoff, Norman. 2000. *Wake the Town and Tell the People. Dancehall Culture in Jamaica*. Durham, NC: Duke University Press.
Styron, William. 1992 [1967]. *The Confessions of Nat Turner*. New York: Vintage.
Tafari, Jabulani I. 1980. "The Rastafari: Successors of Marcus Garvey." *Caribbean Quarterly*: 26 (4), pp. 1–12.
Taylor, Anne-Christine. 1993. "Remembering to forget: Identity, mourning and memory among the Jivaros." *Man*: 28 (4), pp. 653–678.
Taylor, Patrick. 1990. "Perspectives on history in Rastafari thought." *Studies in Religion*: 19 (2), pp. 191–205.
—— 2001. "Sheba's song: The Bible, the Kebra Nagast and Rastafari." In Taylor (ed.), *In Nation Dance: Religion, Identity and Cultural Difference in the Caribbean*, Bloomington: Indiana University Press, pp. 65–78.
Turner, Terisa E. 1987. "Women, Rastafari and the new society: Caribbean and East African roots of a popular movement against structural adjustment." *Labour, Capital and Society*: 24 (1), pp. 66–89.
Van de Berg, William R. 1998. "Rastafari perceptions of self and symbolism." In Clarke (ed.), *New Trends and Developments in African Religions*, London: Greenwood Press, pp. 159–176.
Van Dijk, Frank Jan. 1988. "The Twelve Tribes of Israel: Rasta and the middle class." *New West Indian Guide*: 62 (1), pp. 1–26.

Veal, Michael E. 2007. *Dub. Soundscapes and Shattered Songs in Jamaican Reggae.* Middletown, CT: Wesleyan University Press.
Vernant, Jean-Pierre. 1996 [1965]. *Mythe et pensée chez les Grecs. Etudes de psychologie historique.* Paris: La Découverte.
—— 2006. *Myth and Thought among the Greeks.* New York: Zone Books.
Wade, Peter. 1999. "Working culture: Making cultural identities in Cali, Colombia." *Current Anthropology*: 40 (4), pp. 449–462.
Warner-Lewis, Maureen. 1987. "African continuities in the Rastafari belief system." *Caribbean Quarterly*: 39 (3/4), pp. 108–123.
Waters, Anita. 1989 [1985]. *Race, Class, and Political Symbols: Rastafari and Reggae in Jamaican Politics.* New Brunswick, NJ / London: Transaction Publishers.
—— 1999. "Half the story: The uses of history in Jamaican political discourse." *Caribbean Quarterly*: 45 (1): 62–77.
Weber, Max. 1949. "Objectivity in social science and social policy," in *The Methodology of the Social Sciences*, New York: Free Press.
—— 1958. "The social psychology of the world religions," in *From Max Weber*, Oxford: Oxford University Press, pp. 267–301.
—— 1978. *Economy and Society.* Two volumes. Berkeley: University of California Press.
—— 2002 [1904–05]. *The Protestant Ethic and the Spirit of Capitalism.* London: Penguin.
West, Cornel. 1982. *Prophesy Deliverance! An Afo-American Revolutionary Christianity.* Philadelphia, PA: Westminster Press.
White, G. 1977. "Master Drummer." *Jamaica Journal*: 11 (1/2), p. 17.
Winders, James A. 1983. "Reggae, Rastafarians and revolution: Rock music in the Third World." *Journal of Popular Culture*: 17 (1), pp. 61–73.
Yawney, Carol. 1976. "Remnants of all nations: Rastafarian attitudes to race and nationality." In Henry (ed.), *Ethnicity in the Americas*, The Hague: Mouton, pp. 231–262.
—— 1987. "Rasta mek a trod: Ambiguity in a globalizing religion." In Bremer and Fleischmann (eds), *Alternative Cultures in the Caribbean*, Frankfurt: Vervuert, pp. 161–168.
—— 1994. "Rastafari sounds of cultural resistance. Ahmaric language training in Trenchtown, Jamaica." In Kremser (ed.), *Ay Bobo. African-Caribbean Religions*, Vienna: 2nd International Conference of the Society for Caribbean Research, pp. 33–48.
—— 1999. "Only visitors here: Representing Rastafari into the 21st century." In Pulis (ed.), *Religion, Diaspora and Cultural Identity: A Reader in the Anglophone Caribbean*, London: Routledge, pp. 153–180.

Zerubavel, Eviatar. 1977. "The French Republican calendar: A case study in the sociology of time." *American Sociology Review*: 42 (6), pp. 868–877.
—— 1982. "The standardization of time: A sociohistorical perspective." *American Journal of Sociology*: 88 (1), pp. 1–23.
—— 1985. *The Seven Day Circle: The History and Meaning of the Week*. Chicago: University of Chicago Press.
—— 2003. *Time Maps. Collective Memory and the Social Shape of the Past*. Chicago: University of Chicago Press.
—— 2006. *The Elephant in the Room: Silence and Denial in Everyday Life*. Oxford: Oxford University Press.
Zips, Werner. 1987. "Sister Nanny a one a we, brother Kojo a one a we, brother Bob Marley a one a we. The continuity of Black resistance in Jamaica." In Bremer and Fleischmann (eds), *Alternative Cultures in the Caribbean*, Frankfurt: Vervuert, pp. 69–76.
—— 1994. "Let's talk about the motherland. Jamaican influences on the African discourses in the diaspora." In Hoggbergen (ed.), *Born out of Resistance: On Caribbean Cultural Creativity*, Utrecht: Isor Publications, pp. 46–62.

Index

Abyssinia *see* Ethiopia
Abyssinians (reggae group) 72, 94, 95, 118, 119
Admiral Bailey 58, 60
Adorno, Theodor W. 11, 12, 49
Africaness 14, 101
Ahmaric 46
Aitken, Laurel 30
Alcapone, Dennis 31, 74, 200
Alleyne, Mervyn C. 27
Andy, Bob 31
Andy, Horace 56
Anthias, Floya 87
Anthony B. 39, 40, 72, 74, 75, 77, 78, 99, 110, 113, 114, 118, 119, 121, 131, 136, 148, 149, 152, 157, 158, 160, 161, 167, 176, 183, 195, 196, 198, 199, 200, 201, 202, 220–225
Anthony Red Rose 65
apartheid 121, 181–183
Arendt, Hannah 9–10
Armstrong, Louis 34
Aswad 40, 69, 134, 161, 162

Baby Cham 56, 58
Babylon 25, 44, 45, 150, 155–163, 206, 248
Back, Les 27 30
Balandier, George 206, 210
Banks, Russell 171, 231, 246
Banton, Buju 35, 38, 39, 44, 56, 57, 58, 61, 63, 65, 67, 70, 74, 75, 77, 78, 99, 110, 111, 112, 117, 119, 120, 122, 132, 142, 161, 162, 176, 183, 195, 199, 201, 202, 205, 210, 223, 228
Barrett, Aston 32, 213
Barrett, Carlton 32, 213
Barrett, Leonard 131
Barrow, Steve 60, 61, 72
Barth, Fredrik 75
Bastide, Roger 86, 134
Baudelaire, Charles 105
Bedward, Alexander 127
Beenie Man 58, 65, 67, 69, 74
Behague, Gerard 13
Besson, Jean 28, 171
Big Youth 34, 64, 72, 114, 115, 116, 141, 172, 213
Biko, Steve 181–182, 184, 219
  see also apartheid
Bilby, Kenneth M. 69, 70, 71
Black Uhuru 38, 60, 62, 97, 162, 181, 193
Blender, Everton 61, 75
Bloch, Ernst 101, 248
Bobo Shanti 25, 37, 136

Bogle, Paul 173
Boothe, Ken 31, 200
Borges, Jorge Luis 9–10
Bounty Killer 56, 57, 58, 74, 75
Bourdieu, Pierre 13
Brown, Barry 112, 115
Brown, Dennis 31, 58, 59, 60, 63, 64, 67, 95, 107, 118, 133, 141, 148, 162, 170, 177, 194, 205, 210
Brown, Overton "Scientist" 184
Burning Spear 31, 62, 97, 98, 99, 100, 130, 131, 132, 174, 175, 178, 183, 191
Burru drums 29
Bushman 117, 195, 198
Byles, Junior 64, 176, 200

Caillois, Roger 2
Campbell, Horace 27, 28, 171, 173, 226, 227
Capleton 56, 57, 61, 65, 74
Caribbean music
Cashmore, Ernest 26, 27, 28, 164
Catholic Church
Central Intelligence Agency (CIA) 211
Chevannes, Barry 14, 26, 27, 28, 211
Chude-Sokei, Louis 30, 34, 47, 98, 101, 204
Clapton, Eric 76
Clarke, Johnny 127, 128
Clarke, Sebastian 32
classic album, definition of 48–50
Cliff, Jimmy 65
Clifford, James 9, 87, 90, 91, 103
Cocoa Tea 65, 179
Confiant, Raphael 171
Constant, Denis 29

Cooper, Carolyn 34, 42, 47, 48, 57
Count Ossie 29
creole societies 87
Cudjoe *see* Maroons
Culture (reggae group) 59, 60, 64, 74, 94, 176
Culture, Louie 225
Culture, Stevie 41

Davie, Grace 14, 52
Déchaux, Jean 80, 96
Desroche, Henri 92, 105, 126, 127, 134, 135, 137, 139, 146, 207, 225, 233, 238
diaspora 86–93, 102–104, 180, 181, 184–187
  centered model 88–90
  multi-centered model 90–91
DJs 34
Dodd, Clement "Coxsone" 30, 31, 32, 33, 213
Dowe, Brent 65
dread locks 172
dread talk 39, 46, 132, 200
dub 32–33
Dunbar, Sly 32
Dunkley, Archibald
Durkheim, Emile 2, 6, 79, 80, 135, 234, 235, 246, 247, 248, 250, 251, 253–256, 257, 258, 261, 263
Dylan, Bob 36

Eccles, Clancy 200
Edmonds, Ennis Barrington 26, 41, 253
elective affinity 22–24
Eliade, Mircea 165, 233, 243, 247, 252, 259
Elliott, Paul 38, 111, 113, 162
Ellis, Alton 31
Emmanuel, Prince *see* Bobo Shanti

Index

Emmanuelites *see* Bobo Shanti
Ethiopia 91, 98, 99, 113
Ethiopians (reggae group) 62

Fashek, Majek 165
forgetting 2
Frazier, Franklin 14
Frith, Simon 36, 37, 46, 47

Gadamer, Hans-Georg 8, 238
Garvey, Marcus 24, 98, 101, 108, 126, 127, 139, 174–176, 184, 186
Gibbs, Joe 33
Gilroy, Paul 87, 91, 184
Gladiators (reggae group) 41, 62
Goethe, Johann Wolfgang von 22, 23
Golding, Bruce 200
Gordon, Edmund 94
Gordon, Vin 32
Gordon, William
Grazian, David 205
Griffith, Marcia 213
  see also I-Threes

Haile Selassie 24, 78, 113, 127–137, 143, 172, 251
Halbwachs, Maurice 1, 3–7, 12, 234, 238, 239, 244
Hall, Stuart 87, 220
Hammond, Beres 65
Hannerz, Ulf 87
Hebdige, Dick 27, 32
Heptones 31, 62
Herskovits, Melville 14, 86, 87
Hervieu-Léger, Danièle 15, 207, 208, 238
Hibbert, Joseph 24
Hinds, Robert 24
Homiak, John 26, 91, 164, 166
Hope, Donna 34, 48
Howbsbawm, Eric 8, 236

Howell, Leonard 24, 25
Hubert, Henri 2, 154, 233, 234, 235, 243–247, 249, 250, 256, 261
Hudson, Keith 33
Hurbon, Laennec 28, 166
Hussey, Dermott 72
Huston, Nancy 232, 233

Inner Circle 60
International Monetary Fund (IMF) 60, 200
I Roy 72
Isaacs, Gregory 63, 64, 72, 95, 192
Israelites (reggae group) 107
Israel Vibration 62, 107, 122, 156, 246
Ital living 164, 226
I-Threes 213

Jackson, George 177, 184, 219
Jackson, Vivian 33, 40, 41, 150
Jah Shaka 172, 183
Jahmali 160, 161, 191, 194, 195, 203, 212
Jamaican independence 28
Jamaican Labour Party (JLP) 60, 200, 211
jazz 30, 34
Jenkins, Richard 208
Jesus 106, 107
Johnson-Hill, Jack 26, 156, 164
Johnson, Linton Kwesi 71
Jules-Rosette, Bennetta 164

Kamoze, Ini 65
Kandinsky, Wassily 11
Kant, Immanuel 254
Kebra Negast 236
King Edwards 31
King Jammy 34
King Tubby 32, 33, 213

King, Martin Luther Jr 178, 184
King, Stephen 43, 44, 47, 213
Knooks, George 67
Kumina 29, 30, 69, 70

Lanternari, Vittorio 126
Lavabre, Marie-Claire 7
Lee, Bunny 33
Lévi-Strauss, Claude 255, 263
Levy, Barrington 65, 183
Lewis, William 27, 196
Llewelyn-Watson, 27
Löwy, Michael 23
Luciano 61, 65, 75, 100, 118, 119, 120, 149, 151, 163, 183, 202, 203, 212, 248

Malcolm X 177, 184
Mandela, Nelson 183, 184
Manley, Michael *see* People's National Party
Manuel, Peter 13, 29, 69
Marley, Bob, and the Wailers 29, 34, 38, 40, 41, 42, 43, 45, 47, 48, 49, 58, 59, 60, 64, 69, 70, 74, 76–78, 95, 96, 97, 98, 112, 115, 116, 117, 119, 121, 130, 142, 156, 157, 158, 159, 160, 162, 169, 173, 177, 180, 181, 185, 191, 192, 193, 196, 200, 209, 211, 212, 213–218, 221, 252
Marley, Damian 179
Marley, Kymani 74
Marley, Rita 213
see also I-Threes
Marley, Stephen 74
Marley, Ziggy 74
Maroons 170–172, 184, 185
Martin, Peter 11, 12, 13
Marxism 196, 200
Masouri, John 67
Mau-Mau 172

Mauss, Marcel 2, 6, 234, 246, 247, 249, 250, 256–259, 261
McCook, Tommy 32
Meillassoux, Claude 86, 104
Memory
  and history 6–7, 85, 169, 186
  and time 231–264
mento 30
Merriam, Alan 13
Messianism 14, 125–140, 154
middle passage *see* slavery
Mighty Diamonds 59, 60, 63, 64, 73, 175, 176
Millenarianism 14, 125–140
Miller, Jacob 64, 74, 211
  see also Culture (reggae band)
Minott, Sugar 65
Mintz, Sydney 170
Misztal, Barbara 1
Mittoo, Jackie 32
Mooney, H.F. 37, 47
Morgan Heritage 65, 74, 106, 110, 111, 112, 118, 131, 132, 133, 142, 143, 159, 160, 162
Morgan, Derrick 74
Mowatt, Judy 65, 213
  see also I-Threes
Mülhmann, Wilhelm 126
Mundell, Hugh 151
music, sociological definition of 11–13
Mutabaruka 225
myal 30

Negus, Keith 184
Nettleford, Rex 28
New Orleans jazz *see* jazz
Ninjaman 74
North Atlantic Treaty Organization (NATO) 203
North-American Free Trade Agreement (NAFTA) 203

Index

nyabinghi 25
Nyabinghi Order 26

Obama, Barack 179
Osbourne, Johnny 65
Owens, Joseph 26, 134

Pablo, Augustus 32
Parks, Lloyd 32, 33
Pascal, Blaise 261
Patterson, Orlando 2, 86
Patterson, P.J. 200
patwa / patois 41, 46
People National Party (PNP) 200, 201, 211
Perry, Lee "Scratch" 32, 33, 213
Prahlad, Sw. Anand 40, 41, 134
Price, Richard 170, 171
Prince Buster 74
Prince Emmanuel 25
Prince Jammy 32, 33
Professor Nut 75
Prophets (reggae band) 158
  see also Jackson, Vivian
Psalms in reggae music 110–116
pukumina see kumina

Raboteau, Albert 105, 108
Ranglin, Ernest 72
Rastafari, scholarship on 26
Reckord, Verena 29
recording studios
  Channel One 32
  Studio One 31, 32, 213
  Randy's Dynamic 32
  Black Ark 32
record labels 69, 70
Redding, Otis 36
reggae
  British reggae 31, 218–220
  definition, origins and emergence 29–30
  digital reggae 34
  reggae dancehall 34, 47
  roots reggae 31
Reid, Arthur "Duke" 31, 32
Reid, Junior 60, 65
Revivalism 27
rhythm and blues 30, 34
Ricoeur, Paul 8
riddim 32, 71–73
  see also version
rockers 32
rock steady 31, 32
Rodney, Walter 226
Romeo, Max 59, 64, 200
Rose, Michael 193
  see also Black Uhuru
Roudinesco, Elisabeth 125
routinization 26, 41, 92, 252, 253

sadhus 172
Safran, William 87, 88–90, 102
Sanchez 65, 75
scat 34
Scotty 72, 74
Seaga, Edward 60, 200, 225
  see also Jamaica Labor Party
Seeger, Anthony 11, 12
Shabba Ranks 60, 74, 223
Shakespeare, Robbie 32
Sharpe, Sam 172, 173, 184
Shashamane 183
Shepherd, John 12
Sherman, Bim 193
Silk, Garnett 39, 61, 65, 74, 75, 78–79, 99, 112, 132, 176, 202
Simpson, George Eaton 25
single records in reggae music 30, 33, 70
Sizzla 37, 41, 58, 61, 65, 72, 74, 75, 76, 77, 105, 106, 119, 120, 127, 128, 134, 145, 146, 149, 159, 160, 161, 162, 175, 201, 209, 223, 224, 225

ska 31
Skatalites 31
slackness 34, 57, 60, 222–223
slavery 2–3, 85, 94–98, 99, 100, 102, 103, 104, 125, 232
  mental slavery 158–160
slave trade *see* slavery
Slickers 73, 74
Smith, Earl 32
sound systems 30, 39
  Downbeat 30
  Dynamic Sounds 30
  Killamanjaro 78, 79
South Africa *see* apartheid
Steel Pulse 40, 121, 142, 169, 173, 176, 177, 178, 179, 181, 182, 185, 193, 218–220
Stephens, Tanya 57, 58
Stokes, Martin 10
Stolzoff, Norman 30, 34, 48
Styron, William 118, 246
Supercat 60
Swahili 46

talk over 33, 34, 71
Taylor, Patrick 28, 165
Taylor, Rod 41, 106
Ten Commandments 35
Thompson, Errol 33
Tiger (artist) 58, 60
Tony Rebel 60, 61, 65, 78, 115, 132, 133, 134
Toots and The Maytals 31, 65
Tosh, Peter 74, 200, 213
  see also Marley, Bob, and the Wailers
Twelve Tribes of Israel (in the Bible) 105, 107–110, 125, 146
Twelve Tribes of Israel (organization) 26, 45, 137

Universal Negro Improvement Association (UNIA) 175
Upsetters 33
U Roy 34, 101, 170
utopia 101, 208, 231–232

Veal, Michael 33
Vernant, Jean-Pierre 259–262, 264
version 32–34, 60, 61, 71–73
  see also riddim

Wade, Peter 101
Wailer, Bunny 65, 200, 213
  see also Marley, Bob, and the Wailers
Wailers *see* Marley, Bob, and the Wailers
Wailing Souls 59
Washington, Glen 61
Waters, Anita 170, 200
Waters, Muddy 36
Weber, Max 9, 22–23, 26, 85, 88, 92, 93, 143, 198, 199, 237, 238, 239, 249, 250, 251
  ideal-types 88
West, Cornel 105
Wilson, Delroy 31, 200
Wong, Dickie 30
World Trade Organization (WTO) 203

Yabby You *see* Jackson, Vivian
Yawney, Carol 26
Yellowman 60

Zebra 56, 67
Zerubavel, Eviatar 2
Zion 101, 114, 150–152, 162–167
Zips, Werner 29, 179

EU authorised representative for GPSR:
Easy Access System Europe, Mustamäe tee 50,
10621 Tallinn, Estonia
gpsr.requests@easproject.com

www.ingramcontent.com/pod-product-compliance
Ingram Content Group UK Ltd.
Pitfield, Milton Keynes, MK11 3LW, UK
UKHW020857160426
5217IPUK00036B/1521